Human–Computer Interaction Series

Editors-in-chief

Desney Tan
Microsoft Research, Redmond, WA, USA

Jean Vanderdonckt
Louvain School of Management, Université catholique de Louvain,
Louvain-la-Neuve, Belgium

More information about this series at http://www.springer.com/series/6033

Jennifer Golbeck
Editor

Online Harassment

 Springer

Editor
Jennifer Golbeck
College of Information Studies
University of Maryland
College Park, MD
USA

ISSN 1571-5035   ISSN 2524-4477   (electronic)
Human–Computer Interaction Series
ISBN 978-3-030-08737-1   ISBN 978-3-319-78583-7   (eBook)
https://doi.org/10.1007/978-3-319-78583-7

Printed on acid-free paper

This Springer imprint is published by the registered company Springer International Publishing AG
part of Springer Nature
The registered company address is: Gewerbestrasse 11, 6330 Cham, Switzerland

Contents

Contributors

Sarah A. Aghazadeh University of Maryland, College Park, USA

Aitalohi Amaize University of Maryland, College Park, MD, USA

Zahra Ashktorab IBM T.J. Watson Research Center, Yorktown Heights, NY, USA

Joachim Bingel University of Copenhagen, Copenhagen, Denmark

Cody Buntain University of Maryland, College Park, USA

Alison Burns University of Maryland, College Park, USA

Andrea Castillo University of Maryland, College Park, MD, USA

Jun Chu University of Maryland, College Park, USA

Isobelle Clarke University of Birmingham, Birmingham, UK

Benjamin J. Cooper University of Maryland, College Park, MD, USA

Nicole Demme University of Maryland, College Park, MD, USA

Edward Dixon Intel Corp, Santa Clara, USA

Hazel Feigenblatt University of Maryland, College Park, USA

Jennifer Golbeck University of Maryland, College Park, MD, USA

Bert Huang Virginia Tech, Blacksburg, VA, USA

Bart P. Knijnenburg Clemson University, Clemson, SC, USA

Emily Kowalczyk University of Maryland, College Park, MD, USA

Elizabeth Laribee University of Maryland, College Park, USA

Paul Lee University of Maryland, College Park, MD, USA

Lucy Maynard University of Maryland, College Park, USA

Amy L. M. Meyers University of Maryland, College Park, USA

Grace Mishkin University of Maryland, College Park, MD, USA

Scott Moses University of Maryland, College Park, MD, USA

Moses Namara Clemson University, Clemson, SC, USA

Jessica L. O'Brien University of Maryland, College Park, USA

Xinru Page Bentley University, Waltham, MA, USA

Abigail L. Phillips School of Information Studies at the University of Wisconsin-Milwaukee, Milwaukee, WI, USA

Elaheh Raisi Virginia Tech, Blacksburg, VA, USA

Taylor B. Rogers University of Maryland, College Park, MD, USA

Leah Rufus University of Maryland, College Park, USA

Jazmine Thomas University of Maryland, College Park, MD, USA

James Thorne University of Sheffield, Sheffield, UK

Melissa Wagner-Riston University of Maryland, College Park, MD, USA

Xiaojing Wang University of Maryland, College Park, MD, USA

Zeerak Waseem University of Sheffield, Sheffield, UK

Julia WheelerGareth T. Williams University of Maryland, College Park, MD, USA

Pamela Wisniewski University of Central Florida, Orlando, FL, USA

Chapter 1
Online Harassment: A Research Challenge for HCI

Jennifer Golbeck

The scourge of online harassment has become a problem so severe that it threatens all that is good about social media. Platforms that were once lauded as media that could give equal voices to all, that would improve transparency and access, and that would help keep us all in contact over time and distance are now riddled with humans and bots that spew hate, threats and vitriol at anyone, but especially at women, people of color, and the vulnerable. Pew reports that as of 2017, 41% of Americans have been subjected to online harassment and 66% have witnessed it.[1] We have already seen harassment drive people off social media and transition into offline harassment. If we are to preserve these platforms as open, productive spaces, there must be a solution to the online harassment problem.

That solution is not going to come as one action, but a set of tools to attack the problem, both social and technical. Human-computer interaction as a field, poised at the intersection of people and technology, has a unique opportunity to create solutions both to stop harassers and support their targets. To do so, however, requires an expansive view of HCI and its connections across the spectrum from its overlap with artificial intelligence to key sociological insights.

Artificial intelligence, specifically for automated detection of harassing content, is going to be a critical part of the solution. Many HCI researchers treat AI as a wholly separate field, but in many ways, AI has been at the core of a lot of great HCI work. Intelligent interfaces, personalization, recommender systems, predictive interfaces all leverage AI to fundamentally influence the human experience. We believe strongly that an HCI approach to solving online harassment will include intelligent interfaces and AI on the back end that will assist with building datasets, identifying harassing content, and eventually filtering it. The problem is not one that can be solved solely or even primarily with automation, but any interface approach is likely to leverage some form of automated detection. As such, we include several chapters in this book that present challenges and approaches to the automated detection problem which in turn will connect directly to interfaces and the human experience.

---

[1] http://www.pewinternet.org/2017/07/11/online-harassment-2017/.

J. Golbeck (✉)
University of Maryland, College Park, MA, USA
e-mail: jgolbeck@umd.edu

© Springer International Publishing AG, part of Springer Nature 2018
J. Golbeck (ed.), *Online Harassment*, Human–Computer Interaction Series,
https://doi.org/10.1007/978-3-319-78583-7_1

1

To eventually deal with the problem of online harassment requires understanding how it manifests, how it impacts targets, and how they react. Thoroughly tackling that subject is far beyond the scope of one book; we will need volumes of research that look at the various types and manifestations of harassment, different categories of users, and various impacts. However, while we cannot address the entire problem here, we do include chapters that address these issues. This includes a deep dive on GamerGate and an entire section on how targets respond to harassment. Going forward, it will be critical for HCI researchers to embrace the behavioral and psychological elements of the field to understand manifestations of online harassment, the motivations of harassers, and the wide range of responses that follow.

Online harassment a social problem that has manifested online. The current state of social media is one that supports harassers, both with technology and policy, and largely ignores their targets. The weak-minded advice to "Just stay offline if you can't handle it" reveals a moral and ethical stance that minimizes the impacts of this harassment while strongly valuing the (largely worthless) content generated by harassers. That attitude is imbued with disdain for groups who have been tradition-ally marginalized and silenced in all parts of society; women and minorities are targeted with online harassment more frequently, and telling them to leave social media echoes the societal forces that have always tried to silence their voices. From an HCI perspective, the usability of these platforms is largely dictated by a user's ability to interact and speak freely, not necessarily without criticism and debate, but without threats, intimidation, and harassment. Thus, harassment becomes an ethical problem *and* a usability problem.

As a research field that has traditionally embraced inclusivity, access, and usabil-ity for all, HCI is positioned to lead the effort against online harassment. Going forward, we must research technology to identify harassing content, to consider optimal mechanisms to handle it both technologically and within online communi-ties, to understand the impacts on targets and how to mitigate them, and how to build technology and policy that is inclusive and considers the ability of all users to interact freely. This book offers glimpses at work in all these areas, but it will require years of coordinated efforts to solve this problem. We hope readers come away from this volume inspired to take on the challenge.

Part I
Detection

Chapter 2
Weak Supervision and Machine Learning for Online Harassment Detection

Bert Huang and Elaheh Raisi

Abstract Automated detection tools can enable both the study of online harassment and technology that mitigates its harm. Machine learning methods allow these tools to adapt and improve using data. Yet current well-established machine learning approaches require amounts of data that are often unmanageable by practitioners aiming to train harassment detectors. Emerging methods that learn models from weak supervision represent one important avenue to address this challenge. In contrast to the full supervision used in most traditional machine learning methods, weak supervision does not require annotators to label individual examples of the target concept. Instead, annotators provide approximate descriptions of the target concept, sucsh as rule-of-thumb indicators. In this chapter, we describe the weak supervision paradigm and some general principles that drive emerging methods. And we detail a weakly supervised method for detection of online harassment that uses key-phrase indicators as the form of weak supervision. This method considers multiple aspects of the online harassment phenomenon, using interplay between these aspects to bolster the weak supervision into a useful model. We describe experimental results demonstrating this approach on detecting harassment in social media data. Finally, we discuss the ongoing challenges for using machine learning methods to build harassment detectors.

2.1 Introduction

This chapter discusses the sustainable usage of machine learning for detection of online harassment. Specifically, we highlight the importance of weak supervision to mitigate the need for expert data annotation in the machine learning process. Machine learning is the process through which computer programs adapt to data to improve at some task. It is especially useful for building software that identifies concepts that are difficult to encode manually, such as complex social ideas. Various

B. Huang (✉) · E. Raisi
Virginia Tech, Blacksburg, VA 24061, USA
e-mail: bhuang@vt.edu

E. Raisi
e-mail: elaheh@vt.edu

© Springer International Publishing AG, part of Springer Nature 2018
J. Golbeck (ed.), *Online Harassment*, Human–Computer Interaction Series,
https://doi.org/10.1007/978-3-319-78583-7_2

groups across industry and academia are using machine learning to build detectors of concepts related to online harassment, including harassment itself, cyberbullying, and toxicity (Dadvar et al. 2012; Dinakar et al. 2011; Hosseinmardi et al. 2015b; Raisi and Huang 2017a; Reynolds et al. 2011; Yin et al. 2009; Blackburn and Kwak 2014).

Automated detection of online harassment is an important goal. Software tools that can read massive corpora of social media data and extract instances of harassment can be used as part of intervention strategies or for large-scale data-driven study of the phenomenon. In both of these use cases, automated tools can be either integrated with human experts or used alone to detect instances of online harassment. Machine learning can therefore catalyze significant advances in our understanding of online harassment and our ability to mitigate the damage it causes.

Yet various challenges related to the detection of online harassment have not been met by current machine learning technology. Computers do not understand human social phenomena, and to enable them to gain enough understanding to be useful, machine learning algorithms often need to ingest massive amounts of examples. Moreover, the manner in which these examples are represented must include enough information to allow computers to differentiate the target idea, harassment, from non-harassment. This need for sufficiently rich representation necessarily requires that the automated detectors have access to social information; examining the language of a message sent over social media is not enough to identify harassment. Any entity, whether a computer or a human, must also consider who is messaging whom, their tendencies, the social statuses of those involved, and various other forms of context.

Together, these challenges suggest that machine learning for training detectors of online harassment would require significant human effort to collect and annotate richly represented examples of social media interactions. Yet there is

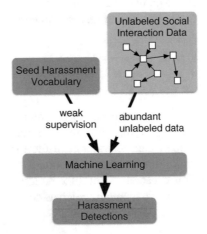

Fig. 2.1 Diagram of weakly supervised machine learning for training harassment detectors. Expert annotators provide approximate indicators of harassment, such as a vocabulary of phrases commonly indicative of harassment. The machine learning algorithm analyzes this weak supervision with a large corpus of unlabeled social media data to identify instances of harassment within the corpus

hope for more efficient and economical approaches. Researchers are developing machine learning methods that learn from weak supervision, which provides feedback to the machine learning not as individual examples one at a time, but as approximate labeling indicators—i.e., rules of thumb—of the target concept. These imperfect and approximate labelings, while noisy, can apply to much larger amounts of data than can be covered by the one-at-a-time supervision of traditional machine learning (see Fig. 2.1).

Moreover, the multifaceted nature of online harassment makes it a target application that can benefit from a key principle in the design of weakly supervised machine learning methods. Various approaches have found success in allowing detectors that consider different aspects of the same underlying concept to train each other. Computers are able to take noisy and weak supervision and extract the most value out of that supervision by considering the idea that the true underlying, real-world concept can be described in multiple different ways. For example, while language alone is not enough to characterize online harassment, considering language certainly can provide a characterization close to the true idea. Analogously, considering social structure alone is not enough to characterize online harassment, but social structure can help describe it. Therefore, the intuition is that good models that describe online harassment using either language or social structure should tend to agree with each other, while bad models for each have no reason to agree with each other.

So far, we have discussed challenges presented by the need for more data-efficient approaches and the need for online harassment detectors to consider multiple aspects of the concept. Fortunately, these challenges complement each other to suggest a strategy toward a technological solution. Online social interaction data is inherently multimodal, in the sense that it is captured through different data representations or modes. This multi-modality actually enables weak supervision to successfully train machine learning models.

In this chapter, we describe one approach for weakly supervised machine learning of online harassment detectors, which we call *participant-vocabulary consistency* (PVC). This method was introduced in our paper at the 2017 IEEE/ACM International Conference on Advances in Social Network Analysis and Mining (ASONAM) Raisi and Huang (2017b). We present the method here as an example of emerging approaches that will begin to make machine learning tools more feasible for tasks involving harassment detection. We describe experiments demonstrating the effectiveness of PVC, and we additionally describe new analyses of the sensitivity of machine-learned detectors to social group profiling. Finally, we conclude with discussion of where machine-learning-based automated detection fits into the role technology can play in mitigating the harm of online harassment.

2.2 Related Work

We briefly review some work related to the methods we describe here. The main relevant bodies of knowledge are other machine learning approaches for detecting online harassment and other existing knowledge on machine learning with weak supervision. We summarize some of the literature on these topics below.

2.2.1 Machine Learning for Detection of Online Harassment and Related Phenomena

A variety of machine learning methods have been proposed for detection of online harassment. These methods mostly approach the problem by training detectors with full supervision. Many of the research contributions in this space involve the specialized design of language features for supervised learning. Feature design is complementary to our approach and could be seamlessly incorporated into our framework.

Many contributions consider specially designed features based on known topics used in bullying (Dadvar et al. 2012; Chen et al. 2012; Dinakar et al. 2011; Reynolds et al. 2011). Others use sentiment features Yin et al. (2009), features learned by topic models Nahar et al. (2013), vulgar language expansion using string similarity Ptaszynski et al. (2010), features based on association rule techniques Margono et al. (2014), and static, social structure features Huang and Singh (2014). Researchers have applied machine learning methods to better understand social-psychological issues surrounding the idea of bullying Bellmore et al. (2015). By extracting social media posts containing the word "bully," they collect a dataset of people talking about their experiences with bullying. They also investigate different forms of bullying, why people post about bullying, and other questions.

Hosseinmardi et al. (2014a, b, 2015a, b) conducted several studies analyzing forms of cyberbullying, including harassment, on the Ask.fm and Instagram platforms. They studied negative user behavior in the Ask.fm social network, finding that properties of the interaction graph—such as in-degree and out-degree—are strongly related to the negative or positive user behaviors Hosseinmardi et al. (2014a). They compared users across Instagram and Ask.fm to see how negative user behavior varies across different venues. Based on their experiments, Ask.fm users show more negativity than Instagram users, and anonymity on Ask.fm tends to foster more negativity Hosseinmardi et al. (2014b). They also studied the detection of cyberbullying incidents over images in Instagram, focusing on the distinction between cyberbullying and cyber-aggression Hosseinmardi et al. (2015b), noting that bullying occurs over multiple interactions with particular social structures. Additionally, some studies have extensively involved firsthand accounts of young persons, yielding insights on new features for bullying detection and strategies for mitigation Ashktorab and Vitak (2016).

Related research on data-driven methods for analysis and detection of cyberviolence in general includes detection of hate speech (Warner and Hirschberg 2012; Djuric et al. 2015) and online predation McGhee et al. (2011), and the analysis of gang activity on social media Patton et al. (2016), among many other emerging projects.

2.2.2   Weakly Supervised Machine Learning

Weak supervision is a machine learning paradigm that is receiving increasing attention. With the growth of "big data," fully annotated data is inherently much more expensive to curate than unlabeled data. Machine learning algorithms are being developed to accept weak supervision, in which experts provide soft, often noisy indicators of the target concept to be learned, and the learning algorithm extrapolates from the weak supervision to form a more specified model. The intuition behind weak supervision is that the learning algorithm should be able to find patterns in the unlabeled data to integrate with the weak supervision, leading to a more refined characterization of the concept being learned.

Weakly supervised approaches have been explored for relation extraction in text (Bunescu and Mooney 2007; Mintz et al. 2009; Riedel et al. 2010; Yao et al. 2010; Hoffmann et al. 2011), especially in the domain of knowledge extraction from the Web. They have also been used for computer vision tasks such as semantic segmentation (Chen et al. 2014; Xu et al. 2014) and in automated healthcare tasks such as clinical tagging of medical conditions from electronic health records Halpern et al. (2016), both cases where human annotation is expensive. General approaches for weakly supervised learning have also been proposed for classification (Nigam et al. 2006; Zhu et al. 2014; Ravi and Diao 2015).

Various contributions have related weak supervision to co-training. Of note, Blum and Mitchell (1998) showed that one can estimate the error of an ensemble of classifiers by measuring their disagreement in a fully unsupervised manner. They proposed a method for unsupervised learning based on co-training, and these ideas have been applied to language-understanding tasks such as semantic parsing Krishnamurthy and Mitchell (2012).

A new line of research on *data programming* has produced a new paradigm for weak supervision where data scientists write labeling functions that create noisy labels Ratner et al. (2016). The approach then discovers relationships among the noisy labeling functions and is able to combine them and train data-hungry models. The data programming concept—much like our approach—is designed to help solve a critical problem in machine learning in a manner that aligns with how practitioners operate. Another related mechanism for weak supervision is *distant supervision* Shin et al. (2015), which uses external data about related real-world objects to generate weak supervision signals for the target concept. Progress on general-purpose methods for weak supervision will improve tools for automated harassment detection.

2.3   Participant-Vocabulary Consistency

Weakly supervised machine learning is motivated by the idea that it should be inexpensive for human experts to provide weak indicators of the target concept. In the case of online harassment, the annotator's task is to provide a vocabulary of phrases commonly used in harassing communications. The machine learning algorithm then takes this weak supervision and a large corpus of unlabeled social media data and extrapolates to form a richer model of harassment and estimates of harassment detections in the data.

The algorithm can be summarized as an iterative process that first uses the weak indicators to find possible instances of harassment in the data. The algorithm then uses these discovered instances to identify users who tend to be harassers or victims of harassment. The process then repeats, finding new vocabulary that is commonly used by these suspected harassers and victims. This feedback loop runs until the algorithm converges on a consistent set of scores for how much the model considers each user to be a harasser or a victim, and a set of scores for how much each vocabulary key-phrase is an indicator of harassment. The algorithm can therefore expand upon the language provided from the weak supervision to related terminology. The algorithm considers the entire communication network present in the social media data, propagating its estimates of harassment roles through the messaging structure and the language used in each message, leading to a joint, collective estimation of harassment roles across the network.

We use a general data representation that is applicable to a wide variety of social media platforms. To formalize the observable data from such platforms, we first consider a set of users U and a set of messages M. Each message $m \in M$ is sent from user $s(m)$ to user $r(m)$. The lookup functions s and r return the sender and receiver, respectively, of their input message. Each message m is described by a set of feature occurrences $f(m) := \{x_k, \ldots, x_\ell\}$. Each feature represents the existence of some descriptor in the message. In our experiments and in many natural instantiations of this model, these descriptors represent the presence of n-grams in the message text, so we will interchangeably refer to them as vocabulary features.

For example, if m is a Twitter message from user @alice with the text "@bob hello world", then

$$s(m) = \text{@alice}, \quad r(m) = \text{@bob}$$
$$f(m) = \{\text{hello, world, hello world}\}.$$

In this representation, a dataset can contain multiple messages from or to any user, and multiple messages involving the same pair of users. For example, @alice may send more messages to @bob, and they may contain completely different features.

2.3.1 Model Details

To model harassment roles, we attribute each user u_i with a harasser score h_i and a victim score v_i. The harasser score encodes how much our model believes a user has a tendency to harass others, and the victim score encodes how much our model believes a user has a tendency to be harassed. We attribute to each feature x_k a harassment-vocabulary score w_k, which encodes how much the presence of that feature indicates an instance of harassment.

For each message sent from user u_i to user u_j, we use an additive *participant score* combining the sender's harasser score and the receiver's victim score $(h_i + v_j)$. The more the model believes u_i is a harasser and u_j is a victim, the more it should believe this message is an instance of harassment. To predict the harassment score for each interaction, we combine the total average word score of the message with the participant score:

$$\underbrace{\left(h_{s(m)} + v_{r(m)}\right)}_{\text{participant score}} + \underbrace{\frac{1}{|f(m)|} \sum_{k \in f(m)} w_k}_{\text{vocabulary score}} . \tag{2.1}$$

We then define a regularized objective function that penalizes disagreement between the participant-based harassment score and each of the message's vocabulary-based harassment scores:

$$J(\mathbf{h}, \mathbf{v}, \mathbf{w}) = \frac{\lambda}{2} \left(||\mathbf{h}||^2 + ||\mathbf{v}||^2 + ||\mathbf{w}||^2 \right) +$$

$$\frac{1}{2} \sum_{m \in M} \left(\sum_{k \in f(m)} (h_{s(m)} + v_{r(m)} - w_k)^2 \right) . \tag{2.2}$$

The learning algorithm seeks settings for the $\mathbf{h}$, $\mathbf{v}$, and $\mathbf{w}$ vectors that are consistent with the observed social data and initial *seed features*. For simplicity, we use a shared regularization parameter for the word scores, harasser scores, and victim scores, but it is easy to use separate parameters for each parameter vector. We found in our experiments that the learner is not very sensitive to these hyperparameters, so we use a single parameter λ. We constrain the seed features to have a high score and minimize Eq. (2.2), i.e.,

$$\min_{\mathbf{h}, \mathbf{v}, \mathbf{w}} J(\mathbf{h}, \mathbf{v}, \mathbf{w}; \lambda) \text{ s.t. } w_k = 1.0, \; \forall k : x_k \in S, \tag{2.3}$$

where S is the set of seed phrases. By solving for these parameters, we optimize the consistency of scores computed based on the participants in each social interaction as well as the vocabulary used in each interaction. Thus, we refer to this model as the participant-vocabulary consistency model.

2.3.2 Learning the Parameters

The type of optimization necessary for solving our learning objective is reminiscent of those used in many recommender systems Koren et al. (2009). It iteratively fits the parameters for different components of the model, treating the rest of the parameters as fixed constants. This iteration repeats until the system reaches a stable state, which represents a local optimum. The objective function in Eq. (2.2) is not jointly convex, but it is convex when optimizing each parameter vector in isolation. In fact, the form of the objective yields an efficient, closed-form minimization for each vector. The minimum for each parameter vector considering the others constant can be found by solving for their zero-gradient conditions. The solution for optimizing with respect to the harasser score vector $\mathbf{h}$ is

$$\underset{h_i}{\arg\min} \, J = \frac{\displaystyle\sum_{m \in M \mid s(m)=i} \left(\sum_{k \in f(m)} w_k - |f(m)| v_{r(m)} \right)}{\lambda + \displaystyle\sum_{m \in M \mid s(m)=i} |f(m)|}, \tag{2.4}$$

where the set $\{m \in M \mid s(m) = i\}$ is the set of messages that are sent by user i, and $|f(m)|$ is the number of n-grams in the message m. The update for the victim scores $\mathbf{v}$ is analogously

$$\underset{v_j}{\arg\min} \, J = \frac{\displaystyle\sum_{m \in M \mid r(m)=j} \left(\sum_{k \in f(m)} w_k - |f(m)| h_i \right)}{\lambda + \displaystyle\sum_{m \in M \mid r(m)=j} |f(m)|}, \tag{2.5}$$

where the set $\{m \in M \mid r(m) = j\}$ is the set of messages sent to user j. Finally, the update for the $\mathbf{w}$ vector is

$$\underset{w_k}{\arg\min} \, J = \frac{\displaystyle\sum_{m \in M \mid k \in f(m)} \left(h_{r(m)} + v_{s(m)} \right)}{\lambda + |\{m \in M \mid k \in f(m)\}|}, \tag{2.6}$$

where the set $\{m \in M \mid k \in f(m)\}$ is the set of messages that contain the kth feature or n-gram.

Each of these minimizations solves a least-squares problem, and when the parameters are updated according to these formulas, the objective is guaranteed to decrease if the current parameters are not a local minimum. Since each formula of the $\mathbf{h}$, $\mathbf{v}$, and $\mathbf{w}$ vectors does not depend on other entries within the same vector, each full vector can be updated in parallel. Thus, we use an alternating least-squares optimization procedure, summarized in Algorithm 1, which iteratively updates each of these vectors until convergence.

Algorithm 1 outputs the harasser and victim scores of all the users and the harassment-vocabulary score of all n-grams. The algorithm is efficient enough to allow it to scale to large datasets. If $|M|$ is the total number of messages and $|W|$ is

---

Algorithm 1 Participant-Vocabulary Consistency using Alternating Least Squares

procedure PVC(h, v, w, λ)

    Initialize $\mathbf{h}$, $\mathbf{v}$, and $\mathbf{w}$ to default values (e.g., 0.1).

    while not converged **do**

        $\mathbf{h} = \left[\arg\min_{h_i} J\right]_{i=1}^{n}$ ▷ update $\mathbf{h}$ using Eq. (2.4)

        $\mathbf{v} = \left[\arg\min_{v_i} J\right]_{i=1}^{n}$ ▷ update $\mathbf{v}$ using Eq. (2.5)

        $\mathbf{w} = \left[\arg\min_{w_k} J\right]_{k=1}^{|\mathbf{w}|}$ ▷ update $\mathbf{w}$ using Eq. (2.6)

    return ($\mathbf{h}, \mathbf{v}, \mathbf{w}$)   ▷ return the final bully, victim score of users and the score of n-grams

---

the total number of n-grams, the time complexity of each alternating least-squares update for the harasser score, victim score, and word score is $O(|M| \cdot |W|)$. No extra space is needed beyond the storage of these vectors and the raw data. Moreover, sparse matrices can be used to perform the indexing necessary to compute these updates efficiently and conveniently, at no extra cost in storage, and the algorithm can be easily implemented using high-level, optimized sparse matrix libraries.

2.4 Experiments

We demonstrate participant-vocabulary consistency on the task of harassment detection using three social media datasets. We evaluate the success of weakly supervised methods on the task of detecting harassing conversations and on discovering new indicators of harassment. To generate a seed set, we collect a dictionary of offensive language—swear words, slurs, etc.—listed on NoSwearing.com NoSwearing (2016). This dictionary contains 3,461 offensive unigrams and bigrams. We then compare human annotations against detections by PVC and baseline methods. We also compare each method's ability to discover new bullying vocabulary against the opinions of human annotators. Finally, we perform qualitative analysis of the behavior of PVC.

We use cross-validation to set PVC's regularization parameter λ. We evaluate the performance of PVC on the task of discovering held-out vocabulary, assuming that the seed words from NoSwearing.com are reasonable indicators of harassment. We randomly partition the set of seed words into three complementary subsets, using each as a seed set in every run. For each split, PVC is given the entire unlabeled social media data corpus, and we measure how well PVC recovers the held-out words, i.e., target words, by ranking all non-seed words by their learned vocabulary score ($\mathbf{w}$). We measure the average area under the receiver order characteristic curve (AUC) for target-word recovery with different values of λ from 0.001 to 20.0. The best value of λ should yield the largest AUC. The average AUC we obtain using these values of λ for three random splits of our Twitter data (described below) ranged between 0.905 and 0.928, showing minor sensitivity to this parameter. Based on these results, we set $\lambda = 8$ in our experiments, and for consistency with this parameter search, we run our experiments using one of these random splits of the seed set. Thus, we begin with just over a thousand seed phrases, randomly sampled from our full list.

2.4.1 Data Processing

We use data from Ask.fm, Instagram, and Twitter, three social networking venues that have been reported to be common venues for cyberbullying and harassment (Ditch 2013; Bifet and Frank 2010; Silva et al. 2013). We describe the datasets we used from these sources in the following paragraphs.

We used a subsample of the **Ask.fm** dataset collected by Hosseinmardi et al. (2014b). Ask.fm is a social question-answering site, where users can post questions on their profiles or other users' profiles to be answered. The original data was collected using snowball sampling, collecting user profile information and a complete list of answered questions. Since our model calculates the harasser and victim scores for every user, it does not readily handle anonymous users, so we removed all the question-answer pairs where the identity of the question poster is hidden. Furthermore, because of the nature of question-answering sites, many of the posts were simply the word "thanks" and nothing else, so we removed these cases. Our filtered dataset contains 260,800 users and 2,863,801 question-answer pairs.

We also used a subset of the **Instagram** dataset collected by Hosseinmardi et al. (2015a), who identified Instagram user IDs using snowball sampling starting from a random seed node. For each user, they collected all the media the user shared, users who commented on the media, and the comments posted on the media. Our Instagram data contains 3,829,756 users and 9,828,760 messages.

We designed a procedure to collect relevant data from **Twitter**'s public API. Our process for collecting our Twitter dataset was as follows:

(1) Using our collected offensive-language dictionary, we extracted tweets containing these words posted between November 1, 2015, and December 14, 2015. For every curse word, we extracted 700 tweets.
(2) Since the extracted tweets in the previous step were often part of a conversation, we extracted all the conversations and reply chains these tweets were part of.
(3) To avoid collecting skewed a dataset, we applied snowball sampling to expand the size of the dataset, gathering tweets on a wide range of topics. To do so, we randomly selected 1,000 users; then for 50 of their followers, we extracted their most recent 200 tweets. We continued expanding to followers of followers in a depth-10 breadth-first search.

Many users had small follower counts, so we needed a depth of 10 to obtain a reasonable number of these background tweets. We filtered the data to include only public, directed messages, i.e., @-messages. And we removed all retweets and duplicate tweets. After this preprocessing, our Twitter data contains 180,355 users and 296,308 tweets.

For all three datasets, we processed the message text by removing emojis, mentions, and all types of URLs, punctuation, and stop words.

2.4.2 Baselines

The task we are considering is one where the harassment detector must use weak supervision to identify instances of harassment. To measure the success of PVC on this task, we compare against a variety of other approaches. The most straightforward of these approaches is to treat the seed phrase set as a key-phrase search query.

Since much of PVC's modeling power comes from the inference of user roles, we compare against a baseline method that extracts participant and vocabulary scores using only the seed query, but does not iteratively adapt the vocabulary as PVC does. For each user, we compute a harasser score as the fraction of outgoing messages that contain at least one seed term over all messages sent by that user, and a victim score as the fraction of all incoming messages that contain at least one seed term over all messages received by that user. For each message, the participant score is the summation of the sender's harasser score and the receiver's victim score. We also assign each message a vocabulary score computed as the fraction of seed terms in the message. As in PVC, we sum the participant and vocabulary scores to compute the score of each message. We refer to this method in our results as the *naive participant* method.

We also compare against standard approaches for expanding search queries. This expansion is important for improving the recall of detections, since the seed set may not include new slang or may exclude indicators for forms of harassment the expert annotators neglected. We compare PVC to two standard heuristic approaches for growing a vocabulary from an initial seed query. The *co-occurrence* (CO) approach extracts all messages containing any of the seed words and considers any other words in these messages to be new, relevant key-phrases. *Dynamic query expansion* (DQE) is a more robust variation of co-occurrence that iteratively grows a query dictionary by considering both co-occurrence and frequency Ramakrishnan et al. (2014). We use a variation based on phrase relevance. Starting from the seed query, DQE first extracts the messages containing seed phrases; then for every term in the extracted messages, it computes a relevance score (based on Lavrenko and Croft 2001) as the rate of occurrence in relevant messages: relevance$(w_i, d, D) = |d \in D : w_i \in d|/|D|$, where $|D|$ indicates the number of documents (in our case, messages) with at least one seed term. Next, DQE picks k of the highest-scoring keywords for the second iteration. It continues this process until the set of keywords and their relevance scores become stable. Because DQE seeks more precise vocabulary expansion by limiting the added words with a parameter k, we expect it to be a more precise baseline, but in the extreme, it will behave similarly to the co-occurrence baseline. In our experiments, we use $k = 4,000$.

2.4.3 Human Annotation Comparisons

Since our learning setting is weakly supervised, we evaluate the detections made by our approach and the baselines by asking human annotators to manually inspect them. We asked crowdsourcing workers from Amazon Mechanical Turk to evaluate the outputs of the various approaches from two perspectives: the discovery of cyber-bullying relationships and the discovery of additional language indicators. First, we extracted the 100 directed user pairs most indicated to be bullying by each method. For the PVC and naive-participant methods, we averaged the combined participant and vocabulary scores, as in Eq. (2.1), of all messages from one user to the other. For the dictionary-based baselines, we scored each user pair by the concentration of detected harassment words in messages between the pair. Then we collected all inter-actions between each user pair in our data. We showed the annotators the anonymized conversations and asked them, "Do you think either user 1 or user 2 is harassing the other?" The annotators indicated either "yes," "no," or "uncertain." We collected five annotations per conversation.

To evaluate the ability of the methods to identify new harassment indicators, we asked the annotators to rate the 1,000 highest-scoring terms from each method, excluding the seed words. These represent newly discovered vocabulary the meth-ods believe to be indicators of harassment. For co-occurrence, we randomly selected 1,000 co-occurring terms among the total co-occurring phrases. We asked the annota-tors, "Do you think use of this word or phrase is a potential indicator of harassment?" We collected five annotations per key-phrase.

In Fig. 2.2, we plot the precision@k of the top 100 interactions for each dataset and each method. The precision@k is the proportion of the top k interactions returned by each method that the majority of annotators agreed were harassment. For each of the five annotators, we score a positive response as $+1$, a negative response as -1, and an uncertain response as 0. We sum these annotation scores for each interaction, and we consider the interaction to be harassment if the score is greater than or equal to 3. In the Ask.fm data, PVC significantly dominates the other methods for all thresholds. On the Twitter data, PVC is better than baselines until approximately interaction 70, when it gets close to the performance of the naive-participant baseline. In the Instagram data, PVC is below the precision of the naive-participation score until around interaction 65, but after that it improves to be the same as naive-participant. Co-occurrence, while simple to implement, appears to expand the dictionary too liberally, leading to very poor precision. DQE expands the dictionary more selectively, but still leads to worse precision than using the seed set alone.

In Fig. 2.3, we plot the precision@k for indicators that the majority of annota-tors agreed were indicators of bullying. On all three datasets, PVC detects bullying words significantly more frequently than the two baselines, again demonstrating the importance of the model's simultaneous consideration of the entire communication network.

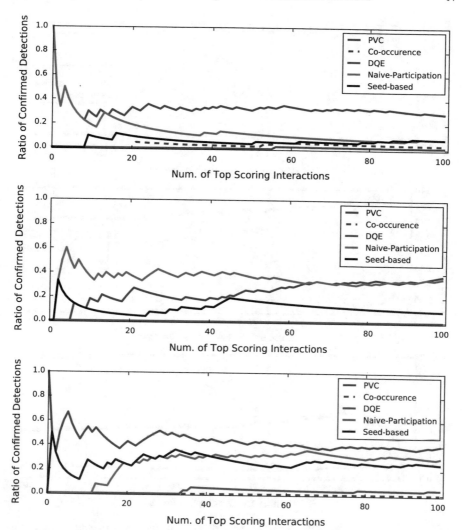

Fig. 2.2 Precision@k for bullying interactions on Ask.fm (top), Instagram (middle), and Twitter (bottom)

These evaluations suggest that the iterative process that seeks to make participant-based and vocabulary-based detection agree with each other enables improved detection of harassment over more naive query-based methods. The amount of human effort is similar to running a search query, but the PVC algorithm is able to consider the coherence of the social concept of online harassment and how individuals tend to play particular roles in the behavior to make more accurate detections.

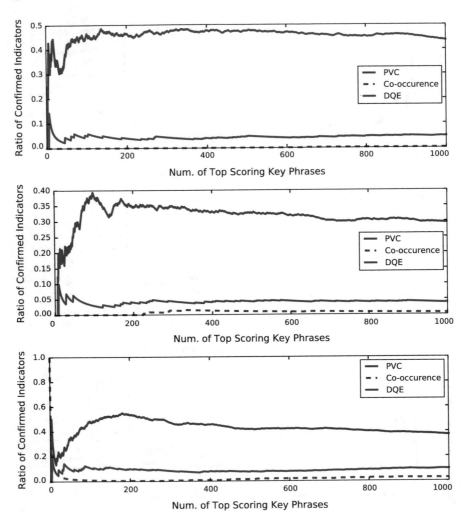

Fig. 2.3 Precision@k for bullying phrases on Ask.fm (top), Instagram (middle), and Twitter (bottom)

Table 2.1 Color-coded bullying bigrams detected in Ask.fm data by PVC and baselines. Terms are categorized according to the aggregate score of annotations. "Bullying" (2 or greater), "Likely Bullying" (1), "Uncertain" (0), and "Not Bullying" (negative) bigrams are shown in red, orange, gray, and blue, respectively

Method	Detected Bullying Words Color-Coded by Annotation: Bullying, Likely Bullying, Uncertain, Not Bullying
PVC	oreo nice, massive bear, bear c*ck, f*cking anus, ure lucky, f*g f*g, d*ck b*tch, ew creep, f*cking bothering, rupture, f*cking p*ssy, support gay, house f*ggot, family idiot, b*tch b*tch, p*ssy b*tch, loveeeeeee d*ck, f*cking c*nt, penis penis, gross bye, taste nasty, f*cking f*cking, dumb hoe, yellow attractive, b*tch p*ssy, songcried, songcried lika, lika b*tch, b*tch stupid, um b*tch, f*cking obv, nice butt, rate f*g, f*cking stupid, juicy red, soft juicy, f*cking d*ck, cm punk, d*ck p*ssy, stupid f*cking, gay bestfriend, eat d*ck, ihy f*g, gay gay, b*tch f*cking, dumb wh*re, s*ck c*ck, gay bi, fight p*ssy, stupid hoe
DQE	lol, haha, love, tbh, hey, yeah, good, kik, ya, talk, nice, pretty, idk, text, hahaha, rate, omg, xd, follow, xx, ty, funny, cute, people, cool, f*ck, best, likes, ily, sh*t, beautiful, perfect, girl, time, going, hot, truth, friends, lmao, answers, hate, ik, thoughts, friend, day, gonna, ma, gorgeous, anon, school
CO	bby, ana, cutie, ikr, ja, thnx, mee, profile, bs, feature, plz, age, add, pls, wat, ka, favourite, s*cks, si, pap, promise, mooi, hii, noo, nu, blue, ben, ook, mn, merci, meh, men, okk, okayy, hbu, zelf, du, dp rate, mooie, fansign, english, best feature, basketball, meisje, yesss, tyy, shu, een, return, follow follow

2.4.4 Qualitative Analysis

We examine a variety of the outputs from the PVC algorithm to qualitatively analyze its behavior. First, we examine the vocabulary it discovers beyond the initial seed set and compare against the vocabulary discovered by the more naive query-expansion approaches. We analyzed the 1,000 highest-scoring, non-seed terms produced by PVC, DQE, and co-occurrence and categorized them based on the annotations. Tables 2.1, 2.2, and 2.3 list the first 50 words (manually censored to obscure especially offensive terms) for Ask.fm, Instagram, and Twitter. Using a scoring system of +1 for when an annotator believes the word is a bullying indicator, 0 when an annotator is uncertain, and −1 when an annotator believes the word is not a bullying indicator, we print a word in red if it scored 2 or greater, orange if it scored a 1, gray if it scored a 0, and blue if it scored any negative value. The fact that there are more red terms in PVC's top phrases suggests that it is capable of detecting new slang that the annotators agreed were reasonable to use as harassment indicators. On the other hand, the expanded vocabulary includes many examples of irrelevant phrases, so there is much room for improvement.

Table 2.2 Color-coded bullying bigrams detected in Instagram data by PVC and baselines

Method	Detected Bullying Words Color-Coded by Annotation: Bullying, Likely Bullying, Uncertain, Not Bullying
PVC	b*tch yas, yas b*tch, b*tch reported, *ss *ss, treated ariana, kitty warm, warm kitty, chicken butt, happy sl*t, jenette s*cking, kitty sleepy, follower thirsty, ariana hope, *ss b*tch, tart deco, sleepy kitty, hatejennette, *ss hoe, b*tch b*tch, sl*t hatejennette, pays leads, deco, happy kitty, fur happy, black yellow, bad *ss, bad b*tch, yellow black, pur pur, kitty pur, black black, d*ck b*tch, boss *ss, b*tch s*ck, soft kitty, nasty *ss, kitty purr, stupid *ss, *sss *ss, stupid b*tch, puff puff, bad bad, b*tch *ss, *ss foo, d*ck *ss, ignorant b*tch, hoe hoe, *ss bio, nasty b*tch, big d*ck
DQE	love, lol, cute, omg, beautiful, haha, good, nice, amazing, pretty, happy, wow, awesome, great, cool, perfect, best, guys, day, time, hahaha, gorgeous, god, pic, girl, people, birthday, tttt, life, man, follow, hair, lmao, hot, yeah, going, happy birthday, wait, better, hope, picture, baby, hey, sexy, ya, damn, sh*t, work, adorable, f*ck
CO	hermoso, sdv, sigo, troco, meu deus, troco likes, lindaaa, eu quero, fofo, perfect body, kinds, music video, girls love, allow, lls, spray, shoulders, wait guys, jet, niners, good sh*t, wie, damnnn, garden, post comments, stalk, rail, captain, belieber, sweety, convo, orders, smash, hahaha true, good girl, spider, au, best night, emotional, afternoon, gallery, degrees, hahahahahahah, oui, big time, por favor, beautiful photo, artwork, sb, drooling

We manually inspected some of the interactions PVC identified in the three datasets and found various categories of note. The first and most common category

Table 2.3 Color-coded bullying bigrams detected in Twitter data by PVC and baselines

Method	Detected Bullying Words Color-Coded by Annotation: Bullying, Likely Bullying, Uncertain, Not Bullying
PVC	singlemost biggest, singlemost, delusional prick, existent *ss, biggest jerk, karma bites, hope karma, jerk milly, rock freestyle, jay jerk, worldpremiere, existent, milly rock, milly, freestyle, *ss b*tch, d*ck *ss, *ss hoe, b*tch *ss, adore black, c*mming f*ck, tgurl, tgurl sl*t, black males, rt super, super annoying, sl*t love, bap babyz, love rt, f*ck follow, babyz, jerk *ss, love s*ck, hoe *ss, c*nt *ss, *ss c*nt, stupid *ss, bap, karma, *ss *ss, f*ggot *ss, weak *ss, bad *ss, nasty *ss, lick *ss, d*ck s*cker, wh*re *ss, ugly *ss, s*ck *ss, f*ck *ss
DQE	don, lol, good, amp, f*ck, love, sh*t, ll, time, people, yeah, ve, man, going, f*cking, head, didn, day, better, free, ya, face, great, hey, best, follow, haha, big, happy, gt, hope, check, gonna, thing, nice, feel, god, work, game, doesn, thought, lmao, life, c*ck, help, lt, play, hate, real, today
CO	drink sh*tfaced, juuust, sh*tfaced tm4l, tm4l, tm4l br, br directed, subscribe, follow check, music video, check youtube, checkout, generate, comment subscribe, rt checkout, ada, follback, marketing, featured, unlimited, pls favorite, video rob, beats amp, untagged, instrumentals, spying, download free, free beats, absolutely free, amp free, free untagged, submit music, untagged beats, free instrumentals, unlimited cs, creative gt, free exposure, followers likes, music chance, soundcloud followers, spying tool, chakras, whatsapp spying, gaming channel, telepaths, telepaths people, youtube gaming, dir, nightclub, link amp, mana

contained conversations that were clearly toxic and possible harassment based on the prevalence of highly charged, offensive language. Two such examples follow.

User1:	lmao don't call me a b*tch. I don't know you, the tweet was just funny, b*tch
User2:	Then you @ her and not me you little instigating *ss irrelevant hoe. Run along, b*tch
User1:	Hy you mad? Lmao you're irrelevant as f*ck, b*tch. You can get out of my mentions you're a piece of sh*t
User2:	Whden dumb random *ss irrelevant hoes mention me, they get response. Now get your c*nt *ss on somewhere bruh

User1:	IS A FAKE *SS B*TCH WHO DOESNT DESERVE A MAN
User2:	b*tch you gave a BJ to a manager at McDonalds so you could get a free BigMac
User1:	B*TCH YOU SRE CONFUSING ME WITH YOUR MOTHER
User2:	YOUR MOM HAS BEEN IN THE PORN INDUSTRY LONGER THAN I HAVE BEEN ALIVE
User1:	B*TCH TAKE THAT BACK
User2:	TAKE WHAT BACK?
User1:	YOUR RUDE DISRESPECTFUL COMMENTS
User2:	I ONLY SEE THE TRUTH YOU HOE
User1:	TBH DONT GET ME STARTED. I CAN BREAK YOU IN TWO MINUTES
User2:	DO IT B*TCH, YOUR FAT *SS WILL GET TIRED OF TYPING IN 1 MINUTE

The second category contained conversations with little prototypical harassment language, such as the slurs from the seed query and beyond. Yet they appear to be examples of harassment. We hypothesize that PVC discovered these because of a combination of discovering new language and considering the typical roles of the conversation participants. Two such cases follow.

User1:	You don't get to call me stupid for missing my point
User2:	I said you're being stupid, because you're being stupid. Who are you to say who gets to mourn whom? Read the link
User1:	You miss my point, again, and I'm the stupid one? Look inwards, f*ckwad

User1:	Stupid she doesnt control the show she cant put it back on you idiot
User1:	She isnt going to answer you stupid
User1:	Its spelled Carly stupid
User1:	She wont answer you stupid

Finally, there were various interactions that PVC mistakenly identified as harassment, where both we and the annotators consider the interactions to be non-harassment. We grouped these false positives into five classes. First, some false positives involved users discussing other people, not addressing each other in their messages. The false positives of this type reveal the importance of considering the presence of words that specify the target of the harassing language such as "you," "you are," and "your"—words that are stripped out by our removal of common so-called stop words. One example of such a case is the following.

User1:	LOL he's so nasty, he has a banana shaped faced
User2:	Lmao . No comment
User1:	L**** is a whore
User2:	Yeah, I'm over him so he can go whore around on his new girlfriend

A second type of false positive occurs when two users are joking with each other using offensive words, which is common at least among young users. One such example is the following.

User1:	Your f*cking awesome then (:
User2:	Damn f*cking right <333333
User1:	Pretty good looking and seem cool (:
User2:	I seem f*cking awesome

A third type of false positive occurs when two users have a conversation about potentially offensive topics. In the following example mistakenly flagged by PVC, the users are discussing sexual promiscuity, and while they are not being completely civil to each other, the conversation is not necessarily an example of harassment.

User1:	If they act like hoes then they getting called hoes
User2:	That's awful thing to say
User1:	What! it's true so if a girls a hoe, acts like a hoe and cheats like a hoe she isn't a hoe?
User2:	And what exactly is a hoe? And what do you call men who cheat? Hoes too?
User1:	Lets just end this conversation because I feel like you're gonna block me soon and I'd rather not lose another friend
User2:	No, I mean, if you can say "if she act like a hoe then she gets called a hoe" then I would like to know what a hoe is
User1:	Could mean wh*re, could imply she sleeps around, could mean she's just a evil f*ck face that flirts with you and then goes

A fourth common form of false positive occurs when there is no apparent justification for the error. Negative words are not used in the conversation, nor is there any other indicator of harassment. These could be explained by spurious vocabulary learned by PVC, or by the fact that the users involved may be estimated to take on roles in harassment. One example follows, where there is nothing particularly obvious about the conversation that should indicate harassment.

User1:	Are u a vegetarian
User2:	My parents are rude and wont let me but i dont like meat rip
User1:	Same dont like it that much but cant live without chicken :/
User2:	I hate chicken what
User1:	Chicken is lyf wyd :/
User2:	The only good thing about chicken are nuggets :/
User1:	Im not demanding i love all shapes and sizes : /
User2:	Chicken is gross :/

Finally, an important category of false positives are ones based on race, gender, sexual orientation, and religion. Because harassment on social media often involves such ideas of identity, PVC will identify some messages containing keywords describing sensitive groups as harassment. These can be problematic because these words may often be used in innocuous contexts. We call these mistakes *unfair false positives*, meaning that non-bullying conversations containing sensitive keywords are falsely identified as bullying. These mistakes may unfairly impact certain social groups more than others. Two such cases follow, where these messages containing the keyword "black" were flagged seemingly incorrectly.

User1:	Owwww sexy
User1:	Lets do that
User1:	Black and yellow hard

User1:	Beef Or Chicken ? Coke Or Pepsi ? White Or Black ? Mercedes Or BMW ? Friendship Or Love ? Yummy! Or Tasty ? Traditional Or Love Marriage ? Sister Or Brother ? Action Or Comedy ? Sweet Or Sour ? Chocolate Or Vanilla ? Strawberry Or Raspberry ? Lemon Or Orange ? Money Or Health?
User2:	Chicken, coke, grey;), Mercedes, love, tasty, traditional, neither, comedy, sour, chocolate, raspberry, lemon, both probably:)

These qualitative examples illustrate that, while PVC is able to learn to identify harassment with better accuracy than naive query methods, there is plenty of room for improvement. In the next section, we describe some ongoing work to improve on PVC and open problems that we and the research community should aim to address.

2.5 Discussion, Extensions, and Open Problems

So far in this chapter, we discussed the need for machine learning algorithms that can use weak supervision to train detectors of online harassment, detailed one such approach, and demonstrated its effectiveness. We called the method the participant-vocabulary consistency approach, because it learns to identify harassment by considering the social participants as well as language used in social media interactions, seeking to make these two views of the detection task consistent with each other. This consistency enables it to be able to learn from only noisy, low-cost annotation in the form of key-phrase indicators of harassment. In addition to demonstrating its strengths, we also pointed out some of the method's weaknesses, especially in the types of incorrect detections it can make.

It is reasonable to consider our particular method to be a proof of concept of the general strategy. In the next subsection, we detail our ongoing research on extending the participant-vocabulary consistency concept. We then describe one of the most important challenges for automated harassment detection and the ethics of its deployment: fairness. We also discuss an important direction of ongoing research on how best to enable interaction between machine learning algorithms and their annotators who provide weak (or full) supervision. Finally, we discuss the role machine learning and automated detection can play in building technology that can mitigate the harm of online harassment.

2.5.1 Deep Learning

In recent years, deep learning methods have been shown to excel at text-mining tasks LeCun et al. (2015). At the same time, their notorious complexity makes their need for large-scale data severely demanding. Weak supervision can be a valuable tool for alleviating this data need.

We have begun investigating the use of deep learning models to build participant-vocabulary consistency ensembles. For each message in an unlabeled training corpus of social media data, we apply one classifier that attempts to identify harassment based on the graph nodes representing the users and another classifier that attempts to identify harassment using the language in the message. We have constructed a set of deep learning models for each participant classifier and for each language classifier. We train the classifiers to agree with one another on all unlabeled messages within the training corpus and to agree with weak supervision provided again as key-phrase indicators. Our initial results are promising Raisi and Huang (2017a), indicating that the paradigm of weak supervision by seeking consistency across representations can in fact train deep harassment detectors.

2.5.2 Fairness

As we mentioned in Sect. 2.4.4, a key concern in the development and adoption of machine learning for building harassment detectors is whether the learned detectors are fair. Machine learning can inherit or amplify biases present in training data, or it can fabricate biases that are not present in the data. Biases in this context could take the form of harassment detectors being more sensitive to harassment committed by or against particular groups of individuals, such as members of ethnic, gender, or age groups. In some cases, such imbalanced sensitivity may be warranted, for example if some identity groups are more frequently targeted by online harassment.[1] However, more likely, imbalanced sensitivity manifests itself as a tendency to make more false detections on particular identity groups.

Recent reactions to a Google Jigsaw-released tool for quantifying toxicity of online conversations (see, e.g., Sinders 2017) have highlighted such concerns. Various users have found examples where the tool flags language used by or about particular groups of people, even if they are used in non-harassing statements. Sinders (2017) illustrated that the tool flagged the single-word message "arabs" as 64% similar to toxic language. Examples such as these illustrate the need for methods that can avoid treating particular identity groups unfairly.

Various machine learning researchers are actively investigating techniques to improve the fairness of machine learning methods. (See, for example, http://fatml. org and http://fatconference.org.) As machine learning is being more readily incorporated into systems that directly affect human lives, tools to measure and mitigate unfairness are becoming more important. Whether machine learning is used to help study online harassment or to attempt to mitigate its harm, the impact it may have on people's lives makes fairness a critical requirement and an imperative open question for researchers.

2.5.3 Weak Supervision Interface

One strategy for improving the performance of our learned harassment detectors is the refinement of the weak supervision. In our experiments, we used a somewhat crude approach of including a list of curated offensive language. In practice, if an analyst were interested in building a detector geared more specifically to their notion of harassment, or to a particular form of harassment, they could do so by choosing a different seed set as the weak supervision. Upon examining the results from the learning procedure, the analyst could then adjust the seed set to guide the learning toward the desired concept. This type of procedure is often thought of as "human-in-the-loop machine learning," and designing the human-computer interface to facilitate such interaction between the human expert and the machine learning algorithm is an important task.

---

[1] Studies have found evidence that certain identity groups do experience online harassment at different rates, especially when considering different forms of harassment Duggan (2017); Lenhart et al. (2016).

2.5.4 Automated Interventions

Like many other researchers studying phenomena related to online harassment, we are motivated to conduct this research because we want to help mitigate the harm caused by this phenomenon. Online harassment and other forms of cyberbullying exist because of technology, yet there is hope that technology can help reduce or prevent the damage they inflict on society. One mode through which machine learning can help in this goal is to aid the study of online harassment. However, eventually, we believe automated detection can enable automated interventions that can help individuals involved in harassment on a case-by-case basis. But before we deploy such interventions, many questions must be answered.

What type of interventions are effective at preventing future harassment? When is it safe and useful to hide online harassment from victims? What is the harm caused by various interventions on false positive detections? Can we identify when human intervention is necessary? These are among the open questions on this topic. Answers to these open questions require studies that will benefit from interdisciplinary collaboration across sub-disciplines of computer science and various social sciences.

Despite the various unanswered questions about how best to use automated detection to benefit those affected by online harassment, it is clear that automated detection is a critical need. And machine learning—especially with weak supervision—is the technology that can enable it.

References

Ashktorab Z, Vitak J (2016) Designing cyberbullying mitigation and prevention solutions through participatory design with teenagers. In: Proceedings of the CHI conference on human factors in computing systems, pp 3895–3905

Bellmore A, Calvin AJ, Xu JM, Zhu X (2015) The five W's of bullying on Twitter: who, what, why, where, and when. Comput. Hum. Behav. 44:305–314

Bifet A, Frank E (2010) Sentiment knowledge discovery in Twitter streaming data. In: Proceedings of the international conference on discovery science, pp 1–15

Blackburn J, Kwak H (2014) STFU NOOB!: predicting crowdsourced decisions on toxic behavior in online games. In: Proceedings of the 23rd international conference on world wide web, ACM, WWW '14, pp 877–888. https://doi.org/10.1145/2566486.2567987. http://doi.acm.org/10.1145/2566486.2567987

Blum A, Mitchell T (1998) Combining labeled and unlabeled data with co-training. In: Proceedings of the conference on computational learning theory, ACM, pp 92–100

Bunescu RC, Mooney R (2007) Learning to extract relations from the web using minimal supervision. Proc. Ann. Meet. Assoc. Comput. Linguist. 45:576–583

Chen LC, Fidler S, Yuille AL, Urtasun R (2014) Beat the mturkers: automatic image labeling from weak 3D supervision. In: Proceedings of the IEEE conference on computer vision and pattern recognition, pp 3198–3205

Chen Y, Zhou Y, Zhu S, Xu H (2012) Detecting offensive language in social media to protect adolescent online safety. In: Proceedings of the international conference on social computing, pp 71–80

Dadvar M, de Jong F, Ordelman R, Trieschnigg D (2012) Improved cyberbullying detection using gender information. In: Dutch-Belgian information retrieval workshop, pp 23–25

Dinakar K, Reichart R, Lieberman H (2011) Modeling the detection of textual cyberbullying. In: ICWSM workshop on social mobile web

Ditch the Label (2013) The annual cyberbullying survey. http://www.ditchthelabelorg/

Djuric N, Zhou J, Morris R, Grbovic M, Radosavljevic V, Bhamidipati N (2015) Hate speech detection with comment embeddings. In: International conference on world wide web, pp 29–30

Duggan M (2017) Online harassment. Technical report, Pew Research Center

Halpern Y, Horng S, Sontag D (2016) Clinical tagging with joint probabilistic models. In: Proceedings of the conference on machine learning for healthcare, pp 209–225

Hoffmann R, Zhang C, Ling X, Zettlemoyer L, Weld DS (2011) Knowledge-based weak supervision for information extraction of overlapping relations. In: Proceedings of the annual meeting of the association for computational linguistics: human language technologies. Association for Computational Linguistics, pp 541–550

Hosseinmardi H, Ghasemianlangroodi A, Han R, Lv Q, Mishra S (2014a) Towards understanding cyberbullying behavior in a semi-anonymous social network. In: Proceedings of the IEEE/ACM international conference on advances in social networks analysis and mining (ASONAM), pp 244–252

Hosseinmardi H, Li S, Yang Z, Lv Q, Rafiq RI, Han R, Mishra S (2014b) A comparison of common users across Instagram and Ask.fm to better understand cyberbullying. In: Proceedings of the IEEE international conference on big data and cloud computing

Hosseinmardi H, Mattson SA, Rafiq RI, Han R, Lv Q, Mishra S (2015a) Analyzing labeled cyberbullying incidents on the Instagram social network. In: International conference on social informatics, pp 49–66

Hosseinmardi H, Mattson SA, Rafiq RI, Han R, Lv Q, Mishra S (2015b) Detection of cyberbullying incidents on the Instagram social network. Association for the Advancement of Artificial Intelligence

Huang Q, Singh VK (2014) Cyber bullying detection using social and textual analysis. In: Proceedings of the international workshop on socially-aware multimedia, pp 3–6

Koren Y, Bell R, Volinsky C (2009) Matrix factorization techniques for recommender systems. Computer 42(8):30–37

Krishnamurthy J, Mitchell TM (2012) Weakly supervised training of semantic parsers. In: Proceedings of the 2012 joint conference on empirical methods in natural language processing and computational natural language learning. Association for Computational Linguistics, pp 754–765

Lavrenko V, Croft WB (2001) Relevance based language models. In: Proceedings of the international ACM SIGIR conference on research and development in information retrieval, pp 120–127

LeCun Y, Bengio Y, Hinton G (2015) Deep learning. Nature 521(7553):436–444

Lenhart A, Ybarra M, Zickurh K, Price-Feeney M (2016) Online harassment, digital abuse, and cyberstalking in america. Technical report, Data & Society Research Institute

Margono H, Yi X, Raikundalia GK (2014) Mining Indonesian cyber bullying patterns in social networks. In: Proceedings of the Australasian computer science conference, vol 147

McGhee I, Bayzick J, Kontostathis A, Edwards L, McBride A, Jakubowski E (2011) Learning to identify internet sexual predation. Int J Electron Commer 15(3):103–122

Mintz M, Bills S, Snow R, Jurafsky D (2009) Distant supervision for relation extraction without labeled data. In: Proceedings of the joint conference of the 47th annual meeting of the ACL and the 4th international joint conference on natural language processing of the AFNLP. Association for Computational Linguistics, pp 1003–1011

Nahar V, Li X, Pang C (2013) An effective approach for cyberbullying detection. Commun. Inf. Sci. Manag. Eng. 3(5):238–247

Nigam K, McCallum A, Mitchell T (2006) Semi-supervised text classification using EM. Semi-Supervised Learning, pp 33–56

NoSwearing (2016) List of swear words & curse words. http://wwwnoswearingcom/dictionary

Patton DU, McKeown K, Rambow O, Macbeth J (2016) Using natural language processing and qualitative analysis to intervene in gang violence. arXiv:160908779

Ptaszynski M, Dybala P, Matsuba T, Masui F, Rzepka R, Araki K (2010) Machine learning and affect analysis against cyber-bullying. In: Linguistic and cognitive approaches to dialog agents symposium, pp 7–16

Raisi E, Huang B (2017a) Co-trained ensemble models for weakly supervised cyberbullying detection. In: NIPS 2017 workshop on learning with limited labeled data

Raisi E, Huang B (2017b) Cyberbullying detection with weakly supervised machine learning. In: Proceedings of the IEEE/ACM international conference on social networks analysis and mining, pp 409–416

Ramakrishnan N, Butler P, Self N, Khandpur R, Saraf P, Wang W, Cadena J, Vullikanti A, Korkmaz G, Kuhlman C, Marathe A, Zhao L, Ting H, Huang B, Srinivasan A, Trinh K, Getoor L, Katz G, Doyle A, Ackermann C, Zavorin I, Ford J, Summers K, Fayed Y, Arredondo J, Gupta D, Mares D (2014) 'Beating the news' with EMBERS: forecasting civil unrest using open source indicators. In: ACM SIGKDD conference on knowledge discovery and data mining, pp 1799–1808

Ratner AJ, De Sa CM, Wu S, Selsam D, Ré C (2016) Data programming: creating large training sets, quickly. Adv Neural Inf Process Syst 29:3567–3575

Ravi S, Diao Q (2015) Large scale distributed semi-supervised learning using streaming approximation. arXiv:151201752

Reynolds K, Kontostathis A, Edwards L (2011) Using machine learning to detect cyberbullying. In: Proceedings of the international conference on machine learning and applications and workshops (ICMLA), vol 2. pp 241–244

Riedel S, Yao L, McCallum A (2010) Modeling relations and their mentions without labeled text. In: Joint European conference on machine learning and knowledge discovery in databases. Springer, pp 148–163

Shin J, Wu S, Wang F, De Sa C, Zhang C, Ré C (2015) Incremental knowledge base construction using DeepDive. Proc VLDB Endow 8(11):1310–1321

Silva TH, de Melo PO, Almeida JM, Salles J, Loureiro AA (2013) A picture of Instagram is worth more than a thousand words: workload characterization and application. DCOSS, pp 123–132

Sinders C (2017) Toxicity and tone are not the same thing: analyzing the new Google API on toxicity, PerspectiveAPI. https://medium.com/@carolinesinders/toxicity-and-tone-are-not-the-same-thing-analyzing-the-new-google-api-on-toxicity-perspectiveapi-14abe4e728b3. https://medium.com/@carolinesinders/toxicity-and-tone-are-not-the-same-thing-analyzing-the-new-google-api-on-toxicity-perspectiveapi-14abe4e728b3

Warner W, Hirschberg J (2012) Detecting hate speech on the world wide web. In: Workshop on language in social media, pp 19–26

Xu J, Schwing AG, Urtasun R (2014) Tell me what you see and I will show you where it is. In: Proceedings of the IEEE conference on computer vision and pattern recognition, pp 3190–3197

Yao L, Riedel S, McCallum A (2010) Collective cross-document relation extraction without labelled data. In: Proceedings of the 2010 conference on empirical methods in natural language processing. Association for Computational Linguistics, pp 1013–1023

Yin D, Xue Z, Hong L, Davison BD, Kontostathis A, Edwards L (2009) Detection of harassment on Web 2.0. Content Analysis in the WEB 20

Zhu J, Mao J, Yuille AL (2014) Learning from weakly supervised data by the expectation loss SVM (e-SVM) algorithm. In: Advances in neural information processing systems, pp 1125–1133

Chapter 3
Bridging the Gaps: Multi Task Learning for Domain Transfer of Hate Speech Detection

Zeerak Waseem, James Thorne and Joachim Bingel

Abstract Accurately detecting hate speech using supervised classification is dependent on data that is annotated by humans. Attaining high agreement amongst annotators though is difficult due to the subjective nature of the task, and different cultural, geographic and social backgrounds of the annotators. Furthermore, existing datasets capture only single types of hate speech such as sexism or racism; or single demographics such as people living in the United States, which negatively affects the recall when classifying data that are not captured in the training examples. End users of websites where hate speech may occur are exposed to risk of being exposed to explicit content due to the shortcomings in the training of automatic hate speech detection systems where unseen forms of hate speech or hate speech towards unseen groups are not captured. In this paper, we investigate methods for bridging differences in annotation and data collection of abusive language tweets such as different annotation schemes, labels, or geographic and cultural influences from data sampling. We consider three distinct sets of annotations, namely the annotations provided by Waseem (2016), Waseem and Hovy (2016), and Davidson et al. (2017). Specifically, we train a machine learning model using a multi-task learning (MTL) framework, where typically some auxiliary task is learned alongside a main task in order to gain better performance on the latter. Our approach distinguishes itself from most previous work in that we aim to train a model that is robust across data originating from different distributions and labeled under differing annotation guidelines, and that we understand these different datasets as different learning objectives in the way that classical work in multi-task learning does with different tasks. Here, we experiment with using fine-grained tags for annotation. Aided by the predictions in our models

---

All the authors contributed equally.

Z. Waseem (✉) · J. Thorne
University of Sheffield, Sheffield, UK
e-mail: z.w.butt@sheffield.ac.uk

J. Thorne
e-mail: j.thorne@sheffield.ac.uk

J. Bingel
University of Copenhagen, Copenhagen, Denmark
e-mail: bingel@di.ku.dk

© Springer International Publishing AG, part of Springer Nature 2018
J. Golbeck (ed.), *Online Harassment*, Human–Computer Interaction Series,
https://doi.org/10.1007/978-3-319-78583-7_3

as well as the baseline models, we seek to show that it is possible to utilize distinct domains for classification as well as showing how cultural contexts influence classifier performance as the datasets we use are collected either exclusively from the U.S. Davidson et al. (2017) or collected globally with no geographic restriction (Waseem 2016; Waseem and Hovy 2016). Our choice for a multi-task learning set-up is motivated by a number of factors. Most importantly, MTL allows us to share knowledge between two or more objectives, such that we can leverage information encoded in one dataset to better fit another. As shown by Bingel and Søgaard (2017) and Martínez Alonso and Plank (2017), this is particularly promising when the auxiliary task has a more coarse-grained set of labels in comparison to the main task. Another benefit of MTL is that it lets us learn lower-level representations from greater amounts of data when compared to a single-task setup. This, in connection with MTL being known to work as a regularizer, is not only promising when it comes to fitting the training data, but also helps to prevent overfitting, especially when we have to deal with small datasets.

Keywords Multi-task learning · Abusive language detection · Social media analysis · Domain transfer

3.1 Introduction

With the growing amount of user-generated content online, issues such as online abuse become more important to tackle as they affect a great number of people. A recent study undertaken by the Pew Research Center found that 73% of online adult users had witnessed online harassment, and 40% had been personally targeted (Pew Research Center 2017). Given staggering numbers such as these, it is clear that current methods of detecting abuse deployed on internet platforms are not effective in shielding users from witnessing or experiencing these forms of violence or harassment.

Alongside the pressure generated by public outcry (Crawford and Gillespie 2014), multiple government agencies have applied political pressure on social media companies to tackle the threat of online hate speech and abuse (The Guardian 2017). For example: the British Home Office created an action plan to deal with hate crime, in which online hate speech is explicitly mentioned (Home Office 2016); Germany has introduced a €50 million fine for social media companies systematically failing to remove hate speech within 24 h (The Guardian 2017); and the European Commission has set released a code of conduct for dealing with hate speech online (European Commission 2016).

As it stands, a vast majority of the moderation of abusive language and hate speech for these platforms is performed by human moderators, in spite of the exposure to online abuse having a profound impact on mental wellbeing (Levin 2017; Smith et al. 2008; Boeckmann and Liew 2002). Notably, two previous moderators have sued Microsoft for negligent infliction of emotional distress resulting in post traumatic stress disorder for being tasked with moderating child abuse (Levin 2017). Studies have shown the adverse effects of cyberbullying on youth (Smith et al. 2008) and negative effects on self-esteem of adults that were exposed to online hate speech (Boeckmann and Liew 2002). Exposing moderation staff to every abusive post reported on an online platform has the potential to cause harm. Not only is it possible to mitigate this risk through detection of the explicit materials using automated means, automatically detecting and auto-moderating content containing hate speech will limit exposure of offensive materials to the end users, thereby reducing risk the negative consequences. For example, it could be possible to shield children from cyberbullying.

Furthermore, correlations between increases in hate speech online and increases in hate crime have been shown Müller and Schwarz (2017). Thus, not only are online safety and mental health compromised by hate speech, but offline safety can be ensured by being able to detect such increases and alerting authorities of potential risks of increase in hate crime.

3.1.1 Hate Speech Detection

Considering the task of detecting hate speech, it is important to recall that word senses may change as the dialect, sociolect, language, and culture changes (Rahman 2012; Boyle 2001). Currently, computational methods for hate speech detection cannot and do not try to consider the influence of socio-demographic variables. Furthermore, the issue of cultural and sociodemographic influences on the data sample are not considered, nor has the consideration of how to overcome these cultural differences in datasets collection.

The influence of these issues culminate in models that are guaranteed to have poor generalization when they are applied to different socio-demographic or cultural contexts. For example, a model trained on Standard American English (SAE) on a Twitter data sample will be likely to evaluate the use of the *n-word* as being offensive when applied to a sample of tweets that are written in African American Vernacular English (AAVE) in spite of the cultural context and acceptability of the use of the word being completely different as it is likely to primarily be African Americans writing in this dialect.

A further issue that affects generalization is the data sampling and annotation methodology. When considering data samples that are collected from two similar but different cultures, hate speech directed to one particular demographic may contain targeted locutions that may only appear offensive to one community. Distinct sets of annotation guidelines may be generated that are specific to the task (Waseem 2016; Waseem and Hovy 2016; Davidson et al. 2017; Wulczyn et al. 2017). This in turn increases the barrier for combining the datasets and using them to train models on hate speech that can detect multiple forms of abuse.

Finally, given a number of datasets sampled from distinct cultural contexts, a possible approach for inducing a joint model from these might be to concatenate the datasets.[1] However, differences in size between these datasets may lead to a bias for the larger dataset, and by extension a bias for the culture captured within it. In this case, the detection of hate speech would be biased towards the cultural assumptions that this dataset makes. In contrast to simply merging datasets, multi-task learning allows us to differentiate between them while still training a common model that exploits their commonalities. Careful optimization of hyperparameters, e.g. pertaining to model topology or differing learning rates for the individual datasets, further allows us to explicitly control and correct for a potential bias, or to introduce a certain bias if we deem this desirable. We discuss multi-task learning in more detail below.

3.1.2   Multi-task Learning

In this work, we seek to address the shortcoming of the previous work by considering issues of generalizability of models to accurately classify hate speech and offensive language across datasets and cultural contexts. To tackle these problems, we make use of multi-task learning (MTL), a machine learning framework that seeks to utilize the similarities and subtle differences in annotations and datasets to improve performance on and regularize against another. To the best of our knowledge, this is the first work exploring the utility of multi-task learning for abusive language.

3.1.2.1   Motivation

Multi-task learning has its origins in the seminal works by Caruana (1993, 1998) and has since been applied to a wide range of areas in machine learning, including computer vision (Girshick 2015), bio-informatics (Ramsundar et al. 2015) and numerous subfields of natural language processing (Klerke et al. 2016; Bingel and Søgaard 2017; Martínez Alonso and Plank 2017). The core idea in multi-task learning is to train a model that generates outputs for several related tasks from a single common input. We contrast this against classical machine learning approaches where typically a model is a function from one input to a single output space.

The rationale behind this idea is that certain information, which is encoded in the training data of some task, may help the model generalize better when learning how to make predictions for another related task. We can draw parallels to intuitions and observations we can make about human learning: whenever we learn a new skill, we build on other skills that we may have gained earlier. For example, when learning a foreign language, we benefit from other languages that we have learned in the past. This benefit is particularly strong when the languages in question are closely related, i.e. when they share a lot of their vocabulary or structure.[2]

---

[1] After re-annotation to unify class labels, if necessary.

[2] The fact that in MTL we tend to learn both tasks simultaneously rather than in succession weakens this analogy to some degree. In fact, the simultaneous learning of two languages could actually

From a more theoretical point of view, multi-task learning has the benefit of serving as a regularizer to a certain task which allows models to be constructed that can generalize better to unseen data. More specifically, because we simultaneously optimize parameters for several tasks, the additional information that is encoded in the auxiliary tasks acts as a mechanism which prevents the model from over-fitting to the training data and becoming so specific that new data, while from the same domain and general distribution, cannot be modeled well. Previous work (Bingel and Søgaard 2017) also suggests that MTL can help a model escape from local optima, i.e. suboptimal solutions, in which it would get stuck in a single-task scenario. It has also been observed that in sequence-to-sequence architectures, the inductive bias introduced by MTL tends to have strikingly similar effects to an attention mechanism typically found in neural decoders (Bollmann et al. 2017), suggesting that MTL helps to focus attention on relevant parts of the input.

Another advantage of MTL that we exploit in this work is the ability to learn from multiple disjoint datasets. This means that we can combine datasets from more or less different tasks without the need for re-annotating the other data so that the label spaces are the same. This is because, as explained in Sect. 3.3.3, we can alternate between optimizing for different tasks during the training process. A consequence of this is that we can benefit from both an augmented data source while ensuring the model to generalize better across different kinds of input (e.g. tweets which originate from different domains and demographics).

3.1.2.2 Task Choices

While the simultaneous language learning analogy above illustrates an approach to MTL that has received relatively large popularity in natural language processing, one is often only concerned with one particular task while leveraging other tasks to help this process. In such a scenario, it is common practice to distinguish between these as a *primary task* and one or more *auxiliary tasks*.

The relative importance of the tasks that we specify influences some of the design decisions of the modeling and training our data in a multi-task environment.[3] If, for example, we are ultimately only interested in a single task, we obviously only want to optimize our model architecture (and selection of auxiliary tasks) to yield the best possible performance for that primary task. If, however, we are equally interested in good performance across all tasks, our job becomes considerably harder, as we potentially need to find a compromise between performance scores across all tasks.

As discussed in Bjerva (2017), there are two distinct approaches to choosing an auxiliary task in the language processing architecture. The first is to select one or several tasks that are similar in their linguistic annotations to the main task (e.g. to induce

---

make learning harder for humans. For a machine, however, the temporal order is less critical given its far superior memory when compared to humans.

[3] Such choices include the number and width of the hidden layers, input representations, task-specific learning rates, training schedules, among others.

better dependency parsing models by also letting the model learn syntactic categories such as parts-of-speech). The second approach is to use some non-linguistic auxiliary task whose annotations encode some signal that could be useful for the main task. A particularly interesting example is that of Klerke et al. (2016), where eye-tracking data is used to inform sentence compression.

3.1.2.3   Limits of Multi-task Learning

Multi-task learning may not always be beneficial in improving the accuracy of a classifier. Besides increasing model complexity and training time, the relation between the tasks and the respective datasets are critical for the success of MTL. Previous studies (Martínez Alonso and Plank 2017; Bingel and Søgaard 2017; Bjerva 2017) have shown systematically that MTL may lead to detrimental performance on the main task compared to training a single-task model, and have explored the conditions under which some task may aid another. While those findings are not always compatible, a common denominator of these studies is that a high entropy in the label distribution of the auxiliary task is beneficial for the main task. In other words, if the auxiliary task has very predictable labels, performance gains on the main task become less likely.

3.1.3   Utility of Multi-task Learning for Hate Speech Detection

Training a classifier to detect hate speech in a supervised setting requires training data that has been annotated by humans. Currently available resources (e.g. Waseem 2016; Waseem and Hovy 2016; Davidson et al. 2017) only capture types of hate speech, or single geographies meaning that a system to detect hate speech based on these data may not correctly identify hate speech outside of this domain. Generating new training data is expensive and exposes the annotator to explicit content. By applying a multi-task learning framework, we aim to provide a method which can easily be extended and allow for generalization onto unseen forms and targets of hate speech minimizing the cost of generating new datasets.

Considering classification confidence, our approach may be used for a automated content approval system which relies on detecting multiple forms of hate speech and abuse. In such a system, documents which are predicted to be hate speech with a high confidence may be automatically rejected, whereas comments for which the prediction has low confidence may be subject to human moderation. In this way, such a system would allow for human moderators to focus on borderline cases where human cognition and ability to consider context is required, exposing the moderators to explicit materials only when absolutely necessary.

3.2 Data

In this work, we utilize three previously published datasets for hate speech detection on Twitter data (Waseem 2016; Waseem and Hovy 2016; Davidson et al. 2017). As Waseem (2016) and Waseem and Hovy (2016) are annotated using the same definition of hate speech and are in fact partially overlapping datasets, we collapse these into a single composite dataset. Below, we give a comprehensive comparison of the three datasets and their annotation methods.

Intersectionality Before we begin with our introduction to the datasets, it is important that we define a key concept: "intersectionality". Intersectionality was originally coined by Crenshaw (1989) to describe how multiple forms of oppression may intersect and create new forms of oppression that draw on the intersecting oppressions. One important note is that being on the intersection of several forms oppression is multiplicative of the separate forms of oppression, not additive. This is seen for instance in the near invisibility of the deaths of black women perpetrated by law enforcement contrasted with the deaths of black men at the hands of law enforcement (Crenshaw 2016).

3.2.1 Understandings of "Hate Speech"

In this work, we make use of existing definitions of hate speech and offensive language and do not introduce or modify the definitions of these concepts. Rather, we provide a discussion of the annotation methods and the definitions used in the previously published datasets.

The definition of hate speech proposed in Waseem and Hovy (2016) (and subsequently in Waseem (2016)) is an 11-point test whereby a tweet is classified as hate speech if any one of the test conditions (provided in Fig. 3.1) are met. This test is based on work in the fields of Gender Studies and Critical Race Theory (CRT). Specifically, Waseem and Hovy (2016) draw on the work of McIntosh (1988) and Crenshaw (1989) to create their test. While intersectionality is not explicitly considered in Waseem and Hovy (2016), it is specifically addressed in Waseem (2016) through the selection of intersectional feminists annotators. In addition, in Waseem (2016), annotators are asked to select between "racism", "sexism", "neither", and "both" while (Waseem and Hovy 2016) do not annotate for "both".

In the criteria for a tweet to be annotated as hate speech in Waseem and Hovy (2016) and Waseem (2016), we observe there are three different groups of tests (see Table 3.1).

Considering the guidelines presented in Fig. 3.1 and the categorization in Table 3.1 in further detail, it is apparent that the aim of these guidelines was to capture a broad spectrum of the hostile experiences that oppressed groups in society face. We can visualize a quadrant describing the types of abuse these guidelines capture. Along one axis, abuse can range from explicit to implicit. And the second axis, abuse can

Fig. 3.1 11-point test for hate speech provided by Waseem and Hovy

A tweet is offensive if it

1. uses a sexist or racial slur.
2. attacks a minority.
3. seeks to silence a minority.
4. criticizes a minority (without a well founded argument).
5. promotes, but does not directly use, hate speech or violent crime.
6. criticizes a minority and uses a straw man argument.
7. blatantly misrepresents truth or seeks to distort views on a minority with unfounded claims.
8. shows support of problematic hash tags. E.g. "#BanIslam", "#whoriental", "#whitegenocide"
9. negatively stereotypes a minority.
10. defends xenophobia or sexism.
11. contains a screen name that is offensive, as per the previous criteria, the tweet is ambiguous (at best), and the tweet is on a topic that satisfies any of the above criteria.

Table 3.1 Types of hate speech in annotation guidelines of Waseem and Hovy (2016), Waseem (2016)

Group description	Test numbers
Overt aggression	1, 2, 9, 11
Defense/Support of hate speech	5, 8, 10
Subversive aggression	3, 4, 6, 7

range from directed to generalized (Waseem 2017). These two datasets (Waseem 2016; Waseem and Hovy 2016) attempt to capture both explicit and implicit hate speech that can be either directed or generalized.

In consideration of hate speech, offensive language, and more generally abusive language, it is important to note that the use of slurs and profanity may not be indicators of abuse. For instance (Rahman 2012) argues that while the *n-word* is considered an offensive term in many contexts, it is not an offensive term when used within the African American community, instead it can function as a way of communicating solidarity and framing oneself within the historical context of the oppression of African Americans in the United States, and as Rahman (2012) writes:

> Using nigga to address and refer can contribute to the construction of a speakers identity, but as in the segment above, it can also ascribe identity (Coupland 2007) to a referent or addressee as a coparticipant in the diaspora.

Waseem and Hovy's annotation method does not explicitly afford context dependent annotation, seen through test 1. As such, any use of the *n-word* may be annotated as hate speech.

In comparison (Davidson et al. 2017), employ a different definition, in which they move away from the categories of sexism and racism and employ the term "target group", which suggests a move away from the literature in Gender studies and CRT. Further, they more clearly move away from the literature by basing their definition of hate speech in the user guidelines of Facebook and Twitter. Thus, they reach a definition that erases the societal context within which hate speech occurs and those who are most frequently targets of it:

> language that is used to expresses hatred towards a targeted group or is intended to be derogatory, to humiliate, or to insult the members of the group.

Using this definition (Davidson et al. 2017), ask their annotators to distinguish between "hate speech", "offensive", and "neither". They allow for distinguishing between these by instructing their annotators to take context in which the message was sent into account and explicitly state that the use of profanity or slurs does not necessarily indicate hate speech, it may simply be offensive depending on the context. Thus they seek to reintroduce *a context* after erasing a societal context from their definition.[4] Considering the case of the *n-word* and AAVE, this annotation method allows for it not to be tagged as hate speech:

> Users were asked to think not just about the words appearing in a given tweet but about the context in which they were used. They were instructed that the presence of a particular word, however offensive, did not necessarily indicate a tweet is hate speech

Thus suggesting that while the use of a term may not be hate speech, it is still offensive and as such the *n-word* may still be flagged as offensive when used within the African-American community. Interestingly (Davidson et al. 2017), find that annotators tend to regard homophobic and racist language more likely to be hate speech whereas sexist language is more often flagged as offensive.

In this work, we do not distinguish between the two definitions and annotation methods as our aim is to investigate methods for domain adaptation from one datasets onto the other.

3.2.2   Commonalities and Differences

Here we give a brief overview of several of the commonalities and differences that are found amongst the three utilized datasets.

---

[4]Context is not defined more clearly in their paper.

In Waseem (2016) and Waseem and Hovy (2016), the same annotation guidelines are used. However, there are also key differences to be found between the two datatsets: in Waseem and Hovy (2016), two annotators label the datasets, whereas in Waseem (2016) the datasets is annotated by a group of activist intersectional feminists and another set of annotations is obtained by crowdsourcing the annotation efforts on CrowdFlower. The annotations from Waseem (2016) that we employ are the feminist annotations. In Davidson et al. (2017) the annotations are similarly crowdsourced on CrowdFlower.

All three datasets are collected from Twitter. However, while Davidson et al. (2017) collect tweets written within the United States of America, Waseem and Hovy (2016) and Waseem (2016) do not limit by geographic location. To mitigate the different geographical (and thereby cultural) biases that arise from the different sampling of these datasets is one of the contributions we seek to make with our work.

One of the key differences between the two definitions of hate speech is its positioning of within societal structures. By basing their test in Gender Studies and CRT (Waseem and Hovy 2016) implicitly place their work within the notion of structural inequality, By using charged terms such as "sexist and racial slur" and "attacks a minority", they explicitly frame their work within the context of abuse not being equally distributed amongst all groups.

On the other hand, (Davidson et al. 2017) do not frame their work within this context nor do they base their definitions in the previous literature. Given that they base their definition in the guidelines of social media companies, it is based in law, as their guidelines are placed within the context of corporations that seek to react to a user base that highlights their discomfort on their platform while simultaneously navigating the legal realities of multiple nations. One such reality is that, within the U.S.A. anti-subordination is a complicated area to navigate, and for a corporation it is unnecessary to do so when it is possible to frame within an anti-discrimination context.

Beyond these differences, another difference occurs in the targets within the "hate speech" and "racism" classes. As previously noted, annotators were more likely to find "hate speech" to be racist or homophobic speech, while sexist speech was more likely to be "offensive" (Davidson et al. 2017). Thus considering the targets of racism between the datasets, the main targets of racism in Waseem (2016) and Waseem and Hovy (2016) are Muslims, whereas the main targets of racism in Davidson et al. (2017) are African Americans.

Finally, the definitions, labels, and the annotation scheme differ slightly as covered in Sect. 3.2.1.

3.3   Model

We use a deep multi-task model to transfer knowledge between different tasks. While a number of different approaches to MTL have been explored in the past, the paradigm that has attracted most attention in deep learning and natural language processing

(NLP) in particular is *hard parameter sharing*. As its name suggests, this MTL paradigm works by sharing a subset of a model's parameters between different tasks. From a different but equivalent perspective, this is building distinct models for each task, with these models sharing (and jointly optimizing) some of their parameters.

We will compare the performance of these MTL models against simple baseline models without hard parameter sharing. We first introduce and define the multi-layer perceptron feed forward neural network and then discuss modifications that allow hard sharing of parameters.

3.3.1 Baseline Model Definition

We build a very simple feed-forward neural network without any parameter sharing. This model which takes as its input some fixed-size representation x of a tweet and computes a hidden latent representation h, which is a linear projection of x using a matrix of weights W_0 and a bias term b_0, followed by a non-linear transformation:

$$h_0 = \tanh(x W_0 + b_0) \tag{3.1}$$

For a deeper model, further hidden representations h_l are computed accordingly by stacking these layers. The respective previous hidden layer output h_{l-1} is provided as the inputs to following layer.

$$h_l = \tanh(h_{l-1} W_l + b_l) \tag{3.2}$$

The final hidden representation h_L is then used to compute the model output:

$$y = \sigma(h_L W_{out} + b_{out}) \tag{3.3}$$

Typically, σ is the softmax function which, for a k-dimensional input, normalizes the output to the range [0, 1] such that its sum is 1, representing a categorical distribution over outputs.

$$\sigma(z) = \frac{e^{z_j}}{\sum_{k=1}^{K} e^{z_k}} \tag{3.4}$$

3.3.2 Multi-task Model Definition

In Eq. 3.3, the model uses the parameters W_{out} and b_{out} to predict outputs for a single classification task. This model can be extended to predict outputs for more than one task, with the use of hard parameter sharing through the introduction of additional parameters that are specific for each task t:

$$y_t = \sigma(h_L W_t + b_t) \tag{3.5}$$

In this setup, the weights W_l and bias terms b_l are thus the parameters that are shared between the tasks and learned jointly. In constrast, the weights W_t and bias terms b_t at the output layer are specific to only one task.[5]

3.3.3 Training

Our goal is to learn parameters for the model in a supervised learning scenario using labeled training data. We assume that training data is provided as set labeled pairs of instances x_i and labels y_i: $\{(x_i, y_i)\}_{i=1}^{N}$. Training the neural network is the process of optimizing the parameters with the objective of reducing the error rate of predicted outputs $\hat{y}_i$ with respect to the annotated labels y_i.

The common way to optimize a deep learning model is via the so-called forward-backward algorithm, where we first compute some guess that the model produces for a given input example (following Eq. 3.5) and then compare this to the ground truth that is annotated in our training data. This comparison is a quantity that measures the error (or *loss*), which we then use to inform our model how strongly it should change its parameters during the backward pass in order to arrive at a better guess in the next iteration. This is typically done using some flavor of gradient descent.

A challenge that multi-task learning now poses in comparison to a classical single-task scenario is that we do not have a single loss that we can use to optimize our model, but one for every task. This raises the question of how to schedule the training across the different tasks. A common technique is to flip a coin at every training iteration (i.e. for every forward-backward pass) that decides for which task we are going to train. Depending on the outcome, we then sample a batch of training data for this task and optimize the parameters that are involved in predicting the respective output for this task. An obvious alternative to flipping a coin would be a strictly defined schedule that alternates between the tasks at every iteration, or a biased coin or schedule that gives preference to some tasks over others.

In this work, we select the coin-flipping strategy and sample training data for a task that we choose randomly with equal probability. We also follow standard practice in employing a dropout regularizer on each hidden layer during training, where we randomly set units in the hidden representations computed in Eq. 3.1 to zero with 0.2 probability.

---

[5]Note that in principle, hard parameter sharing also allows us to predict the different tasks at different depths of the model, e.g. to compute the output for task A from some hidden representation h_m and task B from h_n (with $m \neq n$). Yet another possible variation is to compute further hidden representations that are task-specific and not shared, but ultimately draw on some common lower-level representation.

3.3.4   Features

Our model utilizes fixed-size representations of the input (thereby differing from more complex deep learning architectures like recurrent or convolutional neural networks). We use two classes of features representation: (1) a Bag-of-Words representation of tweet words, bigrams and character n-grams, and (2) continuous word representations. We perform an evaluation of both in isolation as well as a combination of the two.

3.3.4.1   Bag-of-Words (BoW) Representation of Features

We construct a vocabulary of words occurring within our corpus of tweets and restrict our Bag-of-Words representation to the 5000 most frequently occurring words to prevent our model from overfitting the Zipf long tail. Each occurrence of a word is modeled as a one-hot vector that is summed for each tweet.[6]

In addition, we collect word pairs (bigrams) and concatenate these into a single word and also add the most frequent 5000 to our vocabulary. For example: "go away" would be added to the vocabulary as the token "go_away". The intuition behind this is that multi-word expressions that have a meaning that is distinct from their constituent words can be more accurately represented as its their own tokens rather than having the meaning diluted by other training examples.

As we are expecting to classify less formal and non-standard uses of English on Twitter, we must also account for word mis-spellings, alterations and colloquial style. For example: the words "yeah", "ye", "yep", "yea" and "yes" all convey similar meaning but would be represented as five distinct tokens using a Bag-of-Words model. We account for this through character segmentation as well as word segmentation. The segment "ye" appears 5 times and (in conjunction with other observed features) convey part of the meaning. We extract character bigrams (character pairs) and character trigrams (groups of three letters) and treat these as words in our vocabulary. Again, we only use the 5000 most common in our vocabulary.

3.3.4.2   Sub-word Embeddings

Rather than encoding the meaning of a word as a single one-hot vector that is the size of the vocabulary, word embeddings represent the meaning of tokens as low-dimensional real-valued vector. Typically, this vector may be between 100 and 300 dimensions. These dense meaning representations can be designed such that words which convey similar meanings or appear in similar contexts also have similar vector-based representations.

---

[6]A one-hot vector is a binary vector of indicator features that are 1 if that feature occurs in the document otherwise 0 in the feature does not occur in document.

We choose to use embeddings because this allows us to capture from different, but related concepts that occur in our data that cannot so easily be represented with the symbolic Bag-of-Words representation. For example, the encoding of a tweet containing the word 'football' will be entirely different from the a tweet containing the word 'soccer' using a BoW representation—even though these are similar concepts. Using continuous representations enables some cross talk between different concepts encountered during training. We hypothesize this may yield a classifier that is less prone to over-fitting the distribution of data that it observed during training and more accurate for unseen out of domain data.

Our multi-layer perceptron models are designed with a fixed input representation size. However, the size of tweets is variable. To train our model, we must make a fixed size representation of a variable size input. While it is normal in text classification problems perform convolutions (Kim 2014) over the input data or to train train a time-series model such as a Recurrent Neural Network, the limited size of the training data available for this task prevents use from using these techniques. Instead we a perform a pooling operation by averaging all the vectors in the tweet which is shown to yield an acceptable (yet suboptimal) performance on other text classification tasks (Socher et al. 2013).

Because language on Twitter is informal, we expect to encounter unseen words and variations of known words. Rather than using word representations, we use vector representations of sub-word units similar to morphemes (Heinzerling and Strube 2017) which will allow us to better capture common word units that are occurring in this informal language.

3.3.5   Pre-processing

We pre-process all tweets with the following steps: usernames and mentions are converted to a single type to aid anonymity and to also prevent bias in the training that may occur by learning associations between usernames rather than language. URLs and Hashtags are filtered out for the same reason. Furthermore, we convert all text to lower case and normalize numbers to a special digit symbol. Finally, all line breaks in tweets are replaced with spaces.

3.4   Experiments

To test our hypothesis, we construct three experimental configurations which we test out using our models. For our configurations we use the same two datasets described in Sect. 3.2, namely the composition of the datasets from Waseem and Hovy (2016) and Waseem (2016), and the dataset from Davidson et al. (2017). For all three configurations we test our models using each dataset as the training dataset in turn. Further, we conduct three different experiments with different features for each configuration, a lexical model using BoW, a model using only embeddings, and a model using both BoW and embeddings. In each case, we train our models on a total of 45 iterations over the available training data and finally test it using the parameters which yield the best performance on the held-out development set, preventing overfitting on the training data.

3.4.1 Baseline Models

We construct our baseline models using by training a model on a single datasets and predicting on another as has been attempted in previous work (Waseem 2016). We select this as our baseline as it has been been attempted in previous work with low success and therefore will highlight the issues with attempting to predict on one dataset given that a model is trained on another. Consistent with previous work, we expect these models to have poor performance on out of domain data. By using each dataset in turn for training and predicting on the other, we show that it is not simply a questions of which dataset our models are trained on but rather that regardless of which dataset we train on, the capabilities of a model to predict on a dataset which is collected in a different culture, with different ways of using language, and with different targets and topics will be poor unless we specifically seek to address this.

To evaluate the performance of the classifier on the out of domain data, we defined a deterministic class mapping between the two datasets based on observations. We map the "Neither" class from Waseem (2016),Waseem and Hovy (2016) to the "Not Offensive" class in Davidson et al. (2017). We also observe that in Davidson et al. (2017), a large majority of the tweets annotated as offensive language are sexist so we map the "Offensive" class to "Sexist". A large majority of the tweets labeled as hate-speech contain racist slurs and remarks, so we map the "Hate Speech" in Davidson et al. (2017) class to the "Racism" class in Waseem (2016); Waseem and Hovy (2016).

3.4.2 Composite Data Models

In this configuration, we build a composite of all three datasets into a single training set and test set. With this model we seek to build a strong baseline as we expect this will outperform the simple baseline models and simultaneously will allow for us to test the performance of a model where a composition of all known datasets is performed. Additionally, this method allows us to test whether the influence of using a multi-task learning configuration only shows benefits due to the model being exposed to all available datasets. Finally, using the composite datasets we test whether the distribution of documents from each dataset influences which evaluation dataset the model performs best on.

3.4.3   Multi-task Learning Models

Our third configuration uses a multi-task learning framework, in which we test for whether simultaneously learning to predict on two different datasets with a shared representation can outperform a strong baseline. Furthermore, by utilizing this approach, we test the potential of domain transfer for abusive language via multi-tasking. Finally, this setup allows us to test whether cultural influences and differences can be utilized such that prediction is improved on a dataset whose collection is based in a different cultural context. Given that it differentiates between the primary and auxiliary tasks while still learning from both datasets, we expect this configuration to outperform the other two model types. Specifically, we expect it to outperform our simple baseline models by a large margin and, to a lesser degree, our composite data models.

We test two conditions for this set of experiments, alternating between which of the two datasets we use as a main task, with the other serving as the auxiliary training data. While our model internally treats both tasks equally, the difference between these two scenarios is that we only tune the model on the development set of the respective main task.

3.4.4   Dataset Statistics

We construct a dataset for "racism"/"sexism" detection by merging the Waseem (2016) and Waseem and Hovy (2016) datasets. In Waseem and Hovy (2016), only the classes "racism", "sexism", and "neither" are utilized, however due to the focus on intersectional abuse Waseem (2016) also annotate for "both". In our experiments we augment the "racism" class with documents labeled as "both" as there are only 49 documents labeled as "both" and because Davidson et al. (2017) is not annotated for the intersections but rather "hate speech" and "offensive." Therefore, training to detect this composite class, regardless of which dataset is trained on or is used as the primary task, would hardly be successful. Furthermore, the issues with detecting the class would become greater as we create splits in our dataset for training and testing purposes. Finally, we augment the "racism" class with the documents from the "both" class, as "racism" is the class with the fewest documents, and as such increasing the number of documents is more likely to improve performance on the class rather than the "sexism" class which has more documents, even if the increase in number of documents is negligible.

To build our model, we create stratified splits of our dataset to ensure that class balance across different splits remains the same. We generate a split for training our model, a split for development evaluation, and a final evaluation (see Tables 3.2 and 3.3 for dataset statistics across the splits) dataset which is entirely unseen for our models at test time.

Table 3.2 Dataset statistics of the Waseem (2016)/Waseem-Hovy (2016) and splits produced for training, developing and evaluating the models

Dataset split	Racism	Sexism	Neither
Training	1697	3365	11688
Development	211	420	1461
Test	214	423	1461
Total	2122	4208	14610

Table 3.3 Dataset statistics of the Davidson (2017) and splits produced for training, developing and evaluating the models

Dataset split	Hate speech	Offensive	Not offensive
Training	1144	15352	3330
Development	143	1919	416
Test	143	1919	417
Total	1430	19190	4163

3.4.5 Evaluation Metrics

Given the high imbalance between positive classes seen in Tables 3.2 and 3.3, that is the "racist", "sexist", "offensive", or "hate speech" classes, it is important that we evaluate using metrics that are not susceptible to class imbalances. For instance, a metric that would be susceptible to class imbalances is accuracy, which simply calculates the fraction of all correct predictions over all documents in the evaluation set. Thus, if one class dominates the dataset, and a classifier performs well on that class but poorly on all other classes, the accuracy score would still show a quite high score. For this reason, we provide precision, recall, and weighted-average F1-scores for each class as well as their average. As such we can show the actual performance on our task, rather than a biased sample. Below we provide definitions and explanations of our metrics.

3.4.5.1 Precision, Recall, and F1-Score

We compute the precision, recall, and F_1-score, and report F_1-scores, as these measures are robust against class imbalance while providing insight into the performance of our models. For all three, in the class-based representation the "positive" class refers to the class which we are predicting for.

Precision describes the fraction of how many of the examples which our model predicted to belong to one of the positive classes actually belonged to those positive classes. Thus, it provides us with a insight of how often other classes are misclassified as this class.

$$Precision = \frac{True\ Positive}{True\ Positive + False\ Positive} \qquad (3.6)$$

Recall, on the other hand, describes how often our models predicted the correct class as a proportion of all predictions; providing insight how often the classifier misclassifies the this class as another class.

$$Recall = \frac{True\ Positive}{True\ Positive + False\ Negative} \qquad (3.7)$$

The F_1-score is the harmonic mean between precision and recall which penalizes imbalance between precision and recall.

$$F_1\text{-score} = 2 \cdot \frac{Precision \cdot Recall}{Precision + Recall} \qquad (3.8)$$

3.5 Experimental Results

In this section, we present the results of our experiments. Results of all experiments are presented in Table 3.4. Each subsection will highlight one type of model and analyze and discuss the performance of that model. We will be comparing across datasets with respect to the class distributions. Please refer to Tables 3.2 and 3.3 for class distributions.

3.5.1 Single-Task Baseline Models

Our single-task baseline models are built using the same method that has been used in previous work to predict on out-of-domain data, namely training on an in-domain training set and predicting on an out-of-domain test set (Waseem 2016). In this we show findings consistent with previous work, namely that in-domain prediction performs reliably when using simple features and models such as our MLP with BoW features.

Considering the results of out of domain classification presented in the first six rows in Table 3.4, we observe that the performance is extremely poor. While the F_1-scores for minority classes performs below chance, the *Offensive* class out of domain the F_1-scores for the majority class are, in some instances, slightly more respectable.

Considering the average performance over all classes, we observe significant drop in F_1-score from the in-domain dataset to the out-of-domain dataset. This baseline shows that performance on out-of-domain datasets will be poor regardless of which single-domain dataset is used as the training set when the datasets have different underlying distributions and label schemata.

3 Bridging the Gaps: Multi Task Learning for Domain …

Table 3.4 Comparison of test-set performance of within-domain and out-of-domain datasets using models trained only on one dataset (first four rows), models trained by concatenating both datasets (middle two rows), and using both datasets in a multi-task learning environment (final four rows). For each training regime, we compare using Bag-of-Words (BoW), the Average of Subword Embeddings (Emb) and both (B+E) as features for each tweet. Datasets: Davidson (2017), Waseem (2016)/Waseem-Hovy (2016) (W/W + H)

| Training objective | | Features | F_1-scores of predictions on test sets | | | | | | | |
| Primary task | Auxiliary task | | W/W+H | | | | Davidson | | | |
			Racism	Sexism	Neither	Average	Hate speech	Offensive	Neither	Average
W/W+H	–	BoW	0.70	0.65	0.88	0.82	0.00	0.64	0.42	0.57
W/W+H	–	Emb	0.30	0.42	0.85	0.71	0.01	0.04	0.29	0.08
W/W+H	–	B+E	0.00	0.00	0.82	0.57	0.00	0.00	0.29	0.05
Davidson	–	BoW	0.22	0.29	0.69	0.56	0.32	0.94	0.84	0.89
Davidson	–	Emb	0.00	0.32	0.60	0.48	0.19	0.92	0.69	0.84
Davidson	–	B+E	0.25	0.33	0.70	0.58	0.39	0.82	0.94	0.89
Both	–	BoW	0.21	0.54	0.81	0.70	0.20	0.92	0.77	0.86
Both	–	Emb	0.21	0.45	0.76	0.64	0.05	0.90	0.64	0.80
Both	–	B+E	0.17	0.53	0.81	0.69	0.31	0.92	0.77	0.86
W/W+H	Davidson	BoW	0.64	0.63	0.87	0.80	0.39	0.94	0.84	0.89
W/W+H	Davidson	Emb	0.32	0.50	0.84	0.72	0.10	0.91	0.64	0.82
W/W+H	Davidson	B+E	0.51	0.53	0.86	0.75	0.16	0.93	0.78	0.86
Davidson	W/W+H	BoW	0.66	0.62	0.86	0.79	0.37	0.94	0.83	0.89
Davidson	W/W+H	Emb	0.39	0.49	0.84	0.73	0.09	0.91	0.62	0.81
Davidson	W/W+H	B+E	0.60	0.57	0.85	0.77	0.14	0.93	0.78	0.86

3.5.2 Composite Dataset Models

With our composite dataset models, we sought to build a strong baseline which used
both datasets to allow comparison against our multi-task learning models. In our
results, we observe that the performance on the minority classes is around the level
of random chance while the performance of majority class is satisfactory. Considering
the average F_1 score, these models perform well compared to our single-task baseline
models. However, this performance is less than desirable.

We observe that inclusion of the second dataset in training reduces average classification performance of BoW models in comparison to our in-domain baselines
which only use a single dataset. While in comparison the in-domain performance the
accuracy is reduced, in comparison to the out-of-domain performance we observe a
marked rise. This provides evidence to suggest that while the model will be better at
"generalizing" between the multiple datasets, it will do so at the cost of in-domain
performance on the distinct datasets from which it is built.

In our single-task baseline, we observe that for the Waseem/Waseem-Hovy data,
the Embedding-based features yield poor classification performance. This may be
due to data scarcity for the minority classes (racism and sexism). In the composite
dataset, we observe an improvement in classification performance for these values
when using embedding-based features due to the inclusion of the additional data.

3.5.3 Multi-task Learning Models

In all cases, the application of multi-task learning (presented in the final six rows of
Table 3.4) yields clear improvements in the average F_1 classification performance in
comparison to the composite dataset as well as to the cross-domain scenarios, outper-
forming our strong and weak baselines. Notably, these improvements are achieved
with minimal loss of performance compared to the in-domain performance of the single task model. We observe four instances where the score was reduced: the average
reduction in these cases was 0.025.

The choice of a primary versus auxiliary task appears to have little effect on either
test set, which is relatively unsurprising given that the main task choice solely impacts
the final model selection criterion rather than training itself.

Our results imply that the MTL approach can overcome the problems that arise
from differing annotation schemes for hate speech detection stemming from cultural influences and differences. This poses the central contribution of our work
and, extrapolated to a more general case, suggests that the improved generalization
that comes with a multi-task learning approach can bridge gaps between different
domains and annotation schemes in several other tasks. This is, to our knowledge,
an application of multi-task learning that has previously received little attention and
is worth exploring further.

3.5.4 Critiques of Datasets

Referring back to Sect. 3.2, we find one troubling aspect of the data released by Davidson et al. (2017). While their work is interesting and profound there is a serious issue in their data which we discovered quite late in our process of writing this, and had we been aware of it at an earlier stage we would not have used their datasets. The issue that we found is that a large part of their positive classes consist of African American Vernacular English, and while we encourage research to work on abusive language and AAVE, the combination should be handled with care. As a large majority of the datasets is written in AAVE, we consider the use of the *n-word*. The *n-word* occurs with a 'ga' ending 2167 times. It is labeled as either "offensive" or "hate speech" a total of 2161 times. This includes examples such as[7]: "This Niggah Kevin Hart couldn't sit down lmaooooooooooooo My niggah My Niggah", "If I wanted my ex back believe me I'd fucking go get they ass. but I ain't bout to dig through the trash.", and "@user Police just tried to Rodney King a nigga... happen to my nig out here". Considering these examples within the frame of AAVE, it is clear that these are not offensive, nor do they appear to contain other signals of abuse or offensive language, yet they were all labeled as "offensive". We determine that these tweets are in fact AAVE using the references to African American celebrities,[8] the use of phonologically motivated spelling variations and contractions (Jørgensen et al. 2016), and the reference to the police brutality, including the fact that not only is the user describing the threat of police brutality to themselves, but also referring to someone they know who has been a victim of police brutality from which we illicit is AAVE due to the over-policing of black communities (Desmond-Harris 2015). Considering these factors, some of which common to large sets of the dataset it becomes clear that these examples, as so many other in the dataset, are AAVE.

By training models to detect offensive language and hate speech using this dataset, researchers are implicitly also passing judgment on what is deemed acceptable sociolects and dialects. To seek to control the dialect spoken by communities that are marginalized through over-policing (Desmond-Harris 2015), mass incarcerated (Roberts 2004) and under represented in academia (Allen et al. 2000), media (Dixon and Linz 2000), and leadership positions (Cohen and Huffman 2007) is callous at best and malicious at worst. While it is our contention that this dataset in its current state should not be used in terms of abusive language detection research without re-annotation, we encourage a re-annotation of this resource as it can be a valuable resource into the nature of abusive and offensive language within African American communities. Furthermore, it goes to highlight the argument in Waseem (2016), that the identities of annotators is important. We find it unlikely that people from marginalized African-American communities would annotate the examples above, or the many other instances in the dataset as offensive or hate speech. Therefore,

---

[7]Emoticons used in the text are removed, urls are replaced with "<url>" token, and usernames are replaced with "@user".

[8]"My n*ggah my n*ggah" is a reference to Denzel Washington's character in the movie Training Day.

we encourage for a re-annotation with members of marginalized African American communities as the primary annotators.

We acknowledge that through their instruction for annotators to consider context, the fact that AAVE is so frequently annotated as either "hate speech" or "offensive" directly goes against the intentions of Davidson et al. (2017) and the instructions they provided their annotators with. This further highlights the importance of selecting the correct annotators for tasks such as abusive language detection.

3.6   Related Work

3.6.1   Abusive Language

Abusive language research has seen a recent increase in attention from researchers in NLP (Waseem 2017, 2016; Davidson et al. 2017; Jha and Mamidi 2017; Chandrasekharan et al. 2017; Wulczyn et al. 2017; Nobata et al. 2016; Ross et al. 2016) yet the focus of bridging across geographical context, cultural context, or dataset has to our knowledge only been addressed by Waseem (2016), Chandrasekharan et al. (2017), and Nobata et al. (2016). In Waseem (2016), they collapse their annotations and the annotations from Waseem and Hovy (2016) into a "hate speech" and "not hate speech" classes, and train on Waseem (2016) and predict on Waseem and Hovy (2016). In Nobata et al. (2016), they build models using a mixture of lexical features and word embeddings, additionally, they split their dataset up by when the documents were posted and find that by adding data as the model learns improves the performance of the model. Finally, Chandrasekharan et al. (2017) take a very different approach by specifically aiming to make their models function on new datasets. Rather than assigning focus on individual documents, as with a BoW model, Chandrasekharan et al. (2017) choose to approach their task by considering multiple communities, some of which are known to be abusive. Given these abusive and non-abusive communities, they compute the distance of a comment to the communities using a BoW representation of the comment. Using this approach, Chandrasekharan et al. (2017) find that their model outperforms models that are trained within domain using lexical features. One important distinction between Chandrasekharan et al. (2017) and this work, is that Chandrasekharan et al. (2017) requires multiple distinct data sources to perform well. As shown through our use of two datasets, we do not require multiple data sources to obtain generalization.

Other work in the field has dealt with using neural networks for predicting hate speech (Gambäck and Sikdar 2017; Park and Fung 2017; Badjatiya et al. 2017). In all three papers, they experiment with Convolutional Neural Networks (CNN). In Park and Fung (2017) they model the task slightly differently from other previous works by first building a model to detect whether something is hate speech and then classifying it into the specific form of hate speech (Park and Fung (2017) consider "racism", "sexism", and "neither").

3.6.2 Multi-task Learning

As noted above, this is to our knowledge the first work that employs multi-task learning strategies to tackle hate speech detection, aiming at transferring knowledge between domains and differently annotated datasets.

An example of previous work that has used multi-task learning to build models to work well across domains is Yu and Jiang (2016), where sentence representations are learned through auxiliary tasks in order to improve cross-domain sentiment classification. However, this approach critically differs from ours in that the authors do not perceive different annotations as different tasks, but create synthetic data for their auxiliary tasks that are exclusively used to learn better representations of the input.

Another interesting case is that of Luong et al. (2015), which proposes a multi-input and multi-output sequence-to-sequence model for neural machine translation that can handle different source and target languages, encoding input from any language into the same language-independent intermediate representation, from which they decode into any available target language. While fundamentally different in model architecture and learning problem, this work shares our idea of perceiving heterogeneous datasets from different 'domains' as separate tasks to build a robust cross-domain model.

3.7 Conclusion

In this work, we applied the use of multi-task learning to develop classifiers for hate speech and abusive language. We find that utilizing an MTL framework for detecting hate speech allows for vastly improving the ability of a hate speech detection model to generalize to new datasets and distributions. In this work, we specifically chose datasets which were collected with distinct cultural groundings and bias to examine the utility of MTL to overcome such biases. With this in mind, we show that MTL does in fact allow for generalization onto a different cultural context. A particular strength of our MTL approach is that its better generalization allows for a more robust application to completely novel data. In such a scenario, the outputs from the MTL model could act as a mixture of experts that jointly vote on new data. Prior knowledge could be easily integrated here in giving more weight to the sub-model whose training data we believe is closest to our new data.

Our results further show that MTL allows for comparable results to using single task models that predict in-domain, while also allowing for prediction on other datasets. Additionally, we find that a high performance model can be built using composite datasets however, MTL allows for overall improvements over it. Furthermore, we find that in our experiments the choice of primary and auxiliary task had little influence on the performance of the model. We show that applying MTL to classify hate speech on out of domain data is a vast improvement over single-task models and has a slight average improvement over the composite dataset models.

In a more practical sense, our approach simplifies the construction of broad-domain filters for moderation of content by a classifier to learn from examples from multiple different domains and tasks. This minimizes the barrier of entry for detecting hate speech from different domains and communities and thus mitigates the risk of exposing users to previously unseen forms of online hate speech and abuse. By using the confidence from scores from this approach to only expose moderators to borderline content where absolutely necessary, we can reduce the volume of explicit materials that staff members are exposed to which has the potential to reduce harm.

In conclusion, while our method does not guarantee improvements on in-domain prediction of single-task models, we introduce the use of a method that can allow for lower barriers to training and detecting new forms of hate speech and abusive language. Considering the correlation between online hate speech and hate crime, lowering entry barriers for hate speech and abusive language detection may allow for platforms to more easily protect their users from undue harm online and offline.

3.8　Future Work

Our work raises a number of questions on how to deal with domain adaptation and abusive language. First and foremost, future work should seek to address making improvements on the minority classes. Second, this paper explores multi-task learning for domain adaptation, it could therefore be beneficial to consider other methods for domain adaptation. Additionally, future work could seek to address the use of user information and the use of demographic variables such as age, gender, and income as additional signals for detection of abusive language and hate speech across datasets. As far as our multi-task approach is concerned, future work may investigate relationships between the datasets and how they reflect in optimal hyper-parameters for the network architecture and training. For example, specific task combinations could benefit from a more fine-tuned training schedule or learning rate ratio, or the integration of further task-specific hidden layers.

References

Allen WR, Epps EG, Guillory EA, Suh SA, Bonous-Hammarth M (2000) The black academic: faculty status among African Americans in U.S. higher education. J Negro Educ 69(1/2):112–127. http://www.jstor.org/stable/2696268

Badjatiya P, Gupta S, Gupta M, Varma V (2017) Deep learning for hate speech detection in tweets. In: Proceedings of the 26th international conference on world wide web companion, WWW '17 Companion, pp 759–760. International World Wide Web Conferences Steering Committee, Republic and Canton of Geneva, Switzerland. https://doi.org/10.1145/3041021.3054223

Bingel J, Søgaard (2017) A identifying beneficial task relations for multi-task learning in deep neural networks. In: Proceedings of the 15th conference of the European chapter of the association for computational linguistics, short papers, vol 2, pp 164–169. Association for Computational Linguistics, Valencia, Spain. http://www.aclweb.org/anthology/E17-2026

Bjerva J (2017) One model to rule them all: multitask and multilingual modelling for lexical analysis. arXiv:1711.01100

Bjerva J (2017) Will my auxiliary tagging task help? estimating auxiliary tasks effectivity in multitask learning. In: Proceedings of the 21st Nordic conference on computational linguistics, NoDaLiDa, 22–24 May 2017, Gothenburg, Sweden, 131, pp 216–220. Linköping University Electronic Press (2017)

Boeckmann RJ, Liew J (2002) Hate speech: Asian American students justice judgments and psychological responses. J Soc Issues 58(2):363–381. https://doi.org/10.1111/1540-4560.00265

Bollmann M, Bingel J, Søgaard A (2017) Learning attention for historical text normalization by learning to pronounce. In: Proceedings of the 55th annual meeting of the association for computational linguistics, long papers, vol 1, pp 332–344

Boyle K (2001) Hate speech-the united states versus the rest of the world. Maine Law Rev 53(2):487–502

Caruana R (1998) Multitask learning. Learning to learn, pp 95–133. Springer

Caruana RA (1993) Multitask connectionist learning. In: Proceedings of the 1993 connectionist models summer school. CiteSeer

Chandrasekharan E, Samory M, Srinivasan A, Gilbert E (2017) The bag of communities: identifying abusive behavior online with preexisting internet data. In: Proceedings of the 2017 CHI conference on human factors in computing systems, CHI '17, ACM, New York, NY, USA, pp 3175–3187. https://doi.org/10.1145/3025453.3026018

Cohen PN, Huffman ML (2007) Black under-representation in management across U.S. labor markets. Ann Am Acad Polit Soc Sci 609(1):181–199. https://doi.org/10.1177/0002716206296734

Crawford K, Gillespie T (2014) What is a flag for? social media reporting tools and the vocabulary of complaint. New Media Soc 18(3):410–428. https://doi.org/10.1177/1461444814543163

Crenshaw K (1989) Demarginalizing the intersection of race and sex: a black feminist critique of antidiscrimination doctrine, feminist theory and antiracist politics. Univ Chicago Legal Forum 1989(1)

Crenshaw K (2016) The urgency of intersectionality. https://www.ted.com/talks/kimberle_crenshaw_the_urgency_of_intersectionality

Davidson T, Warmsley D, Macy M, Weber I (2017) Automated hate speech detection and the problem of offensive language. In: Proceedings of ICWSM

Desmond-Harris J (2015) Are black communities overpoliced or underpoliced? both. https://www.vox.com/2015/4/14/8411733/black-community-policing-crime

Dixon T, Linz D (2000) Overrepresentation and underrepresentation of African Americans and latinos as lawbreakers on television news. J Commun 50(2):131–154. https://doi.org/10.1111/j.1460-2466.2000.tb02845.x

European Commission (2016) Code of conduct on countering illegal hate speech online. Technical report

Gambäck B, Sikdar UK (2017) Using convolutional neural networks to classify hate-speech. In: Proceedings of the first workshop on abusive language online, pp 85–90. Association for Computational Linguistics. http://aclweb.org/anthology/W17-3013

Girshick R (2015) Fast R-CNN. In: Proceedings of the IEEE international conference on computer vision, pp 1440–1448

Heinzerling B, Strube M (2017) BPEmb: tokenization-free pre-trained subword embeddings in 275 languages. CoRR abs/1710.02187. http://arxiv.org/abs/1710.02187

Home office (2016) Action against hate the UK governments plan for tackling hate crime. Technical report (2016)

Jha A, Mamidi R (2017) When does a compliment become sexist? analysis and classification of ambivalent sexism using twitter data. In: Proceedings of the second workshop on NLP and computational social science, pp 7–16. Association for Computational Linguistics. http://aclweb.org/anthology/W17-2902

Jørgensen A, Hovy D, Søgaard A (2016) Learning a pos tagger for AAVE-like language. In: Proceedings of the 2016 conference of the North American chapter of the association for computational linguistics: human language technologies, pp 1115–1120. Association for Computational Linguistics, San Diego, California. http://www.aclweb.org/anthology/N16-1130

Kim Y (2014) Convolutional neural networks for sentence classification. CoRR abs/1408.5882. http://arxiv.org/abs/1408.5882

Klerke S, Goldberg Y, Søgaard A (2016) Improving sentence compression by learning to predict gaze. In: Proceedings of NAACL-HLT, pp 1528–1533

Levin S (2017) Moderators who had to view child abuse content sue Microsoft, claiming PTSD

Luong MT, Le QV, Sutskever I, Vinyals O, Kaiser L (2015) Multi-task sequence to sequence learning. arXiv:1511.06114

Martínez Alonso H, Plank B (2017) When is multitask learning effective? semantic sequence prediction under varying data conditions. In: Proceedings of the 15th conference of the European chapter of the association for computational linguistics, long papers, vol 1, pp 44–53. Association for Computational Linguistics, Valencia, Spain. http://www.aclweb.org/anthology/E17-1005

McIntosh P (1988) White privilege and male privilege: a personal account of coming to see correspondences through work in women's studies

Müller K, Schwarz C (2017) Fanning the flames of hate: social media and hate crime

Nobata C, Tetreault J, Thomas A, Mehdad Y, Chang Y (2016) Abusive language detection in online user content. In: Proceedings of the 25th international conference on world wide web, WWW '16, pp 145–153. International World Wide Web Conferences Steering Committee, Republic and Canton of Geneva, Switzerland. https://doi.org/10.1145/2872427.2883062

Park JH, Fung P (2017) One-step and two-step classification for abusive language detection on twitter. In: Proceedings of the first workshop on abusive language online, pp 41–45. Association for Computational Linguistics. http://aclweb.org/anthology/W17-3006

Pew Research Center (2017) Online harassment. http://www.pewinternet.org/2014/10/22/online-harassment/

Rahman J (2012) The n word: its history and use in the African American community. J English Linguist 40(2):137–171. https://doi.org/10.1177/0075424211414807

Ramsundar B, Kearnes S, Riley P, Webster D, Konerding D, Pande V (2015) Massively multitask networks for drug discovery. arXiv:1502.02072

Roberts DE (2004) The social and moral cost of mass incarceration in African American communities. Stanf Law Rev 56(5):1271–1306

Ross B, Rist M, Carbonell G, Cabrera B, Kurowsky N, Wojatzki M (2016) Measuring the reliability of hate speech annotations: the case of the European refugee crisis. In: Beißwenger M, Wojatzki M, Zesch T (eds) Proceedings of NLP4CMC III: 3rd workshop on natural language processing for computer-mediated communication, Bochumer Linguistische Arbeitsberichte, vol 17, pp 6–9. Bochum

Smith PK, Mahdavi J, Carvalho M, Fisher S, Russell S, Tippett N (2008) Cyberbullying: its nature and impact in secondary school pupils. J Child Psychol Psychiatry 49(4):376–385. https://doi.org/10.1111/j.1469-7610.2007.01846.x

Socher R, Perelygin A, Wu J, Chuang J, Manning CD, Ng AY, Potts C (2013) Recursive deep models for semantic compositionality over a sentiment treebank. In: Proceedings of the 2013 conference on empirical methods in natural language processing, pp 1631–1642. Association for Computational Linguistics, Stroudsburg, PA

The Guardian (2017) Germany approves plans to fine social media firms up to €50 M (2017)

Waseem Z (2016) Are you a racist or am i seeing things? annotator influence on hate speech detection on twitter. In: Proceedings of the first workshop on NLP and computational social science, pp 138–142. Association for Computational Linguistics, Austin, Texas. http://aclweb.org/anthology/W16-5618

Waseem Z, Davidson T, Warmsley D, Weber I (2017) Understanding abuse: a typology of abusive language detection subtasks. In: Proceedings of the first workshop on abusive language online. Association for Computational Linguistics

Waseem Z, Hovy D (2016) Hateful symbols or hateful people? predictive features for hate speech detection on twitter. In: Proceedings of the NAACL student research workshop. Association for Computational Linguistics, San Diego, California

Wulczyn E, Thain N, Dixon L (2017) Ex machina: personal attacks seen at scale. In: Proceedings of the 26th international conference on world wide web, WWW '17, pp 1391–1399. International World Wide Web Conferences Steering Committee, Republic and Canton of Geneva, Switzerland. https://doi.org/10.1145/3038912.3052591

Yu J, Jiang J (2016) Learning sentence embeddings with auxiliary tasks for cross-domain sentiment classification. Association for Computational Linguistics

Chapter 4
A Network Analysis of the GamerGate Movement

Aitalohi Amaize, Andrea Castillo, Benjamin J. Cooper, Nicole Demme, Emily Kowalczyk, Paul Lee, Grace Mishkin, Scott Moses, Taylor B. Rogers, Jazmine Thomas, Melissa Wagner-Riston, Xiaojing Wang and Julia WheelerGareth T. Williams

In response to the Gamergate harassment phenomenon, Randi Harper developed datamining code that used the twitter account GooberGabber Autoblocker (@ggautoblocker), launched on November 4, 2014 (GitHub 2014). Harper's datamining code (@ggautoblocker) generated a block list of Gamergate harassers, which was made publicly available through an online tool called BlockTogether. Understanding the structural elements of this network can provide valuable insights into semi-organized online harassment movements, how they evolve and manifest, and who is responsible for their growth and actions.

4.1 The Network

For this analysis, a network was built consisting of the accounts on @ggautoblocker's block list. The network consists of nodes that represent a Twitter user and edges which represent a mutual or undirected relationship (following one another) between a pair of nodes. This network is considerably large, consisting of 5,632 nodes and 410,132 edges.

Given the vastness of this network, we found it helpful to identify the most important accounts during our initial analysis. The block list was converted into a.CSV file which was analyzed in Gephi version 0.9.2. To narrow down the network, a degree (i.e., total number of connections to other users within the database) minimum of 1,970 was applied using the topology degree range filter, which reduced the network down to ten nodes. Figure 4.1 displays the network's ten highest-degree Twitter users with a density of 0.867 (i.e., each of them was likely connected to eight or nine of the

A. Amaize (✉) · A. Castillo · B. J. Cooper · N. Demme · E. Kowalczyk · P. Lee · G. Mishkin
S. Moses · T. B. Rogers · J. Thomas · M. Wagner-Riston · X. Wang · J. W. T. Williams
University of Maryland, College Park, MD, USA
e-mail: jgolbeck@umd.edu

© Springer International Publishing AG, part of Springer Nature 2018
J. Golbeck (ed.), *Online Harassment*, Human–Computer Interaction Series,
https://doi.org/10.1007/978-3-319-78583-7_4

57

Fig. 4.1 Top ten
highest-degree users of
#GamerGate (by
Betweenness Centrality)

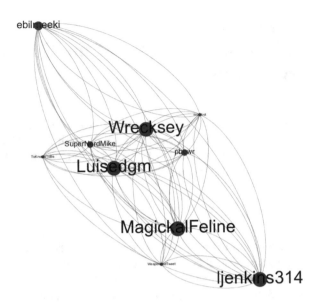

others—this is remarkably high). Their betweenness centrality rank (i.e., how great
a role they play connecting users with other groups) is as follows:

1. Luis Eduardo/@Luisedgm (1.183)
2. nyan/@MagickalFeline (1.183)
3. Tsukkomi/@ljenkins314 (1.183)
4. Wrecks/@wrecksey (1.183)
5. Meeki/@ebilmeeki (0.6)
6. Be Just and Fear Not |Let None Survive/@SuperNerdMike (0.333)
7. Barry/@pbewr (0.333)
8. Limburger Limited/@ToKnowIsToBe (1.33) (2015a, b)
9. Weaponized Tweets/@WeaponizedTweet (2.25)
10. Best Mom Eva/@mombot (1.33) (2018).

4.2   #OpSkynet

The beginning of this network lies with the #OpSkynet movement. The movement
was created as a way to ensure that Gamergate members were working in sync,
with influential figures such as @WeaponizedTweet requesting that members of the
movement all follow each other. In practice, the collection of follows was performed
through the reciprocal following of all new followers by established figures and the
downloading of lists of followers by individuals wishing to join the movement. The
lists of followers—found on Reddit and other message boards, as well as curated lists

within Twitter—were often partial, curated to the creator's connections or leanings within Gamergate.

The @ggautoblocker algorithm, which developed the blocklist analyzed here, adds individuals to its list by determining if that individual follows two or more individuals already on the blocklist (either from the original seed or a previous iteration of the algorithm). This network is tightly connected, particularly at the center. Part of this may be due to the nature of the @ggautoblocker algorithm, which was based upon two mutual connections, inherently ensuring a higher degree. In addition, the most dedicated Gamergate members are all following each other. As a result, seeding any two individuals who were part of the #OpSkyNet activity would likely, after several iterations, capture users with any peripheral connection to Gamergate irrespective of their history of or connection to harassment. Due to this overbreadth, until September of 2017, various individuals connected to @ggautoblocker maintained an appeals process for those who believed they were incorrectly added (Sofaer 2017). That said, analysis of the users with the highest degree within this network (i.e., those with the most connections) found them directly linked with at least one person who engaged in harassment at minimum by constant critical tweeting.

One example user to illustrate this phenomenon is Remi (@RemipunX) (2015), who joined Twitter in June of 2013. Her account is not verified, and she uses her real picture on Twitter. She links to a gaming livestream website in her Twitter profile and also has a YouTube channel where she posts her "Dead Gamers Talking" Podcast every Thursday at 9 pm. She is a supporter rather than a leader in the #GamerGate movement. @RemipunX and @ToKnowIsToBe know each other because of #OpSkyNet on Twitter. @ToKnowIsToBe, as one of the leaders for #GamerGate, mentioned @RemipunX frequently on Twitter. @RemipunX says she will follow anyone who says they are sympathetic to the #GamerGate endeavor, which also means some of the @ggautoblocker stats are skewed by her filling her followers list with people with whom she has nearly no connection. As a result, a number of the clusters of Twitter users in the network may be mathematically significant but are not logically an obvious grouping. Many are likely from the initial list or lists downloaded by the followers and mutual connections of the most influential users. These lists do not illustrate divisions in Gamergate by philosophy or background. Some smaller clusters had more interesting salient features, and those will be discussed later in this chapter.

4.3 #NotYourShield

Who were the blocked individuals on this network? All accounts can be characterized into at least three general types, with some fuzziness at the edges between them. The user accounts used as examples here are discussed in more detail in the class or sub-network analysis that follows.

1. *Movement accounts* exist almost exclusively to broadcast the tactics of Gamergate to other members of the movement. They are anonymous, reveal almost nothing about the user or users behind them, and regularly post and repost objectives, targets, and encouragement to other members of Gamergate. @WeaponizedTweet, one of the originators of this Twitter group, is an archetypal movement account; his account is entirely about coordinating Gamergate and ensuring that it is on message. Limburger Limited (@ToKnowIsToBe) (2015c) is another. Almost all of @ToKnowIsToBe's tweets and retweets are tagged with #PerformanceMatters and/or #GamerGate. Three important items are listed in his profile: the link for #GamerGate, the #GamerGate Current Happenings page, and Mailing goals. @ToKnowIsToBe's posts and retweets are primarily related to movement goals and initiatives, such as which companies to write emails to, or which government bodies to petition. While both accounts communicate significantly within Gamergate, they generally do not tweet to outsiders.

2. *Avatar accounts* are mostly anonymous accounts that are operated by a single individual. The user picture is usually something from a cartoon or video game, and the account itself is short on identifying information. What distinguishes the avatar account from the movement account are tweets with targets outside of Gamergate and its politics. One typical avatar account popular across the network is Best Mom Eva (@mombot), an account with a cartoon profile picture who claims to be a Japanese housewife. @mombot at first look might seem like a movement account—she starts each morning with a tweeted video captioned "Good Morning," which began in 2014 as "Good Morning, #GamerGate." However, she also retweets dozens of unrelated images of aesthetic interest to her, as well as regularly comments on video games and news of the day in Japan. In between all these tweets, @mombot sends critical, insulting, and sometimes rude and borderline racist tweets to individuals with whom she disagrees.

3. *Personal accounts* are individuals who choose to reveal significant information about themselves in their profiles. Within the users surveyed, many of the revelations are related to the #NotYourShield hashtag campaign battling the perception that Gamergate was a young white men's movement; personal accounts often forwent anonymity to show that they were women, LGBTQ, of a minority group, or other nonwhite or non-cisgendered male status. Angela Night (@Angelheartnight) is one of the prototypical personal accounts; she uses her real name, home, and picture of herself in her account details. She also tweets about her personal life. Other users, such as Be Just and Fear Not |Let None Survive (@SuperNerdMike), do not have pictures or identifying information in the profile, but from information in tweets and links to articles written under his real name, it is clear that @SuperNerdMike is not trying to obfuscate his identity like @mombot.

Leaders and followers within the Gamergate network's users cannot be determined reliably by connections alone; since every user part of #OpSkynet is attempting to connect to every other user, even followers may have significant numbers of connections throughout the network. The role the account assumes in the network, based on its activity thereby becomes an important consideration.

1. ***Leader or Follower***: The tweets of a leader influence others to attack, selecting targets for the followers. A leader user like @mombot will tweet something in opposition to, for example, an outsider's critique of Gamergate, and the followers will use @mombot's tweet as a signal to reply both to @mombot and the recipient of @mombot's ire with the follower's own opprobrium. Followers tend to tweet to leaders far more than the leaders tweet back to them, often at a 3:1 ratio or greater. @_WCS_ is an example of a follower who is a prolific tweeter. @_WCS_ has been trying to get more information from the other #GamerGate leaders and supporters. Also, @_WCS_ constantly comments, shares, and interacts with major #GamerGate figures for the purposes of continuing the movement and increasing his notoriety.

2. ***Communication Strategy***: Some accounts take an **offensive strategy**, seeking out perceived opposition with whom to engage. Accounts can also be **defensive**; many of the personal accounts, especially the #NotYourShield ones, tweet in response to criticisms of Gamergate, pushing the **narrative** that the issue was primarily "ethics in gaming journalism," however that user defined it, and that any bad actors were a minority within the movement. Working within the Gamergate community, accounts could serve as **signal boosters** by retweeting other accounts. Some users apply a very active communication strategy, seeking to tweet themselves to relevance in the Gamergate community by mentioning Gamergate's leaders or other followers. Given the closeness of the network, two or three retweets by well-connected accounts would get a message across nearly the entire network. Below are examples of users that employed these communication strategies.

   a. @Wrecksey illustrates the **offensive user**. Along with retweeting Gamergate materials and communicating with other members, @Wrecksey seeks out individuals who have tweeted or posted items critical of Gamergate on the internet. @Wrecksey then tweets back something insulting or derogatory, or retweets the content he finds offensive in a way to hold it up for continued harassment or criticism within Gamergate.

   b. @ljenkins314 is a prime example of the **defensive, alternative narrative user**. As recently as October 2017 he has engaged in lengthy exchanginges with critics of Gamergate, citing the movement as focused on ethics, harassers as an insignificant minority among the Gamergate community, and those opposed to the movement as hypocritical and/or with an ulterior agenda. @pbewr is another example of the defensive, alternative narrative user, whose focus was largely the ways in which media and journalists were portraying the Gamergate movement.

   c. @_WCS_ exemplifies the network **signal booster**. His typical communication strategy is to follow and tweet himself to relevance in the Gamergate movement through sheer quantity of mentions. He is a prolific tweeter (129,000 tweets since joining Twitter in October 2014) and a very active supporter of the #GamerGate movement with a pinned post tagged #GamerGate #NotYourShield. Because Gamergate is a closely aligned community, other users frequently tweet back at him, but not at the same rate. For example, @_WCS_ mentioned @mombot 335 times, but @mombot only mentioned @_WCS_ 18 times. Instead of characterizing this as a relationship between the two users, it is more appropriately thought of as a unilateral interaction with @mombot on the part of @_WCS_. @sloshedtrain2 is another example of a signal booster. Since joining Twitter in September of 2014, 71% of this user's approximately 15,700 posts were retweets. @mombot was the user most retweeted, and users retweeted included those accusing Brianna Wu and Zoe Quinn of lying. All in all, @sloshedtrain2 had very limited direct engagement with other users in the form of replies. This signal boosting role has continued through late 2017, well after the height of the Gamergate controversy.

4.4   #SJWs

There were two sides of how aggression and harassment were viewed in the Gamergate movement. One side said that the members of Gamergate were the aggressors that were sending things like death threats while the other side argued that the members of the anti-Gamergate group (social justice warriors and radical feminists) were the aggressive ones that worked to give the movement a bad name. The tweet above does well to summarize how a large amount of social media users define a social justice warrior (SJW). A SJW is someone who tries to promote an ethical idea or movement but does it in an aggressive manner. When the members of Gamergate are using this hashtag it is usually meant as an insult. However, SJWs tend to be a small subset of a larger group that the media focuses on. Just as the media focused on the negative, aggressive tweets from the members of Gamergate, these members also could have focused on the louder, violent members of the anti-movement.

4.5   #GamerGate

To better understand the network, we ran modularity statistics on the original 5,632 nodes and 410,132 edges. The modularity statistics yielded a number of classes, the

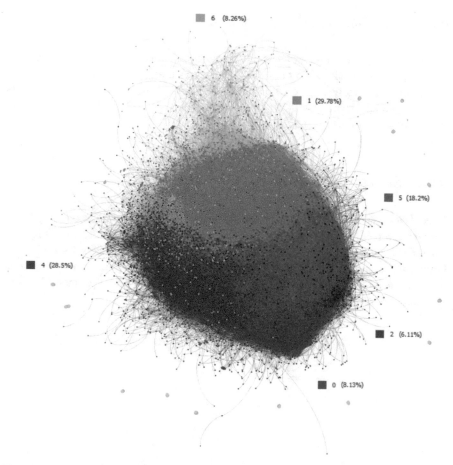

Fig. 4.2 Overview of all nodes in the @ggautoblocker Data Set

top six of which included 98.98% of all nodes. The class breakdown of these six classes is shown below, with color representing each class and node size based on closeness centrality.

Figure 4.2 was produced in Gephi 0.9.2, using Force Atlas layout for 1400+ iterations, running average path length statistics, and setting node size based on closeness centrality. This rendered six primary communities (modularity classes) within the larger set, comprising 98.98% of nodes. In this figure, the six communities are color-coded to illustrate their orientation and interconnection.

4.6   Signal Boosters (Edge Class 0)

Edge class 0 is the second smallest cluster within the overall network. This cluster did not present any significant common themes. Additionally, the users within this cluster did not closely engage with one another but rather, a majority of these users played an integral role in spreading pro-Gamergate message through retweets; hence, they have been deemed *signal boosters.*

4.6.1   Structural Analysis

This class consists of 458 nodes and 34,467 edges. The average degree is 33.35, the network diameter is 6, and the average path length is 2.34. The visualization (Fig. 4.3) was produced by the Yifan Hu layout algorithm and the nodes' sizes are ranked by betweenness centrality and they are color-coded by modularity class. There are five distinct clusters: blue (27.29%), yellow (25.98%), red (27.73%), orange (15.5%), and green (3.49%).

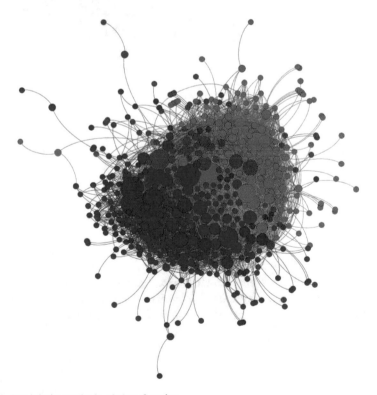

Fig. 4.3 Modularity analysis of class 0 nodes

The top ten nodes (and modularity class) by betweenness centrality are as follows: @paddioche (red), @GarryGaffer (green), @GuardiasKnight (red), @Matchface_(blue), @Maelwaeddau (red), @MeatnTatersShow (red), @Mahogeny_Nerd (blue), @Zakaof (orange), @LapewtanMachine (blue), and @FayzenShok (yellow).

Based on the aforementioned betweenness centrality measures, two important nodes warrant special focus as they were highly ranked on all betweenness centrality, closeness centrality, and degree: @LapewtanMachine (blue) and @Mahogeny_Nerd (blue).

4.6.2   Content Analysis

There are three standout profiles in this group, each representing a different type of role in the Gamergate community. Here we present the individual accounts, the content of their tweets, and a brief overview of how their role fit into the overarching Gamergate movement.

4.6.2.1   Nanomachines, Son! (@LapewtanMachine)

Created in October 2014, during the early heyday of the Gamergate movement, this account immediately jumped into mass retweeting of Gamergate supporters and pro-Gamergate articles. Over a period of two months, the account quickly transmitted over nine thousand tweets, equivalent to about 150 tweets per day. The overwhelming majority of these were retweets of various members of the movement and were sourced from several important Gamergate figureheads (e.g., @WeaponizedTweet, @mombot), as well as less important follower-type accounts. Despite the rigorous pace of the account's activity, there seems to be a legitimate human behind the screen, as @LapewtanMachine can be seen conversing with both supporters and the opposition on a variety of related topics.

Though many movement-follower type accounts focused on only one or two aspects of Gamergate, the user behind @LapewtanMachine indiscriminately retweeted information covering ethical games journalism, video game censorship, anti-SJW retaliation, the nature of journalist/developer relations, perceived slights against men in the industry, and more, to whoever would listen. To build its audience and increase the number of people who would lend an ear, the account retweeted multiple posts that used community building hashtags such as #OpSKYNET, which resulted in @LapewtanMachine and their third-party musings becoming densely integrated into the Gamergate community. With the flood of information going out to their quickly growing follower base, their activities served to facilitate the spread and recognition of pro-Gamergate arguments, classifying them as a signal boosting account.

4.6.2.2   MahoganyNerd (@Mahogeny_Nerd)

@Mahogeny_Nerd is another account created in the early days of Gamergate, as the movement was picking up steam. Like @LapewtanMachine, many of its tweets are actually retweets from other members in the Gamergate community, but this account differs in its focus. There is a decidedly more personal touch to this account, in both the topics of the retweets and the evolution of the account holder's interests over time.

Over the period of about three years, this account tweeted and retweeted over 10,200 times. Unlike other notable accounts in this edge class, @Mahogany_Nerd is still an active member of the Gamergate community and others, though activity has noticeably slowed down since 2016. In the entirety of 2017, there were 47 total tweets from the account, with 44 being retweets and only three being original tweets. The early content from the account resembled many other pro-Gamergate accounts created around the time—retweets en masse, conversations with other community members, and the occasional standalone tweet regarding ethics in game journalism or social justice warrior pushback.

What separates @Mahogeny_Nerd from the rest of the accounts in this edge class is the prominent focus on one particular facet of Gamergate—censorship in video games and in particular, censorship in foreign imports that were applied due to perceived Western sensitivity. The account's tweets touch upon changes in artwork in official video game merchandise, changes made to character poses after public outrage, the creation of censorship patches for sexually explicit games, and more. Throughout these tweets, there is an overarching theme of personal responsibility— time and time again, the account retweets content that harps on the idea that adults should be able to purchase and experience adult content, in the original form that it was intended.

The interests of the owner of @Mahogeny_Nerd result in a more focused, spear-headed effort to raise awareness about this particular issue, a behavior pattern that was rarely seen in this group. In a sense, this account acts as a middle ground between personal and signal boosting accounts. There isn't quite as much public personal information tied to the account as some others, but the personal stakes that the account holder has in the movement clearly affects what topics and messages they spread around the community.

4.6.3   Conclusions: Edge Class 0

As signal boosters, many of the accounts in this edge case were responsible for spreading pro-Gamergate messages to various supporters and to the greater Twitter community. There was, however, very little interaction between the major players of this group. Accounts like @Mahogeny_Nerd, @LapewtanMachine, @Match-Face_, and @Maelwaeddau, rarely responded to or retweeted each other's tweets. Instead, the majority of connections among this group are through the shared retweeting of Flag Bearer and Advocate/Activist type accounts, such as @mombot, @WeaponizedTweet, and @_WCS_. This lack of direct connections mainly stems from the tendency of the accounts to ignore/be unaware of original tweets coming from other, smaller pro-Gamergate accounts and instead focus more on spreading the message of established figureheads.

4.7   Flag Bearers (Edge Class 1)

This sub-network or cluster is not unified by any obvious theme; it's likely primarily people who are connected to one or more of the major figures within this cluster, but not necessarily outside it.

4.7.1   Structural Analysis

The visualization (Fig. 4.4) was created by using Twitter data related to Gamergate. We applied the Yifan Hu proportional layout algorithm and ran the modularity and network diameter statistics. There are 1,677 nodes and 34,467 edges in this network. Each node represents an Twitter user and each edge focuses on the user's interactions with each of the contacts in their Twitter world. The nodes' sizes are based on their degrees and their colors represent their modularity class. This graph includes 6 clusters: purple (25.58%), green (22.96%), blue (18.13%), orange clusters (12.52%), dark green (11.15%), and pink (9.66%). The purple, green, and blue are the three biggest clusters in Class 1.

Immediately evident are some important nodes present in the three biggest groups. In order to identify the central users in Class 1, centralization measures were computed on an individual level. Out of the nodes with highest betweenness centrality and highest degree within this cluster, six users stand out as having both high degrees and high betweenness centrality, which points to their strong influence within the network. These users and their clusters are: @ToKnowlsToBe (orange), @mombot (orange), @_WCS_ (purple), @Angelheartnight (pink), @RemipunX (pink), and @ReLiC71 (purple). While many of them proved influential within Gamergate, none of them were ever Twitter-verified users or otherwise given any imprimatur by Twitter. Their activity and the connections with their most influential contacts (including each other) are examined in the content analysis that follows.

4.7.2   Content Analysis

Even among the top-degree nodes, the individuals do not all have direct connections to each other (Fig 4.5).

Fig. 4.4 Overall structure of the subnetwork

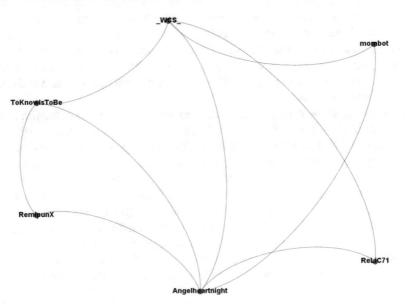

Fig. 4.5 Connections among top-degree nodes in class 1

Fig. 4.6 Egocentric network
of @ToKnowIsToBe

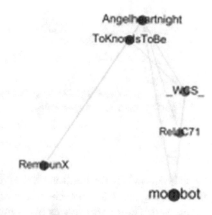

4.7.2.1   Limburger Limited (@ToKnowIsToBe)

The graph below shows @ToKnowIsToBe's 1° egocentric network (degree range
filtered to >384, node size is by degree, color by modularity class). It includes 415
nodes and 10,822 edges. @ToKnowIsToBe has a very high degree and very high
centralities (betweenness and closeness) in Class 1 and connects with other central
nodes in Twitter (Fig. 4.6).

@ToKnowIsToBe joined Twitter in September 2014. He was one of the leaders
of the Gamergate movement, but there is no evidence that shows @ToKnowIsToBe
is a verified account. @ToKnowIsToBe was a very active user but stopped posting
on September 25, 2015. Almost all of his tweets and retweets were tagged with
#PerformanceMatters and/or #GamerGate. There are three important items shown
in his profile. The first one is the link for #GamerGate. When clicking the link, it will
redirect to the homepage of #GamerGate on Twitter. The second is the link for the
#GamerGate Current Happenings page. This link shows not only daily updates about
#GamerGate, but also gives users the ability to share other files regarding #Gamer-
Gate, such as Boycott and Support Lists, How to Contribute, Notices and Pastas, and
Operations. One thing to note is that the #GamerGate's Current Happenings page
stops being updated at the end of September 2015. The last item are the links for
Mailing goals, which is a shared file. In this file, they guide #GamerGate supporters in how to email and protest the companies which are against #GamerGate and
attaches the contact information of these companies.

@ToKnowIsToBe mentions @mombot 28 times on Twitter. All of the interactions were talking about #GamerGate. It is very clear that their interactions are not socially connected. Their purpose was to promote the #GamerGate movement.

@ToKnowIsToBe mentions @Angelheartnight 15 times. @Angelheartnight seems very sensitive and has strong views on female topics related to #GamerGate. We think their relationship may also be purely for the purpose of promoting the #GamerGate movement.

@ToKnowIsToBe mentions @_WCS_ only 7 times. Most of them are @ToKnowIsToBe informing @_WCS_ about #GamerGate updates. While @ToKnowIsToBe only mentions @_WCS_ 7 times, @_WCS_ mentions @ToKnowIsToBe 90 times. This seems to suggest that @_WCS_ is most likely a follower of @ToKnowIsToBe and not a leader for the #GamerGate movement.

@ToKnowIsToBe mentioned @RemipunX frequently on Twitter. After gathering records, there are 54 mentions by @ToKnowIsToBe. They likely know each other from a separate channel named #OpSkyNet and they are often grouped in the same Tweets. This suggests that they may have a closer relationship compared with other users mentioned above.

4.7.2.2   Best Mom Eva (@Mombot)

The account started in December 2014, at the height of #GamerGate; however, it continues to this day with a mix of commentary, sharing of memes, retweeted art, and video game discussion. When asked, @mombot sometimes claims to be a Japanese housewife, but while there's evidence that @mombot is Tweeting from Japan, there is no evidence of her occupation or family status; her avatar is a cutesy version of a giant robot from a 1990s animated show. Whether during the main thrust of #GamerGate or otherwise, @mombot's primary interests on Twitter seem to be Japanese animation, video games, and participating in insult-laden interactions with other Twitter users. @mombot's tweets often have a certain insult comic quality to them, and their cleverness combined with a willingness to interact with people who tweet at her likely contributes to her popularity among other Gamergate members (within the dataset, @mombot has 990 connections, and is the ninth-most significant network by betweenness centrality); there are some accounts whose content even now consists significantly of retweets of @mombot posts, whether about the latest video game or the latest roast of an individual with whom @mombot disagrees.

Although @mombot is willing to reply when mentioned by her "fans," there aren't many major users in her network that she seems close to. The closest appear to be @Angelheartnight and @ToKnowIsToBe; @mombot has extended conversations with both of them. During the height of Gamergate, @mombot was constantly on the attack against critics of the movement, retweeting derogatory information about them and sending insulting tweets.

4.7.2.3   Angela Night (@Angelheartnight)

Angela Night is a British woman with libertarian views who comments on feminism, cultural, political, and video game matters in a variety of online fora. She uses her real name and picture on Twitter. Throughout Gamergate and afterwards, Ms. Night insisted that Gamergate was about the integrity of gaming journalism. Any harassment or other ill behavior by Gamergate was, in Ms. Night's view, the act of a tiny minority attaching themselves to a hashtag movement that by its nature had no gatekeepers to weed out extremists; this position is at least slightly at odds with Ms. Night's friendship with troll accounts such as @ReLiC71.

Ms. Night's ability to sanitize and legitimize Gamergate garnered her many Twitter followers (981 connections in the dataset), and she seemed to appreciate a role as "spokeswoman" for Gamergate (twelfth-most significant individual by betweenness centrality). The simplified graph with connections between the largest nodes makes her look central to the sub-network, this is in no small part due to Ms. Night's liberality with replying to fellow Gamergate members who comment in her mentions.

Within the tweets themselves there does not seem to be significant connection to most of the large-degree fellow users save fellow Brit @ReLiC71, although looking at the tweets shows at least a passing relationship with @mombot, @ToKnowIsToBe, and @RemipunX. There may be deeper relationships that the dataset does not show, as Ms. Night refers in her tweets to both other forms of electronic communication and in-person meetings (although unlikely with @mombot in Japan and @RemipunX in the United States) with other Gamergate members where more consequential messages were relayed.

4.7.2.4   Grand Solar Monarch of the Illuminate Burning Star (@_WCS_)

@_WCS_'s 1° egocentric network is shown in the graph below (degree range filtered to >380, node size is by degree, color by modularity classes). It includes 409 nodes and 13,803 edges. @_WCS_ also has a high degree and high centralities (betweenness and closeness) in Class 1 and connects with other central nodes on Twitter (Fig. 4.7).

@_WCS_ joined Twitter in October 2014. He is a very active supporter of the #GamerGate movement. @_WCS_ is not a verified account, but he is incredibly active and pinned a post which was tagged #GamerGate #NotYourShield.

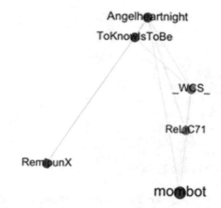

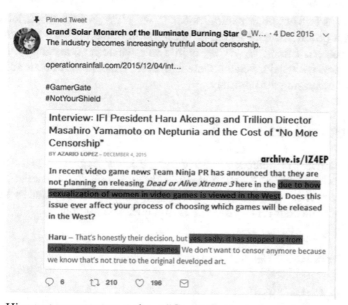

Fig. 4.7 Egocentric network for @_WCS_

His most recent retweet about #GamerGate was from the account named @mombot, where @mombot declared that the #GamerGate movement will never end.

@_WCS_ mentioned @mombot 335 times on Twitter. Rather than calling this a relationship, it is more appropriately characterized as @_WCS_ unilaterally interacting with @mombot. The tweets were not only about #GamerGate, but also mentioned Japanese anime.

Looking at tweets to/from other central nodes in @_WCS_'s network, it looks like @_WCS_ is a prolific tweeter trying to get more information from the other #GamerGate supporters. I think @_WCS_ is in a role where he constantly comments/shares/interacts with major #GamerGate figures for the purpose of continuing the movement and increasing his notoriety.

4.7.2.5 Remi (@RemipunX)

Remi's 1° egocentric network, demonstrated in the graph below (degree range filtered to >380, node size is by degree, color by modularity classes), includes 409 nodes and 5,026 edges. She also has a high degree and high centralities (betweenness and closeness) in Class 1 and connects with other central nodes on Twitter.

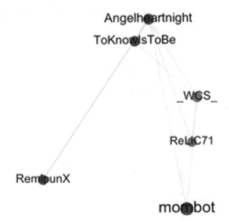

@RemipunX is Remi, who joined Twitter in June 2013, and her account is not verified. She uses her real picture and describes herself is a geek mom on Twitter. She links to a gaming livestream website in her Twitter profile and also has a YouTube channel where she posts her Dead Gamers Talking Podcast every week at 9 pm on Thursday. She is no longer an active user and has stopped posting anything on Twitter as of July 1, 2016. The three most popular tags in her posts were #Fluffy, #DeadGamersTalking, and #GamerGate. She posted a tweet when #GamerGate had been going on for one year. It seems that she was a supporter rather than a leader in the #GamerGate movement.

@RemipunX and @ToknowlsToBe know each other because of #OpSkyNet on Twitter, as mentioned previously. @RemipunX says she will follow anyone who says they are sympathetic to the #GamerGate endeavor, which also means some of the stats are skewed by her filling her followers list with people with whom she has nearly no connection.

4.7.2.6   Rapebert Shekelstein (@ReLiC71)

A human account dedicated primarily to intra-GamerGate banter and subtweet trolling, @ReLiC71 tweets about his personal life only to the extent that he is gay, loves beards, and lives in or around the city of London, England. From a number of pictures he posted on Twitter, it is clear he is using his actual face on his account. The user joined in September 2014, at the same time as Gamergate began, and continued through to August 2016, after which the account became inactive. At the end of his tenure on Twitter, @ReLiC71 was posting mostly current affairs politics unrelated to gaming (a significant portion being British commentary on Islam), indicating against this account being completely purpose-built for Gamergate.

@ReLiC71's account, from the user name through the description to the contents of many of the tweets themselves, means to give offense, making misogynistic, bigoted, and otherwise offensive jokes and insults either directly to other users or to the world at large. Oftentimes, like the more famous celebrity provocateur Milo Yiannopoulos, @ReLiC71 aggressively mentioned his homosexuality in order to claim authority or privilege to say the offensive things he said. In most respects, @ReLiC71 acts like a signal-boosting/attack account; he is like @_WCS_ in that he tweets at fellow accounts multiple times more than they tweet back, and it's likely his high connectivity (851 connections) stems from being an avid follower of others and Gamergate's tendency to encourage following back. Although his discourse is intentionally crude and offensive, the vast majority of his remarks are intra-Gamergate, using crude humor as a form of camaraderie. However, he seems to have a genuine connection with @Angelheartnight; more than just being in the same Twitter mentions clusters, they have conversations indicating knowledge and interest in the others' lives. It's possible that, since they lived in the same geographic region and both participated in Gamergate, they knew each other personally from a Gamergate meetup or similar.

4.7.3 Conclusions: Edge Class 1

In examining the Twitter contacts between the largest nodes, it was clear that most high-degree, high-betweenness users, even though they followed each other, communicated directly only a handful of times. A complicating factor is that much of the coordination for Gamergate did not take place on Twitter; other venues for coordination include Reddit and other forums, Internet Relay Chat (IRC) communications, and in-person meetups to socialize and discuss strategy, and those connections outside Twitter are often not reflected in the network structure or the tweets themselves.

4.8 Activists and Advocates (Edge Class 2)

This sub-network is the network's smallest class, and contains none of the broader network's most central nodes. All of its influential users are followers in the larger network, and many of the central nodes have joined Twitter solely to discuss Gamergate. The class' central nodes include advocates of ethics in journalism as well as several users who host or follow various live streams and radio shows on video games and politics. These users include @rsolgtp, a livestream and radio host based in the UK, as well as advocates such as @The_Sgt_Maj, @Imaconsumer, and @fuzzytoad.

4.8.1 Structural Analysis

Figure 4.8 presents a visualization of the class. The color indicates the modularity class calculated using a resolution of 1.15, and the node size is proportional to each node's betweenness centrality. A large node indicates high centrality, while small nodes indicate less central nodes.

The sub-network consists of only 344 nodes and 2,494 edges, making up roughly 6.11% of the larger network. It has a density of approximately 0.042, an average path length of 2.417, and an average degree of 14.6. Its small size, relatively low density and average degree suggest it's a marginal class of the #GamerGate movement.

The subnetwork is difficult to part into modularity classes, and by a resolution of 1.5 nearly the entire subnetwork (98.61%) is one class. That said,

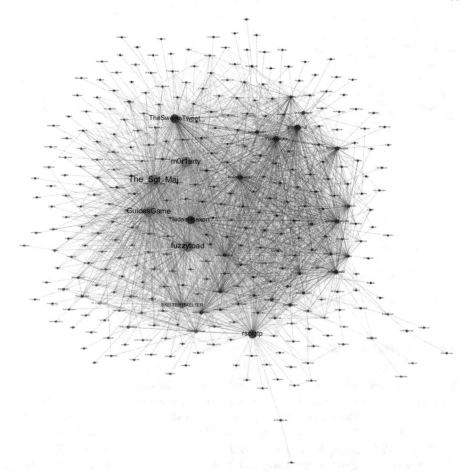

Fig. 4.8 Visualization of class 2. Nodes are colored by modularity class, and sized by betweenness centrality

the figure above shows @rsolgtp is unique among the central users and identifies the accounts with the highest betweenness centrality. The top 12 accounts based on betweenness include @The_Sgt_Maj, @fuzzytoad, @m0ra1rty, @Guides-Game, @rsolgtp, @TheSweetsTweet, @tadashisaxon, @punkerul, @YoloAuntie, @SKELTER1SKELTER, @Imaconsumer, and @ArtistLisaM. Accounts that ranked highly for both betweenness and eigenvector centrality as well as degree include @The_Sgt_Maj, @fuzzytoad, @m0ra1rty, @GuidesGame, @rsolgtp, @TheSweetsTweet, @tadashisaxon, @punkerul, @YoloAuntie, @SKELTER1SKELTER, @Imaconsumer, and @zantagamergate.

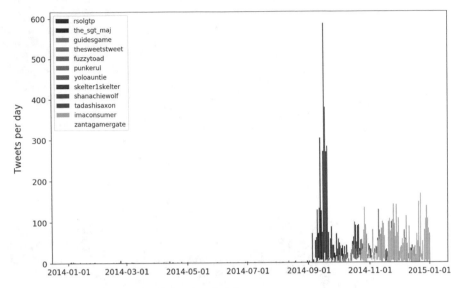

Fig. 4.9 Tweets per day during 2014, class 2 nodes

4.8.2 Content Analysis

To further investigate the class's most central nodes, each account's tweets during the year 2014 were gathered. This was done by using existing Python scripts (Brown 2017), which use Selenium's browser automation to search for all tweets through the Twitter's Advanced Search tool. It gathered all tweets from each user handle from 1/1/2014 to 12/31/2014, the height of Gamergate on Twitter. The returned tweet IDs were gathered and the corresponding metadata was collected using the Twitter API. This provided the text for all original tweets and replies made by the user, as well as the associated metadata such as hashtags, user mentions, and timestamps.

Figure 4.9 displays the tweets per day for the class' most central nodes (note that @m0ra1rty had no saved tweets during this time, and so is excluded from the figure). Of note is the dramatic peak starting in September coinciding with Gamergate's efforts to expand its reach on Twitter. Many of the central nodes (9 of the 15) created Twitter accounts between September-December 2014. Naturally, the number of accounts increased drastically due to no previous tweeting. However, the figure clearly shows that others with existing accounts appear to nearly double their activity during those months.

Fig. 4.10 @rsolgtp 1.5°
egocentric network

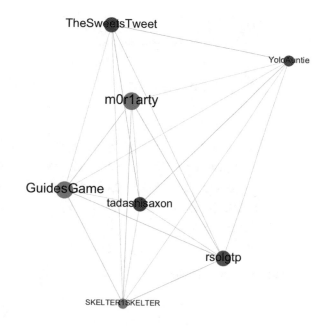

4.8.3   R/TheOpenHouse (@Rsolgtp)

One of the more interesting nodes in the class is @rsolgtp. Not only is he given a unique modularity class in Fig. 4.8, but he is also part of the large blue peak in Fig. 4.9 and the most prolific tweeter in the class. Based on the scraped tweets, he tweeted or replied to approx. 5,131 tweets in 2014, and received moderate interaction from others, recording an average of 0.35 retweets/tweet and 0.41 favorites/tweet. His 1° egocentric network connects him to approximately 30% of the class, and his 1.5° network is shown in Fig. 4.10. The figure shows @rsolgtp egocentric network filtered to contain only nodes which rank in the Top 12 for betweenness centrality. His network spans several modularity classes, and the numerous central nodes appear strongly connected.

The @rsolgtp handle belongs to Robin Gething, a UK-based game developer and graphic artist, who hosts a livestream on YouTube called The Open House, and a radio show. The account is a personal account created in Jan. 2012 and still active today. It appears to have been created to primarily promote The Open House stream, however, seems to attract listeners of all of Robin's programs. Robin's shows vary in topics, with The Open House focusing on open debate and discussion about games and politics, and the radio show primarily discussing gaming. His tweets cover similar topics, typically including promotion for his streams and shows, comments on video games or politics, and replies to his listeners. In addition to promoting his shows, he also tweets members of the larger Gamergate community and asks them to appear on his show. For example, Fig. 4.11 shows a tweet from Oct. 2014 where @rsolgtp asks journalist David Pakman to come on air to discuss his recent interview with Brianna Wu.

David Pakman Show @davidpakmanshow · 27 Oct 2014

Brianna Wu accused me of doing a hit piece attack interview on gamergate today. Interview will be posted later.

   ♡ 93   ⟲ 205   ♡ 237   ✉

r/TheOpenHouse   (Follow)

@rsolgtp

Replying to @davidpakmanshow

@davidpakmanshow hi dave. im live streaming at present and would love to talk about your recent experience. follow me and ill dm you a link

10:36 AM - 27 Oct 2014

♡   ⟲   ♡   ✉

Fig. 4.11 Tweet from @rsolgtp

I'm a consumer   (Follow)

@Imaconsumer

@rsolgtp is there any way that you can be in me I have a smartphone I wish to say something about the events of today

7:13 AM - 28 Nov 2014

♡   ⟲   ♡   ✉

Fig. 4.12 Tweet from @Imaconsumer to @rsolgtp

4.8.4 I'm a Consumer (@Imaconsumer)

Other central nodes in the class are in contact with @rsolgtp about these shows. For example, in Fig. 4.12 @Imaconsumer asks to appear on @rsolgtp's to discuss undisclosed events.

@Imaconsumer is the class' second most prolific tweeter during 2014, and tweeted or replied to approximately 4,253 tweets. Interestingly, his account joined Twitter rather late in October 2014, and his quick rise in activity is shown in Fig. 4.8. He is still active on Twitter today, and tweets with many of the central nodes in the main blocklist network, including @ljenkins314, @ToKnowIsToBe, and @RemipunX.

His account is an avatar account and contains no personal information. His tweets are focused on the importance of transparency and ethics in journalism and promoting #GamerGate. His second tweet on Twitter outlines his intentions for the platform declaring his condemnation of harassment and doxxing, support for women in

Ethan2478 @GuidesGame · 27 Nov 2014
Stop focusing on bullshit but actual equality..> I do not support radical feminism because it supports matriarchy

Ethan2478 @GuidesGame · 4 Dec 2014
The day racism will truly end is when we stop seeing each other as white brown black people but as brothers and sisters as Human beings

Fig. 4.13 Tweets from @GuidesGame on equality

gaming, and general call for ethics in journalism. He is a more directly confrontational tweeter than @rsolgtp, and during his first month, he would often reply to anti-Gamergaters' tweets with Twitter keyword analytics in attempt to prove their statements incorrect. While his tweet rate and association with central nodes in the larger network suggest he may be a signal booster, his tweets are not highly influential—getting only 0.16 retweets on average and 0.34 favorites on average—and he does tweet outside the Gamergate community. These low numbers in combination with his activity suggest he may better be better described as merely a strong advocate or follower of the movement.

4.8.5   Ethan2478 (@GuidesGame)

@GuidesGame is also in contact with @rsolgtp, and is a listener of his show as well other livestreams. He sends @rsolgtp a tweet in December 2014 to tell him how much he enjoys his show, and @rsolgtp replies thanking @GuidesGame. In the tweets, they refer to each other by first name, suggesting they may have spoken before.

@GuidesGame is a young video gamer who decided to join on Oct. 19, 2014, tweeting "I'm in full support of #GamerGate..I've come to my decision and this is my decision….." He uses his account for personal reasons, and is a highly connected user in the class. His 1° ego-centric network contains 183 nodes and 1,285 edges accounting for over 50% of the class including central nodes such as @rsolgtp, @m0ra1rty, @YoloAuntie, and @TheSweetsTweet.

He frequently retweets @oliverbcampell, another live streamer and Gamergate influencer based in Iowa who tweets about games and politics. He posts often about broader political issues, especially the issue of equality. In the tweets in Fig. 4.13, @GuidesGame tries to clarify his own views on equality, which he believes are misunderstood.

Overall, @GuidesGame appears to be a follower with a defensive method of communication. Examples of harassment when analyzing @GuideGame's tweets were unable to be found, and it is suspected that he was blocked due to his association with others. It's unclear how and with whom he was associated with. However, there are several potential reasons, including following fellow listeners of the streams he was partaking in, or taking part in the mass following of #OpSKYNET. The later seems particularly likely since there was a retweeted #OpSKYNET meme in his stream.

4.8.6 A Man in Camouflage (@the_Sgt_Maj), Lalafell Warrior X (@Fuzzytoad), and Frankie Sweets @TheSweetsTweet

In addition to most of these users becoming active on Twitter due to the Gamergate movement, they all take a certain stance on how the movement should be perceived in relation to their opposition. Primarily through replies to other people, they argue that the movement stands for ethics in gaming and journalism. They say that only a small portion of the Gamergate community actually harasses anyone and those that do are probably trying to ruin the movement. This can be seen through tweets by users like @The_Sgt_Maj and @fuzzytoad, two central nodes in this cluster.

@The_Sgt_Maj is one of the most prolific tweeters of this group and joined Twitter in order to be a part of the movement. While he is not influential in the overall movement, he and others appear to act as crowd control for the movement so that others know what Gamergate stands for. Similarly to the first post by @Imaconsumer, they have many posts that say that they condemn harassment and stand for ethics. In addition to this, they speak about the portrayal of Gamergate in media (Fig. 4.14).

@fuzzytoad takes an even more direct approach when talking about Gamergate and the media. He argues that the media won't show how the the Gamergate members are the ones being harrassed and attacked. He had a conversation with @TinyPixel-Block asserting that the media ignored an incident wherein a movement member was assaulted and kicked out of their home due to the media's portrayal of Gamergaters as misogynists.

In addition to talking about their reputation, they pin the blame of Gamergate's negative reputation on others and police the members of the movement that do participate in harrassment. In a tweet, @fuzzytoad tried to convince an anti-Gamergate member that people who are against Gamergate or who are just trying to troll the movement are the ones sending death threats and giving them a bad reputation.

Another user, @TheSweetTweet, actually went as far as reporting another Gamergate member because they were harassing others. The original tweet cannot be seen since the account he reported has been suspended. Despite being a user that often insults others, even if not to them directly, he still argues that members of the movement do not harass others and tries to keep it that way (Fig. 4.15).

Fig. 4.14 Tweet from @The_Sgt_Maj

Ann Hiro @OTDB · 16 Oct 2014
#StopGamerGate2014 Front page NYT. #GamerGate has hurt perception of gamers more than 1000 "gamers are dead" articles

The New York Times

NEW YORK, THURSDAY, OCTOBER 16, 2014

Pull
e Fold

Royals Reach the World Series. Remember Them?
Kansas City completed a sweep of the Orioles, capping a rally after three dry decades. Page B14.

Feminist Critics of Video Games Facing Threats

By NICK WINGFIELD

○ 3   ↻ 1   ♡   ✉

A Man in Camouflage
@The_Sgt_Maj

(Follow) ⌄

Replying to @OTDB

@OTDB you don't understand. Their misrepresentation of us IS the problem. They're the ones who did that. #gamergate is trying to stop it.

6:50 AM - 16 Oct 2014

Frankie Sweets
@TheSweetsTweet

(Follow) ⌄

Replying to @AnitaOfJesus

@AnitaOfJesus @femfreq REPORTED. #GamerGate does not tolerate harassment. This is not condoned or supported by Gamergate. You are sick.

12:16 AM - 12 Oct 2014

2 Retweets 1 Like

○   ↻ 2   ♡ 1   ✉

Fig. 4.15 Tweet from @TheSweetsTweet

4.8.7   Conclusions

Overall, this class appears to contain peripheral nodes in the movement on Twitter, and contains none of the blocklist's most central nodes. The class' most prolific tweeter during Gamergate's height was @rsolgtp, a host of a related livestream on YouTube, who is still active today. The class contains listeners and speakers on the show including the class' second most prolific tweeter, @Imaconsumer, and a young GamerGate supporter, @GuidesGame. In addition to those connected to @rsolgtp, there is a theme among users like @The_Sgt_Maj, @fuzzytoad, and @TheSweetsTweet showing that some members believed very strongly that there were no harassers in the movement and tried to make it stay that way while educating others on Gamergaters' misrepresentation.

4.9   Generals (Edge Class 4)

Edge class 4 is the second largest modularity class. Many leaders of the Gamergate movement can be found within this class, including @WeaponizedTweet, @ebilmeeki, @Luisedgm, @MagickalFeline, @SuperNerdMike, and @StephanieSonmi. The majority of the larger nodes in this class, including @ebilmeeki, @SuperNerdMike and @MagickalFeline, strongly believe Gamergate is a call to hold video game journalists accountable. They do not acknowledge or believe the controversy is about harassment. These users tweet multiple times a day, and frequently engage with other prolific users to recruit for the cause, discuss the issues or talk to others in the movement who disagree with them. Other users, like @radiatastories, frequently tweet about the abuse and doxxing of pro-Gamergate minorities by the "SJWs."

4.9.1   Structural Analysis

Edge class 4 consists of 1,605 nodes with 14,328 edges. This class makes up 28.5% of the Twitters users studied. The average degree is 17.854, which is relatively small considering the highest degree count is 475, and is connected to the largest node, @WeaponizedTweet. The network diameter is 7, and the average path length is 2.882.

Calculations of the degree, betweenness centrality, eigenvector centrality, and closeness centrality highlighted the leaders of edge class 4: @WeaponizedTweet, @ebilmeeki, @Luisedgm, @MagickalFeline, and @SuperNerdMike. When partitioned into modularity classes (Fig. 4.16), 9 distinct communities were produced. These communities are as follows: Purple (22.24%), Green (15.64%), Blue 5 (15.08%), Black (14.52%), Orange (12.83%), Pink (6.54%), Teal (5.92%), Dull Pink (4.8%), and Grey (2.43%). The modularity classes that contain the lead tweeters

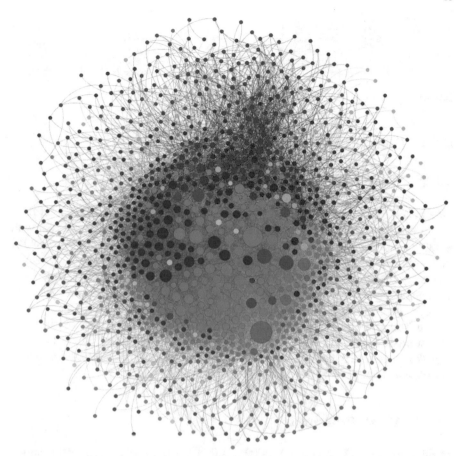

Fig. 4.16 Modularity analysis of class 4 nodes

are purple (@ebilmeeki and @SuperNerdMike), blue (@WeaponizedTweet and @StephanieSonmi), and pink (@Luisedgm and @MagickalFeline). The size of the nodes is determined by degree, and largest node is @WeaponizedTweet.

The user @WeaponizedTweet is the most prolific tweeter in the edge class 4 dataset, with an average of 142.76 tweets per day. The last set of tweets were posted in February 2015. @SuperNerdMike and @Luisedgm averaged about 112.36 and 36.51 tweets per day respectively. Both of these accounts still actively retweet content. The remaining major leaders, @ebilmeeki and @MagickalFeline, have considerably lower daily tweet averages. Both accounts are still active, but @MagickalFeline has an average of 17.35 tweets while @ebilmeeki only has 9.28 tweets.

Fig. 4.17 Tweet from @ebilmeeki regarding #GamerGate

4.9.2 Content Analysis

4.9.2.1 Weaponized Tweets (@WeaponizedTweet)

One of the originators of this network and nearly an archetypal movement user. There is no personally identifiable information on the account, which began with #OpSkynet in September 2014. Before the account went inactive in December 2014 due to infighting among a subset of influential Gamergate members over tactics and other issues, @WeaponizedTweet provided a constant stream of advice and commentary on Gamergate to the user's many connections. Tweets out tended to be within Gamergate and involved tactics or intra-Gamergate politics.

Much of @WeaponizedTweet's true connections are obscured by the fact that they were on Skype and other platforms, not Twitter. From his tweets it's apparent that @WeaponizedTweet had some organizational relationship with @RemipunX, but it's not entirely clear what that was.

4.9.2.2 Meeki (@ebilmeeki)

@ebilmeeki joined Twitter in July 2009. Unlike some of the other prominent Gamergate voices, this user posts primarily original, personal content, with posts in early 2018 including tweets about her cat, other video games, etc., and her profile includes a photo of herself, rather than a cartoon. Many of her Gamergate tweets defend the movement as one that calls for integrity in the gaming world and in gamer journalism. In her tweets, she says those who cry misogyny in the #GamerGate movement don't truly understand the issue. She also denounces misandry and insists that women and men should be treated equally (Fig. 4.17).

She also says that she has been the target of harassment from other women and those who shut her out on the basis of her support for Gamergate (Figs. 4.18 and 4.19).

Along with using the hashtag #GamerGate in her tweets on the topic, she also makes frequent use of #OpSkyNet and #notyourshield. She is actively engaged with other users, with those such as @mombot and @SuperNerdMike among her most recent and regular contacts.

@ebilmeeki also engages with @Angelheartnight, disagreeing with the latter's views (Fig. 4.20).

Fig. 4.18 Tweets from @ebilmeeki regarding initial involvement in gamergate

Fig. 4.19 Tweet from @ebilmeeki regarding @ggautoblocker

Fig. 4.20 Tweet from @ebilmeeki replying to @Angelheartnight concerning misogyny

4.9.2.3   Be Just and Fear Not I Let None Survive (@SuperNerdMike)

@SuperNerdMike joined Twitter in August 2014, as Gamergate was getting underway, and remains active on the platform as of early 2018. During Gamergate, @SuperNerdMike tended to post multi-tweet responses and focused on ethics in game journalism. He, like other Gamergate supporters, talk about video games as a platform that showcases a user's skills and merit, and not their identity politics, railing against SJWs who believe differently (Fig. 4.21).

He has also posted tweets marking the one-year anniversary of #GamerGate. @SuperNerdMike identifies as Native American in his tweets and regularly used the hashtag #notyourshield, posting angry tweets after game developer Tim Schafer used a sock puppet to make a joke about the hashtag at the Game Developer's Choice Awards in March 2015 (Griffin 2015). @SuperNerdMike wrote an op-ed about #GamerGate on Supernerdland.com and tweeted a link to it, which also includes his full name and photo. The website Supernerdland.com is also included in @SuperNerdMike's profile. He tweets to other prolific users like @ebilmeeki, seen recruiting her for the Gamergate cause in this thread (Fig. 4.22):

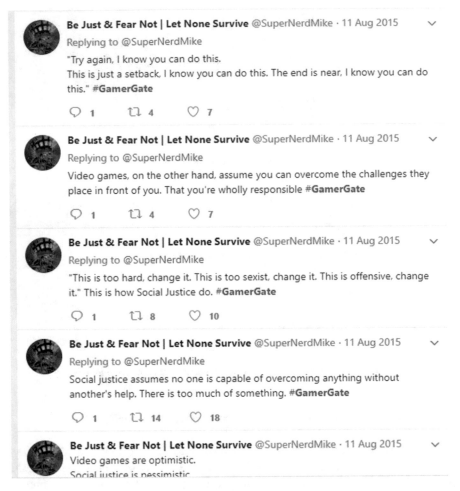

Fig. 4.21 A series of tweets from @SuperNerdMike

@SuperNerdMike maintains back-and-forth Twitter correspondence to users like @mombot, @MagickalFeline and @ebilmeeki, continuing to do this years after the beginning of the movement.

4.9.2.4 Luis Eduardo (@Luisedgm)

@Luisedgm created this Twitter account in August 2014, and remains a very active user as of early 2018. The profile description of this user says, "#GamerGate Supporter, Anti-Feminist and Human Rights Advocate (Men are human too) There's nothing more hypocritical than a journalist." This users here is in line with the image of the belligerent Gamergater who harasses others. This user also maintains a strong

Fig. 4.22 Tweet from @SuperNerdMike recruiting @ebilmeeki

anti-mainstream media stance. Tweets from Jan. 20, 2018, mock the Women's March. @Luisedgm continues to tweet with the #GamerGate hashtag after the movement hit its peak and into 2018. Below is an example around the time of the 2016 presidential election (Fig. 4.23):

Many of @Luisedgm's tweets feature Vivian James, a symbolic Gamergate every-woman, created within the movement as a support for feminists against Gamergate targets Nicole Quinn and others (Vivian 2014). In one tweet, @luisedgm expresses amusement at arguing between anti-Gamergaters and social autopsy, a group that attacks women and SJWs, featuring images of Vivian James (Fig. 4.24).

User @Luisedgm tweets to @ebilmeeki at the peak of Gamergate, between September 2014 and July 2015, but also maintains communication with users like @mombot and @SuperNerdMike into January 2018. When Gamergate supporters were banned from other platforms, @Luisedgm worked to reunite them with their base (Fig. 4.25).

4.9.2.5   Nyan (@MagickalFeline)

@MagickalFeline is a very active Tweeter who joined Twitter in December 2008 and remains active as of early 2018. @MagickalFeline's actual identity remains obscure; he uses an animated image as a profile picture and doesn't discuss other personal details. He frequently uses the hashtags #GamerGate and #notyourshield. His Gamer-

Fig. 4.23 @Luisedgm tweets a Gamergate reminder to journalists

gate content in 2014–2015 focuses on integrity in gamer journalism, expressing interest and enthusiasm in engagement with the Society of Professional Journalists. SPJ
Region 3 Director Michael Koretzky hosted a Gamergate forum in Miami in August
2015, featuring Gamergate personalities Yiannopoulos and Christina Hoff Som-
mers, but was shut down because of a bomb threat (Good 2015). @MagickalFeline
also frequently criticizes media website Gawker, which lost seven figures worth of

Fig. 4.24 Tweet from
@Luisedgm featuring Vivian
James

advertising dollars following pressure from Gamergate supporters angry with the site's coverage and tweets from editorial staff (Sterne 2014).

He tweets to prominent users like @mombot, @SuperNerdMike, @radiatasto-ries and @RemipunX. Among his tweets are a link to a University of Maryland Diamondback editorial by a female student who supported Gamergate. Later tweets include rants about how Gamergate has leaned politically left and he becomes more alt-right, with many misogynistic tweets. He continues to tweet about #GamerGate in 2017. He also tweets about his autism and blames its emergence on Gamergate.

4.9.3   Conclusions: Edge Class 4

The majority of the important nodes (@WeaponizedTweet, @ebilmeeki, @Luisedgm, @MagickalFeline, @SuperNerdMike, @StephanieSonmi) in edge class 4 were integral to the social media network before the dataset was separated by modularity classes. Their strong scores in betweenness centrality, degree, and eigenvector centrality secured their role as leaders, not only in edge class 4, but also in the dataset as a whole. They emphasize Gamergate's pursuit of ethics in journalism, while the lesser nodes share stories of harassment from their opposition. Users like

Fig. 4.25 Tweet from @Luisedgm helping to reunite banned Gamergate supporters

@WeaponizedTweet initiated the #OpSkyNet hashtag to organize and collaborate fellow Gamergate supporters. Even to this day, the leaders in this group frequently tweet between each other and with lead nodes within other edge classes.

4.10 Soldiers (Edge Class 5)

Class 5 comprises "soldiers," split between avatar and personal accounts. Even the most prominent participants in this class seem to take their cues from the more dominant personalities in the database, such as @WeaponizedTweet, @ebilmeeki, @ToKnowIsToBe, and @mombot.

4.10.1 Structural Analysis

This class includes 1,025 nodes, but only a few—@ljenkins314, @pbewr, @WolfpackZX, and @Wresksey—are significant figures in the broader overall network. Graphic depiction of the class as a whole shows that many nodes are tightly connected, and the remainder are very loosely affiliated, tangential connections. Network

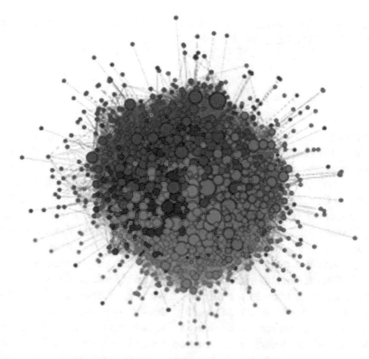

Fig. 4.26 Class 5 nodal map, with color coding by modularity

analysis of the 1,025 nodes and 31,312 edges provided clear patterns regarding some of the central users. The visualization in Fig. 4.26 was created using the Force Atlas 2 layout algorithm and clearly shows six distinct modularity classes, separated by color. Nodes are also sized by degree. Some key statistics regarding these findings are that the average path length is 2.293 and the average degree is 61.097, where the maximum is 443 and the minimum is 1.

The modularity classes are broken down by the following percentages and colors by modularity class size: lavender 27.8%, centered primarily on @WolfpackZX; green 26.15%, centered primarily on @ljenkins314; light blue 22.83%, centered primarily on @pbewr; orange 13.37%, teal 8.68%, and pink 1.17%.

Nodes with the top 10° are the following users (ranked in order by degree), with the modularity class listed: @pbewr: 443, @ljenkins314: 395, @sloshedtrain2: 388, @Wrecksey: 377, @GGHaikus: 361, @auggernaut: 351, @n8vb8: 342, @nat_401: 340, @WolfPackZX: 336, and @RanGa996: 328. Of the top 10 users with the highest degree, 4 (including the node with the highest degree: @pbewr) belong to the 3rd largest modularity class (C: light blue). Nodes with the top 10 betweenness centrality are the following users (in order), with the modularity class listed: @pbewr, @ljenkins314, @WolfPackZX, @Wrecksey, @ShrekBane, @GGHaikus, @n8vb8, @sloshedtrain2, @NorBdelta, and @darthnadar. Nodes with the top 10 closeness centrality are the following users (in order), with the modularity class listed: @pbewr,

@ljenkins314, @sloshedtrain2, @Wrecksey, @GGHaikus, @auggernaut, @n8vb8, @nat_401, @WolfPackZX, and @RanGa996.

4.10.2 Content Analysis

In order to understand the impact of the following accounts on Gamergate, it's important to evaluate their content and usage patterns. One central aspect to this discussion is whether or not the account is even a real human being, since Twitter accounts can easily be created as fake or computer-automated "bot" accounts. Key factors like contacts in the Gamergate network, latest tweet, and notable content can help determine whether or not an account is a human or a bot. Starting with one of the foremost players, @pbewr joined Twitter in September 2014, which is about a month after the beginning of key events in Gamergate. @pbrewr is also a current user, whose most recent tweet was on September 16, 2017. An interesting aspect of @pbrewr in particular is that the total number of tweets is relatively low at 928, considering the fact that more central users in the network have tens of thousands of tweets. This goes to show that number of tweets doesn't necessarily correlate with influence or centrality within the network. Like many other notable players in this edge class, @pbrewr tweeted consistently about Gamergate and the role of media coverage in the discourse, particularly about the false representation of Gamergate members as misogynistic gamers. In contrast, @sloshedtrain2 had 15,666 tweets, 71% of which were retweets of other users' anti-SJW, pro-Gamergate tweets. @mombot was was the user that @sloshedtrain2's retweeted the most.

The node class structure changes dramatically when the top nine betweenness centrality nodes from the overall network are introduced. This group's alignment with the flag-bearers and leaders of the overall movement is thrown into stark relief. Even the most dominant nodes in Class 5 are overwhelmed by the influence of the top nine in the database (nodes that are primarily "Generals" and "Flag Bearers"). This vividly presents the members of this class as "followers" of the most dominant personalities–"soldiers" following the commands of the generals and the lead of the flags (Fig. 4.27).

Figure produced in Gephi 0.9.2, Force Atlas 2 rendering, Approximate Repulsion, Approximation = 1.2, Dissuade Hubs, Edge Weight Influence = 1, Gravity = 400, Prevent Overlap, Scaling = 80, Threads = 3, Tolerance = 1. Filter Degree = 2. Node labels scaled by node degree (size range 1 to 20), node colors by modularity.

Adding the top 9 betweenness centrality nodes from the overall database (i.e., @WeaponizedTweet, @ebilmeeki, @angelheartnight, @RemipunX, @mombot, @ToKnowIsToBe, @MagickalFeline, @Luisedgm, and @StephanieSonmi) replaces all intra-class organization with distinct realignment around these dominant leaders and flag-bearers. Also note that six of these nine nodes are women.

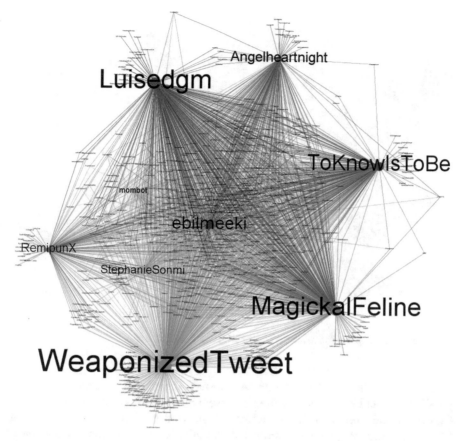

Fig. 4.27 Class 5, Adding the Overall Network's Top 9 Betweenness Nodes

4.10.2.1   Barry (@Pbewr)

One of the most unique nodes in the overall network (7th in betweenness centrality) is Barry, who, like many other Gamergate Twitter users, joined in September of 2014. As of January, 2018, his account showed that he was following 2,035 users, and that he had 1,849 followers. Unlike most of the other prominent nodes of the overall network, his overall number of tweets was very small (928) and he rarely retweeted content from others. In fact, only 39 of his tweets (4%) were retweets. He was, however, mentioned by many others in the network, which could explain his high level of centrality. He also engaged a number of other Twitter users (not at all prominent nodes in the broader Gamergate network) in a string of back-and-forth replies, debating very specific topics related to Gamergate coverage. @pbewr is a key player at the top of the lists for Class 5. As a result, his intra-class 1° egocentric network was established by filtering the degree range as less than 300, and the node size is shown by betweenness centrality (Fig. 4.28).

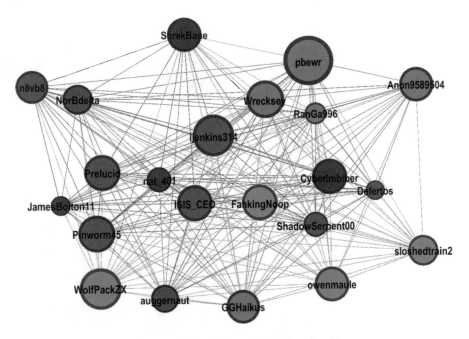

Fig. 4.28 Filtered egocentric network for @pbewr (within class 5 only)

The central themes of his tweets were around the role of media coverage and the discourse and false representation of misogyny of gamers. His tweets defended Gamergate and talked about ethics in journalism. He also offered opinions regarding SJWs being thought police and reiterated on multiple occasions that he and others "are not, in fact, a bunch of misogynists." His tweets seemed to focus on the coverage of Gamergate and debated the nuances of this with other users. Highlights included an "Intel article" and whether ad revenue played a role in the way the article was written to be at odds with Gamergate, the propaganda /megaphone effect of the SJW network, and the ways in which Gamergate was portrayed in the media. His main thesis seemed to be that Gamergate was about journalistic fraud as opposed to representation of women in games, and he objected to the vilification of Gamergate and the shutting down of the flow of information. He also defended games as art and shared links to a handful of articles about Gamergate. Perhaps it was his perspective that garnered him a high number of mentions from other users and thus the relatively high centrality in the overall network. Interestingly, @ToKnowIsToBe is the only user among the top 10 users of the broader network with whom he interacts directly through replies and retweets. Thus, his account may also function a role of linking his followers to the mainstream Gamergate leaders and their content.

Unlike some other notable nodes of the Gamergate network, @pbewr stopped tweeting on 10/7/14. When tweets resumed on 9/27/15, they were not Gamergate-related. Notable tweets from @pbewr's brief burst of Gamergate-related tweets include the following, all from early October, 2014:

- "My focus is trying to understand this media machine that we're up against."
- "Anyone attacks gamers of all people as mIsogynist delusional & needs be critiqued IMO."
- "Corrupt jornos turn to SJW to attack critics. SJW happy to attack games as misogynist."
- "Toxic are the lies told about #GameGate by people who want to stop it before too much of their own dirty laundry is exposed".

4.10.2.2   Tsukkomi (@Ljenkins314)

@ljenkins314 is a prominent avatar account in Class 5. This poster serves as an aligning and motivating force in his network. His profile masks personal details but posts occasionally feature sufficient (apparently) genuine information among memes, attacks, and snark to begin to understand the personality behind the account. His avatar name "Tsukkomi" is drawn from Japanese comedy (owarai), the "straight man" to the *boke*. This role includes correcting the *boke*'s misconceptions, often by smacking the "funny man" *boke* on the head (TV Tropes 2017). In the context of Gamergate, this is a telling label. Further layers of tongue-in-cheek may be seen in his handle itself: ljenkins may be a reference to Leeroy Jenkins, an infamous meme based on World of Warcraft demo character known for "screaming out his name before ignorantly charging into battle" (KnowYourMeme 2018). The suffix 314 is unclear, but may refer to the California Penal Code, Sect. 314: Indecent Exposure, Obscene Exhibitions, and Bawdy and Other Disorderly Houses.

One of the more prolific and thoroughly connected nodes in the network (7th highest degree overall), @ljenkins314 joined Twitter in September of 2014 during the early stages of Gamergate. Analysis of posted content including post-election commentary (Tsukkomi 2016) and frequent references to hurricane recovery (Tsukkomi 2015, 2017a) indicates a location in Florida, probably the Gulf Coast, though the profile nods to Guy Fieri by indicting his location as "Flavortown." Activity continues through recent months, with @ljenkins314's most recent tweet dating November 2, 2017. In contrast with @pbewr, @ljenkins314 has produced a greater amount of content, with a total of more than 32,500 existing tweets. Another difference between the two accounts is the nature of that content; @ljenkins314 includes a greater breadth and variety of subjects and content, including retweeting memes, commentary

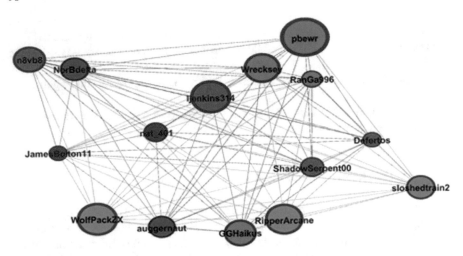

Fig. 4.29 Filtered egocentric network for @ljenkins314

ranging from politics to online harassment to bitcoin, and tweeting at/replying to Milo Yiannopoulos. The dozens of attempted engagements with Yiannopoulos are all the more interesting in light of a recent deflection of Gamergate as an alt-right phenomenon with the response that he has "Been a registered Democrat for 20 years" (Tsukkomi 2017b). Overall, the user seems defensive of the gaming community and often tweets negative comments regarding feminism and those who portray themselves as victims of harassment. The most recent example is an extended exchange with Gamergate critic @lynnxe in which @ljenkins314 sought to bolster his port discussion of the nature of Gamergate (Tsukkomi 2017c).

@ljenkins314 has cultivated sufficient profile to receive dozens of replies from the top-tier personalities, including @mombot, @ebilmeeki, and @WeaponizedTweet. @ljenkins314's 1° egocentric network within Class 5 (Fig. 4.29, degree range filtered to >300, node size is by betweenness centrality) includes the major figures in this class and comprises all subdivisions.

4.10.2.3 Wrecks (@Wrecksey)

@Wrecksey, self-asserting as "utterly invincible to social justice losers," joined Twitter in October of 2014, with an established location of South Carolina. The user's latest tweets were a little older than the previous two, with the most recent tweet dating from August 15th, 2017. While Wrecksey has far fewer tweets than @ljenkins314, the user still has a good deal more than @pbewr at a total of 3,016. @Wrecksey's content focuses on politically charged topics like race, sexuality, hypocrisy, and media bias. However, some of the account's older content largely relates to memes, much like @ljenkins314. The user also retweeted and/or replied directly to other data set nodes, such as: @TheIvyClover1 on 9/15/15, @GamergateSings on 6/2/15 and 5/30/15; @WendigoNasty on 5/31/15; @Eliah_R on 5/30/15; and, most notably, @mombot on 3/16/16.

Illustrating the in-joke humor prevalent in this group, @Wrecksey was allegedly doxxed (i.e., when identifying information about a person is published on the Internet, typically with malicious intent to intimidate). A package of unknown and unspecified origin was delivered to the user's house and several tweets and possibly even a Youtube video were generated in order to evaluate the unexpected box (Wrecks 2015a). The contents ended up including a small strip of paper in a ring-sized jewelry box with the words "Thank You For Your Subscription, Shitlord! → http://bit.ly/surprisefaggot" on it. "Shitlord" or "Shit Lord" is a title appropriated by the Gamergate community for "…a natural enemy of the sjw or, social justice warrior." The term was possibly coined by "Sjws…for people that support the patriarchy and hold views they find contrary" (Reddit 2015). The link was to an audio file that has since been deleted and is unable to be opened. Ultimately, it appears that this was a prank pulled by a peer. Initial appearance of the box, however, appeared to generate genuine alarm among the user's contacts, who encouraged him to open the box from the bottom and to wear gloves and a mask in case it was rigged with a trap or weapon (Wrecks 2015b).

- In Profile: "utterly invincible to social justice losers #PoC #BLM #Drumpf".
- Older (2015) tweet content also featured a lot of memes.
- First few months saw frequent tweeting almost exclusively focused on Gamergate. More recent tweets broader in scope.

4.11   The Spectrum (Edge Class 6)

Edge class 6 belongs to @MT8_9 and @TheGingerarchy, both possessing extremely high betweenness centrality in the network overall. @MT8_9 belongs to the signal booster class, created and used only during Gamergate. @TheGingerarchy is part of the gaming and gaming journalism industry and directly connected to many of the most important nodes in the network. She is a general. Between them is everyone else.

4.11.1   Structural Analysis

The third smallest class in the network, Class 6 consists of 465 nodes and 1715 edges. It is a sparsely connected network with a density of only 0.016. The maximum number of degrees is only 93 and the average is only 7.376, far lower than any of the other classes, suggesting that this class is more of a fringe group than a part of the main cluster. Our analysis divided the group into seven modularity classes,

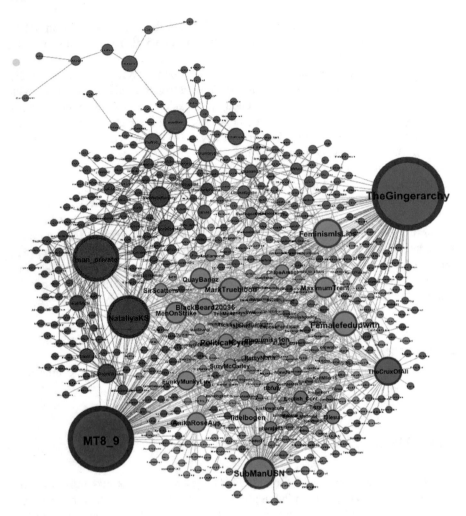

Fig. 4.30 Modularity analysis of class 6 nodes

generally centered on a few major figures such as @TheGingerarchy, @MT8_9, @Femalefedupwith, and @NataliyaKS. We determined who was important by comparing the top ten rankings of degree centrality, closeness centrality, and betweenness centrality and selecting those who appeared on either two or all three lists. Those of particular interest in descending order of betweenness centrality are: @TheGingerarchy, @MT8_9, @man_private, @NataliyaKS, @SubManUSN, @FeminismIsLies, @Femalefedupwith, and @MarkTrueblood.

A Yifan Hu layout of Class 6 and its modularity classes. Nodes are sized according to betweenness, labeled according to degree, and colored according to modularity class (Fig. 4.30).

4.11.2   Content Analysis

Several of the major figures are (or present as) women or other minorities who joined for personal purposes before taking up the Gamergate banner (and have remained active users after the movement's time in the limelight). @TheGingerarchy, @Femalefedupwith, and @NataliyaKS are women, and @PoliticalCynic is a gay man. As an exception to this trend, @MT8_9, while likely a woman, seems to have registered specifically for the purpose of supporting Gamergate in August of 2014, and stopped posting in April of 2015. While several other important figures are/were proudly anti-feminist white men, Gamergate encompasses more than the popular image of angry young right-wingers.

4.11.2.1   Liz Finnegan (@TheGingerarchy)

@TheGingerarchy belongs to Liz Finnegan (also known as @lizzf620), who is still actively tweeting. During Gamergate, Finnegan was a senior editor at *The Escapist* where she reviewed games. In June 2017, Finnegan left *The Escapist* to become director of marketing at Muse Games, a transition that she happened to tweet about with @mombot (Figs. 4.31 and 4.32):

During Gamergate, @TheGingerarchy had several interactions with more than half of the users included in our top 10 of betweenness centrality. In addition to @mombot, she tweeted with @ToKnowIsToBe, @ljenkins314, and @Luisedgm.

@WeaponizedTweet said she was cute (Figs. 4.33 and 4.34):

@ebilmeeki drew a picture of her:

Early in the controversy, Finnegan attempted to enlist other users to write about Gamergate. During this process, she required interested parties to direct message (DM), requiring them to both follow each other, thus increasing her numbers (Fig. 4.35).

Among her many tweets supporting Gamergate, Finnegan produced a 23-point series mocking Anita Sarkeesian (Fig. 4.36).

Finally, Finnegan also claimed to be harassed during the controversy, which she reported to Twitter and discussed with other users (Fig. 4.37).

Among some accounts set up only for Gamergate (@MT8_9) and sock puppets that are still active (@feminismislies), also appearing prominently in the degree and centrality measures in this modularity class are @NataliyaKS, "an antifeminist blogger" from Oslo who stopped tweeting in March 2015 and @femalefedupwithf, "a very proud non feminist female" from London who is still active. Interestingly, neither of these users directly interacted with @TheGingerarchy, nor did they interact with each other. Moreover, neither @NataliyaKS nor @femalefedupwithf interacted with any of the top users for betweenness centrality for the graph, and neither has ever used #GamerGate. While their profiles and other tweets suggest that they align with other pro-Gamergate users, they were not as actively engaged as other seemingly non- or anti-feminist activists like @TheGingerarchy.

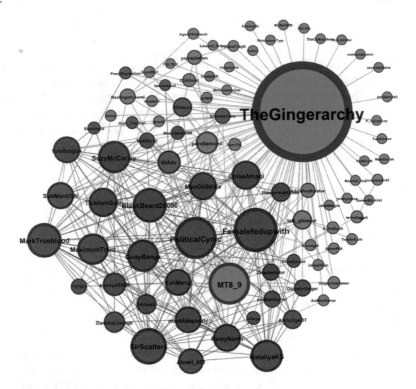

Fig. 4.31 Filtered egocentric network for @TheGingerarchy

Fig. 4.32 Tweets between @mombot and @TheGingerarchy

@SubManUSN and @man_private are former members of the military, though neither had contact with the other. @man_private was a blogger belonging to the men's right subculture. He so strongly adhered to its beliefs that he claimed his video game handle to be "Red Pill," a term used in that movement to represent an

Fig. 4.33 @WeaponizedTweet tweet to @TheGingerarchy

Fig. 4.34 @ebilmeeki tweet to @TheGingerarchy

adoption of the idea that men are actually the ones discriminated against in modern society (Fig. 4.38).

Fig. 4.35 @TheGingerarchy recruiting #notyourshield collaboration

Fig. 4.36 @TheGingerarchy tweets mocking Anita Sarkeesian

While he had no contact with @TheGingerarchy, he did have links to @NataliyaKS and other accounts in her cluster (in orange on the graph), though they did not communicate directly. He appears to have mostly been a hanger-on and cheerleader for the movement rather than a leader or much of a harasser; he claims to have only gotten back into video games with the movement and continued posting after the movement collapsed up until his death in 2017.

@SubManUSN, on the other hand, did have contact with @TheGingerarchy, often either posting flattering comments about her appearance or denigrating popular

Liz Finnegan ✓
@TheGingerarchy

Follow ˅

I support #GamerGate
I do NOT support threats of death/
harassment
I have reported this and suggest you do the
same

~~Thank you for~~
your report.

(e.g. @safety)

Please provide specific Tweets
as evidence of this issue.

Reported Tweet URL

〉 https://mobile.twitter.com/AnitaOfJesus/status/

Please provide at least one direct link to the content you are
reporting, more links are helpful to establish patterns.
Instructions on how to find the direct URL to a Tweet.
If what you are reporting appears outside of a Tweet (e.g.
account bio, profile photo or header), please provide details
in further description of problem.

Your report has been submitted. We may need
additional information before processing your
report. Please check your email. You can print out
a copy of your report at this link.

Add another Tweet

🏠 Home   @ Connect   # Discover

Anita Christian
@AnitaOfJesus

femfreq I WILL KILL YOU

15pm - 11 Oct 14

Fig. 4.37 @TheGingerarchy supporting #GamerGate and reporting harassment

The Private Man @man_private · 6 Oct 2015   ˅
While he is no Godfrey Elfwick, @kylehsimmon is making a PC, genderqueer,
inclusive attempt at it. #GamerGate

💬   ↻   ♡

The Private Man @man_private · 7 Sep 2015   ˅
Thanks to #gamergate, I'm playing some video games again. My online handle is
"Red Pill"

💬 1   ↻ 1   ♡ 1

The Private Man @man_private · 7 Sep 2015   ˅
Replying to @MarkTheBassist

@MarkTheBassist No, I was sidetracked by a video game! #gamergate is getting
me back into video games! #facepalm

💬 1   ↻   ♡

Fig. 4.38 @man_private supporting #GamerGate

Gamergater targets. He developed his own little subcluster while still linking himself to the members of the purple cluster such as @Femalefedupwith.

4.11.3   Conclusions

Despite their lack of interaction, both @SubManUSN and @man_private fit into Gamergate in a couple of interesting ways. Both are/were considerably older than the popular image of a younger man or teen, and both had served in the military. Both were more than happy to at least root for a movement that seemed to match their own beliefs. The diversity and complexity of Gamergate is clear with class 6, with these men supporting or at least following important figures like @TheGingerarchy and other committed anti-feminist women.

4.12   Overall Conclusions

The @ggautoblocker data set, which must necessarily be recognized as a subset of the Gamergate community, defies easy description. Befitting the chan and reddit cultures from which it emerged, this group may be easy to stereotype but stereotyping misses a rich reality. First, caution is necessary to not conflate @ggautoblocker's dataset with Gamergate. The group examined here was caught in a net contrived to identify harassment. Some were clearly participants, while others claim to be collateral casualties of overzealous and overly sensitive crusaders. Second, speaking again to the chan and reddit culture from which much of this group arose, caution must be taken in how literally the texts and accounts are read. The dialogue among these individuals is very rich and dense, employing obscure cultural and pop-cultural references, in-jokes layered on in-jokes, and a carefully veiled lexicon that requires intimate familiarity to accurately and fully glean underlying meaning. Our analysis here skims the surface of these factors. That said, a few arch narratives emerged that may be surprising and confound expectations, and indicate some aspect of the nature of this group.

4.12.1   No Single Narrative

Though often framed as misogynistic basement-dwelling angry young men, the @ggautoblocker group comprises a spectrum of personal identities. In some respect, the Gamergate movement is about gaming journalism; the unifying thread between the trolls, the libertarians, the #NotYourShield spokespeople, and the others is a sense of grievance about how video games are addressed in news media. Some were offended by feminist or intersectional critique of games they love. Others felt condescended to and patronized by a media that in their minds often referred to them as "neckbeards" and "basement-dwelling losers." Others still wanted to hitch their own political hobby-horse to the portrayal of video games. The intentionally decentralized and leaderless Gamergate movement allowed all of these people to share tangible goals even if the reasons for realizing them were completely different. The sense of shared purpose and camaraderie seems to have obscured for many that what one group was doing was antithetical to the politics of another, whether through willful blindness or rationalization.

Interactions among the users profiled here and their antagonists also offer an interesting study of contrasting, multiple narratives. The portrait these gamers paint of themselves and their opposition in journalists, developers, general public, etc., is that of passionate hobbyists defending their chosen entertainment against commercial forces colluding to manipulate and deceive them and an ignorant public that wants to dictate parameters of their world without understanding it. These parameters often engage seemingly arbitrary standards for "decent" behavior, and employ different metrics for those on the opposing side (i.e., the SJWs). The Gamergaters, in turn, are portrayed as a vicious, swarming, no-holds-barred mob ready to bully perceived opponents into submission. This all-out amoral assault on anyone who is different from them is the attributed impetus behind @ggautoblocker. Asking what is/was Gamergate all about is a loaded and problematic proposition, as the answers may be almost as varied as the participants and their motives.

While there is no denying that many members of Gamergate come from diverse backgrounds, the use of anonymous accounts and the #NotYourShield hashtag complicate an attempt to find a true demographic makeup. With the advent of #NotYourShield, non-white and non-male accounts were highlighted, whereas many "stereotypical" gamer accounts may be hiding behind anonymous accounts. Whether organic or intentional, the mix of #NotYourShield and anonymous accounts serves to obscure Gamergate's demographics.

4.12.2   Post-feminist Leadership

Perhaps the most surprising feature of the @ggautoblocker dataset is the prominent–even dominant–role played by women. Four of the top five nodes by betweenness centrality are women (@ebilmeeki, @AngelHeartNight, @RemipunX, and @mombot) and the non-female node in the group, @Weaponized_Tweet, was contrived solely as a rallying point for Gamergate. The other four continue to tweet regularly and about a broad array of subjects besides Gamergate. Expanding the set to the top 14 further includes @MagickalFeline, @StephanieSonmi, and @TheGingerarchy—the latter a prominent and even dominant focal point of Class 6. Why is there such strong female presence and leadership of a mass characterized as misogynistic?

It is possible that these personalities emerged as the dominant voices in the dataset because they were less concerned with obfuscating their identities, leaving them more willing to be honest and open in a way that engaged other users, both within the movement and broadly. Some of these prominent voices also turned to Twitter to discuss their own views and experiences as women in the movement. They insist that Gamergate was never about harassment, although sometimes they themselves are the targets of harassment.

4.12.3 Reports of My Death...

Many of these accounts joined Twitter after Gamergate assumed a semi-coherent identity (to whatever extent the Gamergate identity has ever been coherent). For some, participation lasted through 2015 before burning out or concluding that Gamergate was "over." For example, @ToKnowIsToBe was one of the leaders for #GamerGate, but stopped posting on September 25, 2015, after having not only shared links pertinent to the daily #GamerGate update, but also other files regarding #GamerGate. Others moved on to other movements and activist causes, re-focusing energy into new subjects. Many, however, maintain that Gamergate is ongoing. These tend to be the users asserting that Gamergate is centered on journalistic ethics and collusion between game developers and media. These accounts are still engaging in passionate defense of the ideals of Gamergate, as can be seen in multiple threads from late 2017. The perception of Gamergate being "over" or "ongoing" appears to vary with the user perception of what Gamergate was about. Many who joined in the initial furor either burned out or lost interest as years passed. Those who engaged in the narrative that Gamergate centered on journalistic ethics and disrespect of gamers by gaming journalists, game developers, and factions of society writ large remain as engaged and emphatic as ever. The answer to the question "is Gamergate dead?" is as loaded and will receive as varied and individual an answer as "what is/was Gamergate about?"

4.12.4 Directions for Future Study

This review is both preliminary and executed by researchers with a cursory understanding of the Gamergate phenomenon and the community participating in it. Due to the nature of dialogue and intra-group lexicon, any understanding by outside researchers will likely lack the full depth of meaning present. In addition, due to the structure of the Gamergate movement, it is difficult to pinpoint the reason for its existence. This is something that should be studied further to fully understand what led to the differences between the members' beliefs and actions. While it could have been due to the lack of coherent leadership, the location of the members, the social media site used, or even just the different array of personalities could all have been important contributing factors.

References

Best Mom Eva (2018) "The war never ends." Tweet, @mombot. https://twitter.com/mombot/status/954208852056031232. Accessed 18 Jan 2018

Brown B (2017) Twitter_scraping: Grab All a User's Tweets (and Get Past 3200 Limit). Python. https://github.com/bpb27/twitter_scraping

GitHub: freebsdgirl/ggautoblocker (2014). https://archive.is/78K3G. Accessed 21 Jan 2018

Good OS (2015) Bomb threat shuts down SPJ event discussing GamerGate (Update). Accessed https://www.polygon.com/2015/8/16/9161311/bomb-threat-shuts-down-spj-panel-discussing-Gamergate. 21 Jan 2018

Griffin A (2015) GamerGate: developer Tim Schafer provokes rage with joke about online gaming activists at industry awards. http://www.independent.co.uk/life-style/gadgets-and-tech/news/Gamergate-developer-tim-schafer-provokes-rage-with-joke-about-online-gaming-activists-at-industry-10089124.html. Accessed 21 Jan 2018

KnowYourMeme (2018) "Leeroy Jenkins," Know Your Meme. http://knowyourmeme.com/memes/leeroy-jenkins

Limburger Limited (2015a) "@mombot At least it would be vidya-related conflation. Progress! #GamerGate" Tweet, @ToKnowIsToBe. https://twitter.com/mombot/status/636128912561410049. Accessed 25 Aug 2015

Limburger Limited (2015b) "@angelheartnight we need a vaccine for foot-in-mouth disease. #GamerGate"Tweet, @ToKnowIsToBe. https://twitter.com/ToKnowIsToBe/status/618708295885430784. Accessed 8 July 2015

Limburger Limited (2015c) "@_WCS_just reminds everyone to archive everything. #GamerGate" Tweet, @ToKnowIsToBe. https://twitter.com/ToKnowIsToBe/status/560122260879839232. Accessed 27 Jan 2015

Reddit (2015) "What Is a Shit Lord? What Is a Shitpost? • r/OutOfTheLoop," reddit. https://www.reddit.com/r/OutOfTheLoop/comments/3etz5k/what_is_a_shit_lord_what_is_a_shitpost. Accessed 27 July 2015

Remi (2015) "#Gamergate actually started an Op almost a year ago about rebuilding what the press ruined.:) @taddmencer @Delafina777". Tweet, @RemipunX. https://twitter.com/RemipunX/status/638418401191428096. Accessed 31 Aug 2015

Sofaer A (2017) "Aaron Sofaer, Signing Off." https://www.google.com/url?q=https://groups.google.com/forum/%23!topic/ggautoblocker-appeals/Tvjbj8Xa7o4&sa=D&ust=1516657098623000&usg=AFQjCNGXobgcXs5_HK_6Jk3Uc6qdgTnPBg. Accessed 28 Sept 2017

Sterne P (2014) Gawker discusses cost of 'Gamergate'. https://www.politico.com/media/story/2014/12/gawker-discusses-cost-of-Gamergate-003205. Accessed 21 Jan 2018

Tsukkomi (2015) "@redlianak I Feel Your Pain. I Had to Live without A/C in the Middle of Summer after Hurricane Charlie. It Was Hell.," Tweet, @ljenkins314 (blog). https://twitter.com/ljenkins314/status/62641562418139160. Accessed 8 July 2015

Tsukkomi (2016) "My Vote for Jill Stein Helped Trump Win Florida.," Tweet, @ljenkins314 (blog). https://twitter.com/ljenkins314/status/796394319909363712. Accessed 8 Nov 2016

Tsukkomi (2017a) "I've Been without Power for Four Days Because of a Massive Hurricane, so I Missed That Discussion.," Tweet, @ljenkins314 (blog). https://twitter.com/ljenkins314/status/908687743877812224. Accessed 6 Sept 2017

Tsukkomi (2017b) ">alt-Right Blahblahblah Been a Registered Democrat for 20 Years.," Tweet, @ljenkins314 (blog). https://twitter.com/ljenkins314/status/922163900396789761. Accessed 11 Oct 2017

Tsukkomi (2017c) "I'm Not Ignoring Anything. I Acknowledged Harassment, but It Was Coming from a Tiny Minority.Pic.Twitter.Com/F8OKFKkV7 g," Tweet, @ljenkins314 (blog). https://twitter.com/ljenkins314/status/917403405055877122. Accessed 7 Oct 2017

Vivian J (2014). http://knowyourmeme.com/memes/vivian-james. Accessed 21 Jan 2018

Wrecks (2015a) "WTF WOULD BOTHER DOXXING ME #Gamer-Gatepic.Twitter.Com/KqqVD4jGVs," Tweet, @Wrecksey (blog). https://twitter.com/Wrecksey. Accessed 12 Apr 2015

Wrecks (2015b) "Fuck Th*t, Let's Do It. Should Use Gloves or s/t but Don't Have Any. Need Something to Open This with… #GamerGatepic.Twitter.Com/Do6oE4P7Rh," Tweet, @Wrecksey (blog). https://twitter.com/Wrecksey. Accessed 12 Apr 2015

Chapter 5
Automation and Harassment Detection

Edward Dixon

Abstract Replacing complex and brittle hand-written rules with models trained using machine-learning lead to the first truly effective spam filters, improving the lives of email users and reducing the need for human intervention in detection efforts.

5.1 Introduction

Replacing complex and brittle hand-written rules with models trained using machine-learning lead to the first truly effective spam filters, improving the lives of email users and reducing the need for human intervention in detection efforts. Could similar techniques be used to reduce online harassment? Researchers in both academic and industrial settings have indeed had success with training text classifiers to detect harassment. While machines can learn to model the human consensus on whether a given text is harassing, or not, the work to-date also shows the limitations of this approach: since human raters do not always agree, neither can a machine. This problem is already familiar to spam researchers in the form of "grey mail"—one reader's junk mail is another's valuable special offer. In this chapter, we examine the application of machine learning to harassment detection, using datasets from two of the popular websites built on user-generated content, Wikipedia and Reddit. We conclude with suggested next steps for both application developers and for academic researchers.

5.2 First Attempt: Just Code

From an engineering perspective, online harassment looks a lot like spam detection—how can we detect (and block) harassing messages? In the early years of the Web, rising volumes of spam threatened to make email useless. Engineers trying

E. Dixon (✉)
Intel Corp, Santa Clara, USA
e-mail: edward.dixon@intel.com

© Springer International Publishing AG, part of Springer Nature 2018
J. Golbeck (ed.), *Online Harassment*, Human–Computer Interaction Series,
https://doi.org/10.1007/978-3-319-78583-7_5

to defeat spam compiled lists of keywords and phrases to separate wanted from unwanted messages.

Let's take a really nice public dataset and see if that approach can help us to detect online harassment; a 2016 paper by researchers from Google's Jigsaw project and the Wikimedia foundation[1] describe how their detox project built possibly the best extant open dataset for harassment detection (described at https://meta.wikimedia. org/wiki/Research:Detox/Data_Release). One subset, the "Personal attacks" dataset contains 100,000 samples, each of which have been annotated by 10 human raters. For our purposes, we'll consider comments which *no* rater labellers as attacking to be "benign", and take comments labelled by 4 or more rater to be "attacking". This were 36,647 very benign comments and 10,201 attacking comments from our subset[2] of the "Persona attacks" dataset. Now is a great time to open up your web browser, and use the code we've published at https://github.com/EdwardDixon/Automation-and-Harassment-Detection to follow along.

Picking a few "obvious" candidate words that might be included in a a personal attack, we arrive at the following table.

Word	Benign count	Attack count
Moron	3	158
Hate	84	250
Ass	10	514

At first glance, we might be rather encouraged to see that "moron" is almost (but not quite!) limited to comments that many see as personal attacks. Perhaps we can auto-block comments containing words like "moron" or "ass" ("hate" doesn't seem so selective). There are a few obvious problem with this approach:

- *Sample bias*: the dataset we are using isn't representative in one important way. The authors deliberately include a much larger fraction of attacking comments than would be present if these comments were selected at random. From their paper, we learn that only 3% of anonymous contributions were attacks (for registered users, the number is about 0.5%); since we had only about 3 times as many benign as attacking comments in this dataset, we should assume that "in the wild" we would see 10X–60X as many instances of "moron" in the "benign" column as we did in this sample. It would still be more common in attacking than benign comments, but we would have a much higher "false positive" rate than this table applies.
- *Recall rate*: the recall rate is the fraction of true-positive samples that are actually flagged or captured. Note that even the relatively popular "ass" account for only 512 of our "attack" comments.

---

[1] Ex Machina: Personal Attacks Seen at Scale, https://arxiv.org/pdf/1610.08914.pdf.
[2] Why only a (70,000 sample) subset? This will be explained later in the chapter.

5.3   A Little Help from Statistics

Perhaps we can do better just by finding more good-quality keywords? We can look for words that are very predictive of one class or the other by using a statistical method called the χ^2(chi-squared) score[3]. Essentially, this method ranks items according to how much their distribution varies between classes (ideally, we want words that occur a lot in one class, but not at all in another). The words with the highest scores will be the most class-specific. What is the input for this method? We could use the raw counts of words, but a better choice would be the tf-idf[4] (term frequency-inverse document frequency) score, a statistical score widely used in information retrieval and text classification that accounts for some words have a higher background level of popularity than others. Calculating the χ^2 score based on the tf-idf of each word (statistic piled on statistic!), the top-scoring (most useful-looking) words are as follows:

Rather a depressing list, even from a purely literary perspective! Checking the counts, we can see that although some words are gratifyingly specific—at 25th in the list, "fuck" actually looks like a plausible candidate for exclusion, with nearly 1,502 total usages, and all but 4 involving personal attacks. More positively, gratitude is a strong signal also, with "thanks" a strong hint that comment isn't an attack. Most pejoratives only seem to be present in a few hundred words, but perhaps we can combine them to get an effective detector?

From the list above, let's remove any words with non-negligible "benign" counts to arrive at a shortlist of words that seem to be almost entirely restricted to attacks (faggot, dick, cunt, idiot, asshole, gay, suck, bitch, ass, stupid, shit, fucking, fuck). Now, we can plot the attack score for each comment against its count of words from this shortlist. There is a nice strong correlation between attack score and count; unfortunately, many comments have a count of zero, regardless of attack score.

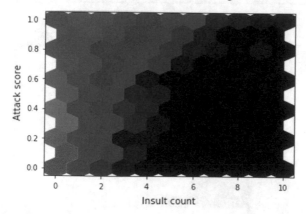

The hexbin plot is great for getting an overall impression. Let's take a closer look at scores for just the attacking comments using a histogram.

---

[3]http://www.statisticshowto.com/probability-and-statistics/chi-square/.

[4]https://lizrush.gitbooks.io/algorithms-for-webdevs-ebook/content/chapters/tf-idf.html.

Word	Attack comments	Benign comments	Rank
Personal	350	780	1
Block	454	558	2
Vandalize	83	111	3
Life	575	498	4
Attack	234	294	5
Thanks	227	2763	6
Hate	250	84	7
Faggot	223	1	8
Vandalism	311	559	9
Hell	310	79	10
Dick	303	20	11
Cunt	262	1	12
Blocked	420	699	13
Idiot	355	6	14
Asshole	326	1	15
Gay	308	39	16
Redirect	13	791	17
Suck	373	5	18
Bitch	401	1	19
Ass	514	10	20
Stupid	568	35	21
Shit	734	11	22
Stop	834	566	23
Fucking	977	4	24
Fuck	1458	4	25

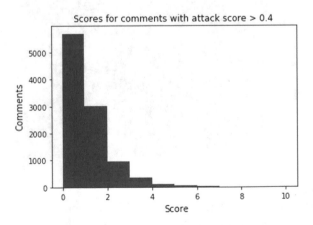

Unfortunately, we can see that, even among these the most common score is 0! Flagging any comment with at least one of our statistically-selected terms turns out to give us a relatively low false positive rate on this dataset (0.18%) on the most benign comments (attack score <0.1) and a *recall rate* of 44% (where a score of 100% would mean that it caught all comments with an attack score above 0.4).

How could we improve on this rule? Of course, we can add more keywords. We would have to be careful, though: remember that the words we used were found using statistical tests which ranked the best candidates first. Still, the next 25 words on our χ^2-sorted list include many promising candidates—'loser', 'bullshit', 'penis', 'fag' 'dumb', 'troll', 'moron', 'kill', 'cock', 'racist', 'crap'—all much more common in posts with a strong "attack" score. When we add these words to our keywords list (doubling its size) our recall rate increases—to 54%—and the false positive rates goes to 0.5%.

Why didn't doubling the size of our keyword list double our recall? Unfortunately, as we move down the list, although we can still find very class-specific words ('fag' and 'cock') appear to be almost perfect "indicators" of a personal attack, we also find that words rapidly become rarer (111 and 171 usages respectively). In fact, *most* words in human languages are comparatively rare. The frequency of words conforms almost perfectly to the Zipf distribution[5], in which the second-most common word is half as common as the post popular word, and so on (bad news in this context, but a big when when one studies a new language—although native-speaker proficiency might require a vocabulary of 20,000 words or more, even 2,000 of the most common words is enough to make sense of a newspaper).

Since most words are comparatively rare, adding a small number of words to our keyword list won't get us very far. Adding a *lot* of words will also present challenges, however, as we'll be forced to add terms that are not only rarer but also less class-specific. Our false positive rate went from 0.18 to 0.5% (about 2.5X more errors) when we added 10% to our recall rate. As we descend our word list, this problem will get worse—we'll have to invent more and more complicated rules as we try to increase recall without blowing up our false positive rate.

This was the path taken by engineers fighting spam at the turn of the millenium; ever-increasing efforts for ever-diminishing rewards. Then, in 2002, the hugely influential technologist and investor Paul Graham published a seminal article "The Plan for Spam"[6], in which he described what happened, when—after 6 months of trying to code his way through the problem—he changed course:

> When I did try statistical analysis, I found immediately that it was much cleverer than I had been. It discovered, of course, that terms like "virtumundo" and "teens" were good indicators of spam. But it also discovered that "per" and "FL" and "ff0000" are good indicators of spam. In fact, "ff0000" (html for bright red) turns out to be as good an indicator of spam as any pornographic term.

The hand-coding approach had made intuitive sense—after all, *humans* easily distinguished spam from non-spam, and certain words ("teen", "click") were "by inspection" far more common in spam. However, as Paul Graham discovered, having the *implicit* understanding required to perform a task is very different from being

---

[5]https://plus.maths.org/content/mystery-zipf.

[6]"A Plan for Spam", Paul Graham, http://www.paulgraham.com/spam.html.

able to give *explicit* instructions for performing the same task (perhaps you have tried to teach a small child to walk or to ride a bicycle?). Like the other engineers tackling this problem, Paul Graham's insights into how he himself identified spam were not enough to reach an acceptable solution. By switching to statistical modelling—we would call it "machine learning" now—he was able to delegate the hardest work to the computer.

5.4   A First Attempt with Machine Learning

We used statistical techniques to find the right words; how does this differ from the "statistical modelling" that Paul Graham talks about? Statistical modelling or statistical learning is what we called machine learning before we got better at marketing. Instead of just using math to find useful keywords (or "features" in machine learning argot), we try to use it to find the rules, too. In place of our rule ("label as 'attacking' any comment with at least one of these keywords"), machines can learn rules of arbitrary complexity—all with empirical roots in our datasets.

What sort of rules might our machines learn? Early model-based spam filters used a type of model called a *linear* model. These have a very straightforward geometric interpretation and work like this:

- Conventional code counts the relative frequencies of words in spam and non-spam documents (or, better, the tf-idf score we discussed earlier).
- Each document gets represented as a list of counts—e.g. a potentially harassing document could be reduced to {"fuck":1, "thanks":0} and a non-spam document might (ideally!) be converted to {"fuck":0, "thanks":1}. If we have just two keywords, then each document is now effectively a point on a plane with two axes—"fuck" and "thanks".
- The machine then finds the line that *best* separates spam from non-spam (or harassment from non-harassment).

Couldn't a human pick those weights (find that line)? If we had a two-word vocabulary, and some metrics or visualisation as guide, this might be viable. However, an effective classifier is likely to need to consider at least *hundreds* of words. If a 2 word vocabulary required us to find a *line* (solving a 2 dimensional problem) then a 3 word vocabulary requires us to find the *plane* that best separates the classes. Anyone who has tried to fix a wobbly four-legged table will appreciate that fitting a plane to just four points isn't always easy! Moving above 3 dimensions, we need to find "best-fit" *hyperplanes*. Viewed from this geometrical perspective, it is easy to see that having humans choose weights for keywords, while superficially appealing (simple! transparent! use the human expertise!) almost always produces very low-quality solutions. Although we "know it when we see it", it turns out that the best way to leverage human expertise is to have humans label sample posts as "harassment" or "not harassment".

So what can a simple linear model do? Using the features we already prepared, the sample code (https://github.com/EdwardDixon/Automation-and-Harassment-Detection) uses Python's popular sklearn[7] library to train a linear model—a "logistic regression" classifier. The resulting model can give us a "yes/no" decision or a "class probability"—the probability of whether a comment is attacking or not.

If you follow along with the sample code (recommended!) you should find that the logistic regression classifier achieves an overall recall rate of about 88%—sklearn gives us a simple way to get a nice report.

	Precision	Recall	f1-score	Support
False	0.94	0.93	0.93	11759
True	0.60	0.63	0.61	1997
Avg/total	0.89	0.88	0.89	13756

You don't have to understand all the numbers here immediately, but let's quickly revise our metrics:

- **Recall** is the fraction of harassing content that we actually catch. Imagine you are trying to catch all the trout in a given stretch of river: 50% recall would mean that you caught half of the trout.
- **Precision** measures how often you "catch the right fish". A precision score of 90% would mean that every time you landed a "trout" it was, in fact, a trout.

The fishing metaphor will perhaps make clear why there is a tension between these two metrics: we could maximize our recall by just diverting the water from our riverbed, then picking up all the fish from the drying mud. 100% recall! However, we would have an enormous bycatch—all the other denizens of the river from nematodes to pike!

Similarly, one could maximize precision by standing, heron-like, at the edge of the water and patiently waiting to spear some luckless passing trout. With a little training, one could imagine learning to catch *only* trout. However, most of the trout would presumably elude us: we would have perfect precision (1 or 2 trout for supper) but very poor recall (hundreds of surviving trout still happily snacking on mayflies).

Catching *all* trout and *only* trout would clearly be a more complex exercise. The Holy Grail of classification is to score very highly *on both metrics at the same time*. This isn't always possible, and in practice, you may well decide to sacrifice some recall for the sake of higher precision.

What about that mysterious F1 score? It is the harmonic mean of precision and recall, and so attempts to provide a single number with which to compare models.

---

[7]http://scikit-learn.org.

5.5   Improving Our Model

There are 4 paths to finding a better model:

1. **More data**: It is important to try to use data from your problem area, and as much of it as possible.
2. **Better models**: linear models, as the name implies, are limited to finding a simple (flat) decision surface. However, a curvier, more complex surface may perform better. You'll need to look at "non-linear" models, like ensembles of decision trees, or even neural networks.
3. **Better features**: the way you represent your text can have large influence on any model's effectiveness; we used tf/idf, but there are many other possibilities; "word vectors" are one especially powerful example.
4. **Experimentation**: if you really need to maximize performance, you'll have to do lots of fine-tuning and tweaking, on both features and model "hyper-parameters" (variables that aren't learned from the data, but must be chosen by the investigator). In particular, *time spent studying samples on which your model failed is rarely wasted*. Remember to slog through the actual text, not just summary statistics like those we just explored.

Collecting and labelling more data is a little out of the scope of this chapter (but has never been easier, and you should not underestimate how many samples you can label—1,000 per person per hour is quite possible in the harassment domain,—look at tools like Prodigy from explosion.ai[8]).

Simply trying different model types is a fast and easy way to find some improvements: a very popular model type called Gradient Boosted Trees is currently the tool of choice for engineers tackling problems relating to structured data (think databases), but can do quite well on messier data like our free-text dataset. If you follow along with our sample code, you'll see that we can train and test a "Gradient Boosted Trees" model with only a few extra lines of code (in fact, most of our effort has gone into loading and preparing the data—this is quite typical of machine learning projects).

	Precision	Recall	f1-score	Support
False	0.90	1.00	0.95	11759
True	0.94	0.37	0.53	1997
Avg/total	0.91	0.90	0.89	13756

Interestingly, our new model is better *and* worse than our old linear model: it has better (perfect!) recall on the harassment-negative samples, and very high precision on the positive samples. There has been a trade-off, though: the recall on harassment-

---

[8]https://prodi.gy/.

positive samples has dropped a lot. The right trade-off will depend heavily on how you plan to apply your detector.

5.6 Domain Matters: A Tail of Two Distributions

Now that we have trained a classifier, let's take it for a test drive—on a different dataset. So far, we've worked only with the WikiMedia "Detox" dataset, which is drawn from the English Wikipedia Talk pages (where editors discuss the content that goes into the actual pages). How confident can we be that our classifier will work well on other datasets? Will the comments on those pages be representative of how internet users in general communicate? We'll explore this question through a different dataset which lacks labels—comments drawn from Reddit, the well known discussion site, for May 2015[9]. Applying one of the models we trained earlier (you are following along with our online example code, aren't you?), we classify content from two different subreddits—"Rangers", a group for ice hockey fans, and "Personal Finance" (what it sounds like).

Let's take a look at the most "attacking" comments from Rangers, as rated by our model:

Attack_probability	Comment
0.98	How do you hop on the guys dick that just got fucking wrecked by kreiders skill skating? that confuses the fuck out of me
0.97	Stop fucking passing it in the slot. holy fuck
0.96	Jesus fuck just put it on the fucking net
0.95	One thing we have to do in this series. ONE FUCKING THING. STAY OFF THE GOD DAMN PENALTY KILL
0.95	Shut the fuck up pierre
0.94	Holy fucking shit
0.92	Fuck you pierre! god damn, that just doesnt look the same without the capslock
0.91	It's the same fucking spot every goddamn fucking time. how can no one stop that fucker. goddammit grandpa boyle
0.89	Garden needs some life, damn people start rooting for the players; chant their name or something. be the extra player on the fucking ice
0.87	Fuck you, ovechkin

What about the nicest, or at least lowest on the "attacking" scale?

In evaluating our results, we should keep in mind the criteria used to create our training set—raters were explicit instructed to watch for comments including a

---

[9]https://www.kaggle.com/reddit/reddit-comments-may-2015 Reddit generously provides dumps of *all* Reddit comments—1 terabyte of text, and rising!

Attack_probability	Comment
0.11	Who is announcing the game, his style seems to be just calling out names. Not a fan
0.11	This guy rules. http://imgur.com/ktGj08v
0.11	No goalie ever seems to make that save... so frustrating
0.11	They will come out flying. Av is going to perform more mystical coaching voodoo, you just wait....\n \nAlso Hank will give them that disapproving look that makes men ashamed and strive for excellence
0.11	Those don't look like the type of people who would be ordering two feet of pizza
0.11	We defiantly deserved a goal this period
0.11	Dan boyle, the words I have for you... dear god they aren't pretty
0.09	Thank you nbcsn... it is possible to fall asleep in your chair during playoff hockey. is it too much to ask from maybe a little tiny bit of excitement from your broadcast? maybe we should get gary thorn to do nantz impressions
0.08	Thanks!
0.07	You can hear the lgr ranger's chant trying to start from the 300 s section

personal attack[10]. In this case, few of highest confidence comments appear to be attacking *someone who is actually part of the conversation*—although one does wince for the teams! Looking at the comments rated *least* likely to be attacking, the model's "judgment" seems plausible.

What about our personal finance folk? "Most attacking" first:

Looking at the "attack probability" column, we see that the top scores on this topic are far lower than for sports. Looking at the lowest-ranked comments in this forum:

Looking at the most and least "attacking" for personal finance, you may notice lots of gratitude—specifically, "thanks" or "thank you" feature heavily. Remember those top-ranked "Rangers" comments? Lots of "fuck" or "fucking"! At this point, we might start to worry that our model might be over-relying on certain words. Recall that that the features the model learns from and predicts on are really just *counts* of words in the document. The models we built so far have no chance to use the sentence structure itself. Of course, this is interpretation is just a theory, but one that you can put to the test in the accompanying code by constructing sentences yourself and seeing how they are rated. For example, "Reader, you fucking rock! Thank you so much for buying my book!" scores an attack probability of 0.65!

---

[10]https://meta.wikimedia.org/wiki/Research:Detox/Data_Release#Personal_Attacks.

Personal finance: Comments with the highest 'attack' score

Attack_probability	Comment
0.85	18% car loan? What the fuck. Do you never pay your debts or did you just sign a loan without looking at the fine print?
0.69	Definitely junk food gotta go grocery shopping and use coupons. apply for help from the state, get food stamps. Its always the junk food that costs the most. The average wages life sucks ass and has plenty of paperwork to stay comfortable
0.53	I used to have very bad anxiety. I went and talked to a physiologist who made me realise no one else actually gives a shit about what I do so why should I worry. Getting help is the best thing
0.42	Realistically, most of the regular, reliable audio engineer gigs out there are for megachurches. Unless the congregation >10 k every sunday, they don't pay shit. \n\nYou might score the odd recording gig or maybe doing the tech behind indie film scoring or folio work, but other than that there…
0.36	jpoysti bought two jet skis, a Martin guitar, and week-long trip to Hawaii with the 15,000 *e saved by buying a* 15,000 he saved by buying a 10,000 car instead of a 25,000 *car. He had* 25,000 car. He had 6,000 left over. He took that 6,000 *invested in for* 30 *years at* 56,000 invested in for 30 years at 534,000—which allowed him to retire 5 months…
0.36	Just be careful about food. I justified moving out as being cheaper because splitting the rent 4 ways and no expensive-ass meal plan meant a big chunk of savings. However, with house-mates never keeping the kitchen clean, and not having a lot of confidence or experience cooking even basic meals,…
0.24	And I probably hate yours:)
0.20	>Although I have a job I have a really hard time not spending money on things like games.\n\nLife's hard. Set a budget, stick to it. Search for jar method or envelope method as two ways to see your budget and if you can spend money. \n\nIf you can't control your spending, you're in for a lif…
0.20	I dont understand either. It's like the apex of your life is working that job, for real? I can kind of understand if it's your own company because then you get into your personal legacy which some care about but if it's someone else's name on the building I don't understand how people get so obs…
0.20	It's a lot more complicated than just living there for a year or two. You need to transfer your whole life over and make enough money to support yourself for that time.\n\nhttp://registrar.berkeley.edu/establish.html?no_server_init

Personal finance: Comments with the lowest 'attack' score

Attack_probability	Comment
0.10	Bigger doesn't always mean better either, it also has to do with the cut, clarity, and color, and usually bigger diamonds are less likely to have a good color/clarity. And if they do, will cost an arm and a leg. The thing I see lately is halo rings, where there are a lot of small diamonds around...
0.08	/r/budgetfood mod here. thanks for the plug!
0.08	Thanks for the replies
0.08	ah, makes sense—thanks
0.08	Thanks!
0.08	thanks!\nYea I dont really want to stretch beyond 3 k/month...thats a little too much going into housing for my preference!!!
0.07	Agreed with Uptown. Luckily Dallas is starting the trolleys again in May and it runs right by my building, so I can go to Uptown for free. I'm not opposed to driving. Thank you for the info!
0.07	I understand your point and my friend has raised this issue as well. I will be sure to keep it in mind.\n\nI am going to see how that works. I am about 10 min from my office and where I am working is pretty relaxed, so hopefully it will be doable. Thank you for the advice!
0.07	Lol you do raise a valid point. I do understand living in my means. \n\nSocal rents are ridiculous (grew up in HB), so I didn't think this was over the top for what I wanted. Thank you kind redditor! I will be visiting SoCal this summer, so please let me know if you want me to bring some water:)
0.05	Just curious if you've looked at WiseBanyan. They were mentioned in a recent WSJ article about robo-advisors along with the commonly mentioned names

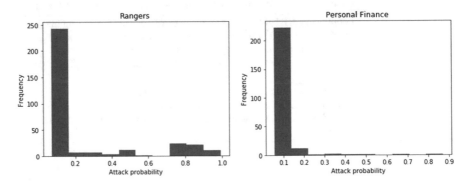

As a final way of comparing the forums, let's have a look at the overall scores for "Rangers" versus "Personal Finance":

As one might hope, *most* comments get quite low score. However, we can clearly see that the Rangers group scores a lot higher than the Personal Finance group.

Comparing Rangers fans and finance folk, it is clear that there are rather noticeable differences in language and tone. Language is simply used differently between these two groups; in fact, those passionate Rangers fans use language common to many sports groups on Reddit, where "fuck" is not so much a signal of exasperation as a warning of an imminent noun. Successful classification needs to into account the wider context.

Remember that our classifier was relatively accurate on the Wikipedia dataset on which we trained it, and did not suffer from the over-sensitivity which it seems to show when reviewing "Rangers" posts. We are encountering two different distributions—which is just a fancy statistician's way of saying that words occur at different frequencies and with different neighbors on Wikipedia versus Reddit. In fact, comparing "Personal Finance" to "Rangers", we might well suspect that Reddit itself is divided into many subcultures.

The implication here is that it might be difficult for a model trained *exclusively* on data from one source to perform really well on another. If our goal was to provide harassment detection for Reddit, we would need to consider adapting our model to the new domain. How would we do this?

- Creating a Reddit benchmark by having humans label comments from Reddit would be a sensible first step, giving us a way to measure quality
- A simple remedy would be to adjust the sensitivity—raise the threshold required for a comment to be labelled as "attacking". However, having reviewed comments from the top end of the spectrum and found many false positives, clearly that alone wouldn't suffice (just look at that "Rangers" histogram).
- Creating labelled training data drawn from Reddit to supplement our Wikipedia set would be a really good idea. If you want to understand sports fans, you may want to train on sports fans!
- Giving our models a way to understand the context around a word would also be good (think "fucking" versus "fucking awesome"). One simple way to do this is by changing how we create features; e.g. instead of using only single words as features, we could use combinations of 2 or even 3 words ("bigrams" and "trigrams").
- We could explore more advanced model types, such as deep neural networks, which can successfully learn to perform more advanced language understanding tasks like machine translation. Models of this type can use the context of a an entire sentence or even a paragraph, to more accurately determine meaning.
- Given the recent success of deep learning-based approaches to machine translation, it is possible that "translating" between styles could be used to present users with suggested re-writes of posts even before they actually post them. The attraction of such an approach is that it could potentially raise the standard of contributions generally.

We began this chapter treating machine learning as a programming problem, and showed how using machine learning has distinct advantages over a manual one. However, it is important to understand that—at the time of writing—machine-learning is not yet a silver bullet for this problem. Harassment is a harder problem than spam, written one comment at a time, rather than mass-produced, and this "artisanal" quality leads to variations that impede detection. Additionally, different norms apply to different communities, even within a single website: our passionate sports fans might not appreciate being held to the same standard as our analytical finance gurus—and vice versa. To successfully train a machine on tasks like these, you'll need to begin by considering exactly what it is that you want your machines to learn, and the context in which you want them to operate, and you'll need to consider how best to integrate such detectors with the work flows of your anti-abuse teams.

Part II
Characteristics

Chapter 6
Characterizing Gender Differences in Misogynistic and Antisocial Microblog Posts

Cody Buntain

Abstract This chapter presents an observational study into the genders of authors posting abusive misogynistic insults and hate speech on Twitter. We first characterize the different uses of potentially abusive and misogynistic expletives in Twitter using a novel diversity-based sampling strategy and use Amazon's Mechanical Turk (MTurk) crowdsourcing platform to construct a labeled dataset of abusive, misogynistic insults. This misogyny dataset and datasets from prior work on harassing and hate speech in Twitter provide datasets for evaluating classification algorithms that can automatically identify this antisocial content. Leveraging 1.8 billion tweets from Twitter's 1% public sample stream between 1 January 2015 to 31 December 2015, results show this antisocial content is relatively rare on Twitter, accounting for less than 1% of English tweets. After applying a gender classifier to this data, results demonstrate the population of English-tweeting Twitter users in 2015 who posted abusive misogynistic content were more likely to be classified as female when compared against a random Twitter sample from the same timeframe. For harassing and hateful speech, however, we find authors are more likely to be classified as male when compared against a random Twitter sample. Though this work does not cover threats of sexual violence, these results are consistent with prior research into misogynistic and hateful insults both on- and offline and have consequences for interventions designed to improve the quality of content in online spaces.

NB: Subject matter in this chapter covers explicit, offensive, degrading, and racist language. Readers should be prepared to encounter such content.

C. Buntain (✉)
University of Maryland, College Park, USA
e-mail: cbuntain@cs.umd.edu

© Springer International Publishing AG, part of Springer Nature 2018   127
J. Golbeck (ed.), *Online Harassment*, Human–Computer Interaction Series,
https://doi.org/10.1007/978-3-319-78583-7_6

6.1   Introduction

Information quality in online social spaces is an increasingly important topic as these spaces become gathering points and major sources of news, especially for younger Internet users. Abuse, misogyny, harassment, and other antisocial behaviors are of particular concern for online platforms like Twitter's microblogging site, YouTube's video service, and Twitch's streaming offering, who want to foster open, welcoming communities and increase their user bases. While such platforms have instituted strict policies for behavior (e.g., Twitter's "Hateful Conduct Policy",[1] YouTube's "Hate Speech"[2] and "Harassment and Cyberbullying" policies, and Twitch's "Community Guidelines"[3]), such guidelines have not dissuaded this behavior. On the contrary, though Microsoft's Xbox Live platform officially prohibits "content that could harm or harass a person",[4] prior research has shown female-sounding gamers are three times more likely to receive insults and offensives messages compared to muted or male-sounding gamers (Kuznekoff and Rose 2013). Such negative content makes these platforms unappealing to female and minority users, which exacerbates the digital divide and restricts the platform's population.

Despite computer science researchers' tendencies, purely technical solutions are unlikely to solve these problems; instead, combined socio-technical interventions are likely necessary. Developing such interventions, however, requires a better understanding of the authors creating anti-social content. To this end, this chapter presents an observational study of the makeup of misogynistic content on Twitter across all of 2015, compares this content to existing studies of hate speech (Davidson et al. 2017; Saleem et al. 2016) and harassment (Golbeck et al. 2017), and examines the gender distributions of this content. Our focus on Twitter as a model platform is motivated by its size and accessibility for data collection, its textual nature, and existing research into gender inference; other platforms deserve attention as well (e.g., Reddit, YouTube, Twitch, Instagram, etc.), but Twitter provides a foundation for an already difficult problem. By elucidating the demographics of authors creating this anti-social content, we can gain a better understanding of their motives and targets and construct interventions tailored to specific content types.

This chapter describes methods for automatically classifying misogynistic and hateful content, inferring author gender, and comparing gender distributions in Twitter against these antisocial messages. One should note this work takes a narrow view of misogynistic content, defining "misogynistic language" in Twitter as **a tweet that contains at least one misogynistic expletive and is meant to be hurtful**; this definition excludes more subtle but equally malicious misogynistic insults like "get back in the kitchen where you belong" or "make me a sandwich." Our results demonstrate first that the majority of content including explicit, misogynistic keywords are classified as aggressive insults (approximately 78% of instances). From a crowdsourced

---

[1] https://help.twitter.com/en/rules-and-policies/hateful-conduct-policy.

[2] https://support.google.com/youtube/answer/2801939?hl=en&ref_topic=2803176.

[3] https://www.twitch.tv/p/legal/community-guidelines/.

[4] https://www.xbox.com/en-US/Legal/CodeOfConduct.

dataset, we construct a classifier for automatically identifying insulting, misogynistic tweets and identify the most significant features in making this determination. For comparison, we construct a similar classifier for identifying harassment and hateful content in Twitter and compare their significant features to our misogyny classifier. This comparison demonstrates misogynistic tweets tend to focus on insults of sexual promiscuity whereas harassing and hateful tweets refer to race and ethnicity. Comparing the genders of these antisocial messages, we find the proportion of female authors of misogynistic content is significantly different from and larger than the proportion of female authors in a random Twitter sample. For harassing/hateful tweets, however, we find the proportion of male authors is both significantly larger than that of male authors in a random Twitter sample and larger than the proportion of female authors. Female-authored misogynistic and male-authored harassment/hateful content is consistent with prior work on characterizing insulting and racist content in other offline and online contexts.

Prior to presenting our methodology, this chapter first discusses the literature in antisocial content and inferring gender in social media. Building on this prior work, Sect. 6.3 present a set of seed keywords for bootstrapping misogyny identification, a method for developing a crowdsourced dataset of aggressive-and-misogynistic insults from Twitter, models for automatically identifying this content, hateful content, and inferring distributions of gender therein. The following section present analysis results on these datasets (Sect. 6.4), as summarized above, before we contextualize our findings in a discussion (Sect. 6.5).

6.2   Related Work

Prior efforts have studied anti-social content in online social spaces, regarding misogynistic, harassing, and hateful speech. While our research is novel in its comparisons of gender distributions across general Twitter and several anti-social behaviors (misogynistic, harassing, and hateful content), these prior efforts provide an important foundation for datasets and expectations. This foundation is presented below followed by a review of relevant literature in inferring gender from Twitter content, on which we heavily rely.

6.2.1   Anti-social Content in Online Spaces

With stories like #GamerGate and the backlash against Caroline Criado-Perez after circulating a petition to maintain a female image on the British five-pound note (Hardaker and McGlashan 2016), one is given the impression that online social spaces are negative places, full of degrading discussion, especially against women (Cole 2015). Work by Kuznekoff and Rose supports this impression in a study of Microsoft's Xbox Live gaming community, wherein gamers with feminine-sounding voices are three times more likely to be insulted for their gender within moments of broadcasting their voices (Kuznekoff and Rose 2013). In open online communication spaces like Twitter, gender also plays a major role in discourse, with many women being targeted for threatening and hateful messages online (Hardaker and McGlashan 2016; Cole 2015). Work by Fulper et al. further find misogynistic language directed at women on Twitter has a significant relationship with rape crime statistics at the state level in the United States, suggesting that such negative online content can mirror the offline world (Fulper et al. 2014).

In an effort to characterize this anti-social, misogynistic content, work by the Demos organization in the United Kingdom (UK) and Barlett et al. sought to identify the gender demographics of authors posting abusive misogynistic content (Barlett et al. 2014; Demos 2016). Their analyses suggests such content is often used casually, and women are more likely to post abusive misogynistic content than men (53% female versus 47% male). The details of this work, however, are opaque, and their sample size is limited to the UK and during a three-week period in the spring of 2016. Further complicating their analysis is the lack of a comparison against the gender distribution in Twitter, so it is unclear whether this larger percentage of female authors is a real effect or merely an artifact of Twitter's demographics in the UK. This chapter improves upon and extends this research by studying a larger timeframe (one year) and population of Twitter, compares gender populations against a random sample of Twitter, and provides additional detail in model development.

As this chapter is clearly not the first effort to study misogyny in Twitter, we also mention work by Hewitt et al. who characterize misogynistic content on Twitter more generally (Hewitt et al. 2016). Like the Demos work, the Hewitt et al. study finds numerous difficulties in identifying instances of this content that are truly anti-social as opposed to affectionate teasing/humor, self-effacing, lyrics, or others. This difficulty is identified in similar efforts relating to online harassment by Golbeck et al. (2017) and hate speech by Davidson et al. (2017) and further expounded on by Saleem et al. who propose alternate socially oriented means for identifying anti-social content (Saleem et al. 2016). The work described in this chapter similarly extends this work and develops a dataset of insulting misogynistic content, accounting for these different types of usage. As misogynistic content is not the only form of anti-social online behavior, we also compare this content with existing datasets on harassment and hate speech in Twitter. Golbeck et al. collect a large dataset of trolling content and potential harassment, and Davidson et al. present a dataset of over 20,000 potentially offensive and hateful tweets from Twitter.

Prior work has studied gender as it relates to misogynistic and hateful content in the offline context, which provides a foundation for expectations in Twitter and a point for comparison and validation for our results. Specifically, Preston and Stanley study gender-directed insults in college students, with finding on what types of insults men and women find the most insulting and what genders tend to use which insults (Preston and Stanley 1987), and Harris follow up this work to include anger-provoking behavior and verbal insults (Harris 1993).

6.2.2   Gender Inferences in Twitter

A key aspect of this chapter's work is the study of gender in Twitter, but the scale we wish to study is too large for manual analysis. Fortunately, a large body of literature exists around studying demographics and automatically inferring gender in Twitter.

Likely the most common approach for gender inference in Twitter leverages a user's self-reported name. Work by Mislove et al. use names and genders provided by the US Census Bureau to construct a naive Bayes classifier that can predict genders based on given names (Mislove et al. 2011). Burger et al. expand on this work by integrating census-backed name-gender pairs with additional user dimensions, finding Twitter to be slightly more female than male for accounts that included gender cues (Burger et al. 2011). Liu and Ruths also study name-gender associations in Twitter, using Amazon's Mechanical Turk to construct a dataset of Twitter user-gender labels, support vector machines (SVMs) to infer these pairs, and also find a female bias in Twitter (Liu and Ruths 2013). At the same time, Rao et al. use sociolinguistic cues like emoticons, punctuation, capitalization, and other features to improve inference over a collection of demographics, from age to gender to political affiliation (Rao et al. 2010). More recently, Tenuto at CrowdFlower[5] posted a public dataset on social media users and their genders (Tenuto 2015). Tenuto's study use the CrowdFlower crowdsourcing platform to generate gender labels from Twitter profiles and a single tweet and leverages the CrowdFlower Artificial Intelligence offering to recover gender labels from a collection of features, including profile descriptions, usernames, profile colors, and tweets. Findings from that work include male references to wrestling, female uses of the heart emoji, and differences in profile color selections. We integrate Tenuto's multi-faceted approach to enable our own automated gender prediction.

Other approaches also exist for inferring gender that we do not leverage here for scalability reasons. Face++[6] is one popular offering that ingests a picture of a person and outputs estimates on demographics (e.g., age and gender); to use this platform, however, we would limit ourselves to Twitter users with profile pictures of themselves, a population that would be difficult to identify at the scale of hundreds of millions of users. Another such approach is outlined in Volkova and Yarowsky, who include a Twitter user's social network in who they follow and who follows them to augment gender prediction (Volkova and Yarowsky 2014). While this social networking approach is performant, our focus on Twitter's public sample stream makes it difficult to extract a user's friend/follower network across the entire dataset.

---

[5]http://www.crowdflower.com.

[6]https://www.faceplusplus.com.

6.3 Methods

Our primary objective in this research is to shed light on the creators of misogynistic and hateful anti-social content in Twitter. To this end, we present the following research questions and describe our methods for answering them. As discussed in the previous section, however, identifying misogynistic and hateful content is more complex than simply searching for offensive keywords. Hence, our research questions are divided into two groups, the first of which concentrates on characterizing and automatically identifying this content:

RQ1.1   What is the proportion of aggressively insulting misogynistic content in Twitter?

RQ1.2   How well does a classifier do at automatically identifying aggressive misogynistic insults?

RQ1.3   What features contribute the most to identifying this insulting content?

RQ1.4   What proportion of harassing and hate-speech tweets are classified as aggressively insulting misogynistic content?

After extracting datasets of misogynistic content from Twitter, we then focus on characterizing the gender of this content's authors in our second set of research questions:

RQ2.1   Does the distribution of misogynistic, insulting messages significantly diverge from the distribution of gendered content in English-language Twitter?

RQ2.2   Does this distribution change across the different offensive, misogynistic words we've selected?

RQ2.3   Are these proportions different than authors of harassing and hateful tweets?

NB: This section introduces explicit, degrading, and potentially insulting language. Please be advised.

6.3.1 Data Sources

To address potential temporal biases and analyze a larger cross section of Twitter (as opposed to the single month analyzed by Demos (2016)), our dataset for this research is a 1% random sample captured from Twitter's Public Sample Stream[7] between 1 January 2015 and 31 December 2015. In total, this dataset contains 365 days at

---

[7]https://developer.twitter.com/en/docs/tweets/sample-realtime/overview/GET_statuse_sample.

approximately 4 million tweets per day, totaling 1,883,534,530 tweets. We focus on 2015 rather than a more recent year given the 2016 US election, in which Hillary Clinton's presidential campaign may have increased the amount of misogynistic content online. From this Twitter sample dataset, we extract all English-language tweets (as identified by Twitter's language inference field), yielding 739,839,678 tweets. Our samples of misogynistic, hateful, and harassing tweets are extracted from this sample.

For characterizing harassing and hateful tweets, we rely on datasets provided by Golbeck et al. (2017) and Davidson et al. (2017) respectively. Our Golbeck dataset contains nearly 20,000 tweets with binary labels for whether the tweet constitutes harassment or not, and the Davidson dataset contains approximately 25,000 tweets labeled as hateful, offensive, or benign. We likewise extracted datasets of potentially harassing and hateful tweets from our 2015 dataset by filtering tweets for the seed keywords used in the Golbeck and Davidson datasets. For the 2015 analog for the Golbeck dataset, we include all tweets in our 2015 set that included:

- "#whitegenocide",
- "#fuckniggers",
- "#whitepower",
- "#whitelivesmatter",
- "you fucking nigger",
- "fucking muslim",
- "fucking faggot",
- "religion of hate",
- "the jews", and
- "feminist".

For the 2015 Davidson analog, we extract tweets from our 2015 dataset that included the 50 most hate-specific phrases from their refined dictionary of n-grams.

6.3.2 Inferring Gender

As described in Sect. 6.2.2, several efforts have studied automated methods to infer gender from Twitter content and user profiles (Liu and Ruths 2013; Mislove et al. 2011; Burger et al. 2011; Pennacchiotti and Popescu 2011). Since one of our objectives is to study large samples of Twitter data, it would be cost prohibitive to use crowdsourcing for evaluating gender in millions of tweets, so we turn to machine learning approaches, which past research has shown can be more effective than crowdsourced labels (Burger et al. 2011). Rather than collect our own dataset, we leverage a publicly available dataset of Twitter users, samples of their tweets, and crowdsourced gender labels presented by CrowdFlower.[8] Following the results presented in Tenuto (2015), we develop a stacked classifier using version 0.19.1 of

---

[8]https://www.crowdflower.com/wp-content/uploads/2016/03/gender-classifier-DFE-791531.csv.

Scikit-learn (Pedregosa et al. 2011) from this 20,000-sample dataset that combines results from three weaker classifiers. These first three classifiers use naive Bayes to predict a user's gender from the text of a sample tweet, from the user's description, and from the user's username. We featurize tweet text and user descriptions through a standard bag-of-words model of both unigrams and bigrams. Our username classifier, however, featurize Twitter handles at the character level, converting a username into a bag of 2- and 3-character strings. We merge results from these classifiers via a random forest and only keep inferred labels with a reported probability $\geq 95\%$. Using 10-fold cross validation, this stacked classifier achieved an accuracy of 71.82%, on par with the gender classifier presented in Rao et al. (2010).

Our decision to exclude self-reported author names despite prior work showing names to be a useful feature (e.g., (Liu and Ruths 2013)) is motivated by two factors: First, our classifier analysis shows including this feature reduces performance for our CrowdFlower dataset. Second and potentially relatedly, many users' self-reported names are blank or ill-formed. Liu and Ruths discuss this omission, finding the majority of users in their dataset did not provide useful name information (Liu and Ruths 2013).

To ensure this classifier does not introduce significant biases towards one gender or another, we apply it to a random sample of 1,000,367 English tweets extracted from the 2015 sample described above. Of this one-million-tweet set, our gender classifier identifies 489,622 users whose labels were more than 90% certain, with a distribution of 47.78% male and 52.22% female. This slight bias towards women in Twitter is consistent with the findings of Burger et al. (2011), whose dataset of blog-based gender labels contained 45% male and 55% female labels. These results are also consistent with those from Pew Research Center (Duggan et al. 2016).

6.3.3 Identifying Misogyny

Unlike studying gender, harassment, and hate speech in Twitter, where prior datasets exist, this research requires constructing a new dataset of misogynistic content from Twitter. As discussed in Hewitt et al. (2016), however, identifying misogynistic content is difficult given its potentially subtle nature (e.g., the hashtag "#GetBackInTheKitchen") and cross-context usage, especially in adult/pornographic content (e.g., "Sexy teenager likes getting her hot shaved cunt fucked [adult website link]") and song lyrics (e.g., references to Rihanna's song "Bitch Better Have My Money"). In some cultural contexts, generally misogynistic words like "bitch" and "cunt" can be used in an affection manner (e.g., "Happy birthday, you beautiful bitch" or "Love ya, cunt!"), further complicating this identification.

The following sections first describe our method for constructing a precise dataset of misogyny before discussing methods for automating this identification at scale.

6.3.3.1   Extracting Potentially Misogynistic Tweets

To restate, this work's objective is to study the gender makeup for authors of misogynistic content in Twitter; we do not attempt to characterize fully the entire spectrum of misogynistic content online. Instead, we focus on building a precise dataset of grossly misogynistic content. For the purposes of this paper, misogyny in Twitter is therefore defined as:

> **Misogynistic Tweet**: A tweet that contains at least one misogynistic expletive and is meant to be hurtful.

This definition includes two important factors: First, we require a set of "misogynistic expletives." Second, by requiring a hurtful or aggressive intent behind the message, we discount affectionate uses of misogynistic words.

For constructing a set of misogynistic expletives, several sources provided insight: the Hatebase.org[9] website for classifying hate speech, the Preston and Stanley paper on gender-directed insults (Preston and Stanley 1987), the Demos paper on gendered misogyny in Twitter, and the recent Hewitt et al. work on identifying misogynistic language in Twitter (Hewitt et al. 2016). Hatebase.org includes a set of English, gender-specific hate-based tokens, and the three papers introduce a collection of insulting and misogynistic terms. From these four sources, we select misogynistic expletives that occurred in two or more of the sets, yielding five keywords:

- Bitch,
- Cunt,
- Hoe,
- Slut, and
- Whore.

To construct our initial dataset, we extract any tweet whose text contains a case-insensitive substring matching one of these keywords (e.g., "Bitches be trippin" matches "bitch"), resulting in a set of 2,705,586 million tweets.

6.3.3.2   Coding Misogynistic Content

We know not all uses of these potentially offensive keywords are actually examples of misogyny. Both the Demos report and Hewitt et al. (2016) discuss this concern, with the Demos report categorizing such content into "pornographic," "aggressive," "self-identity," and "other" (Demos 2016). Rather than taking these categories directly, we randomly sample 300 tweets from our potentially misogynistic dataset on which two researchers performed inductive thematic analysis to determine the different types of data. In addition to the aggressive and self-identifying categories from the Demos

---

[9]www.hatebase.org.

Table 6.1 Inductively generated categories of potentially misogynistic tweets

Category	Includes	Excludes
Abusive remark	Angry, misogynistic, or hateful comments designed to insult, upset, or disparage	Self-deprecation, lyrics, colloquialisms like "life's a bitch", or uses of hateful words in a friendly or humorous way
Affectionate	Humorous references to friends or family that use explicit language	Intentionally insulting and hurtful content
Music lyrics	Quotes from popular songs (e.g., "Brittany Bitch," or "Bitch better have my money")	Comments directed at other people or things
Self-identifying	References to self or self-deprecating comments like "I'm such a bitch"	References to other people or things
Pornographic	Advertisements for adult web sites	References to other people or things
Other	A message that does not fit in a category described above	A category as described above
Not english	A message that is not in english	Tweets in english

report, we also find a number of tweets advertising adult content, many references to song lyrics, affectionate uses (especially of "bitch"), and a large number of Dutch tweets that included the token "hoe". Categories resulting from this thematic analysis are shown in Table 6.1.

6.3.3.3   Subsampling and Labeling with Mechanical Turk

The next step in developing a labeled dataset of hurtful, misogynistic content is to construct a subsample that we can then hand off to humans for manual labeling. For labeling, we use Amazon's Mechanical Turk[10] to obtain several labels for each sample tweet. To construct a high-quality subsample, however, we need to remove tweets that would obviously be excluded from a potentially aggressive sample and construct a set that was sufficiently diverse to cover the linguistic feature space. Twitter's metadata provided some measure of filtering here with its inferred-language field and possibly-sensitive field, which is generally present on tweets with links to potentially adult content. Using these fields, we remove all tweets tagged with a language other than English and all tweets that included the `possibly_sensitive` field, thereby removing obviously negative potential samples.

To increase diversity in our subsample, we opt not to sample randomly from the remaining tweets, as retweets and duplicate content is common in Twitter. Instead,

---

[10]https://www.mturk.com/.

we want each tweet a human labeler may see to be relatively unique and include as much of the potential linguistic feature space as possible. To ensure this diversity, we apply the k-means clustering algorithm against the remaining English, non-sensitive tweets with $k = 1,000$ and extracted the tweets closest to the k-means cluster centers, yielding an approximate subset of the 1,000 most diverse tweets.

We then posted this 1,000-tweet data set to Mechanical Turk as a categorization task. The task was tagged with Mechanical Turk's "potentially explicit or offensive content" tag and included the following warning in its title: "WARNING: This HIT may contain adult content. Worker discretion is advised." We also included qualifications to ensure all Mechanical Turk workers were from the United States and had a high approval rate (>90%) for past work to ensure consistent and high-quality results. Instructions for this task included the category descriptions shown in Table 6.1. For each of these 1,000 tweets, we collected three labels from Turk workers and used the majority label as the tweet's final label, discarding tweets in which labelers tied (i.e., each worker chose a different label).

The resulting dataset contains 849 tweets with a majority label, 459 of which have a unanimous label across all three workers.

6.3.4 Automatically Classifying Misogynistic, Harassing, and Hateful Tweets

Having established a dataset of tweets containing aggressively insulting misogynistic content, we need to scale this identification process up to handle the nearly 800 million tweets in our 2015 Twitter sample. Because our labeled dataset is optimized for diversity rather than representativeness, by using this dataset to identify misogynistic examples automatically in the larger set, we avoid potential sampling biases introduced by clustering this content. Constructing a classifier to classify this content represents a standard text classification task, consisting of tokenizing and featurizing tweet text, evaluating several classifiers through 10-fold cross validation, and training a final classifier for filtering the full 2015 sample.

To convert tweet text into a feature space on which we could train a classifier, we use a bag-of-words model to transform tokenized tweets into a feature space of discrete counts. We also remove infrequent words (words that occur in fewer than five tweets) and collapse frequent pairs of words (words that occurred together in five or more documents) into bigrams. Leveraging Scikit-learn's (Pedregosa et al. 2011) collection of classification algorithms, we evaluate several algorithms for performance via their averaged area under the precision-recall curves (AUPRC) in 10-fold cross validation. This algorithm list includes random forests, naive Bayes, linear SVMs, and logistic regression.

We replicate this procedure for our harassment and hate-based datasets as well to support a consistent comparison across the same timeframe. For the harassment and hate datasets, however, the class imbalance is substantial, with many tweets having a negative label. To address this imbalance, we oversample the minority positive class during cross validation.

6.3.5   Comparing Gender Distributions

While prior work (Demos 2016) has studied gender in misogynistic content in Twitter, these studies did not compare gender proportions against the underlying distribution present in Twitter. As this research's objective is to characterize gender distributions against what one might expect to find in Twitter, we employed a statistical test to compare these distributions in misogynistic, harassing, and hate speech with the gender proportions found in a random Twitter sample. For all such comparisons, we use the χ-square test for equality with gender proportions in a random sample of one million tweets as the expected proportions. Additionally, as this research performs several such statistical tests, all p-values were adjusted using the Bonferroni Correction to ensure a study-wide error rate $\alpha < 0.01$.

For the Bonferroni Correction, m denotes the number of statistical tests; in this research, $m = 8$ (individual tests for misogyny, harassment, and hate, as well as an individual test for each of the tokens in our misogynistic keyword set). Therefore, each statistical test is tested against $\alpha/m = 0.01/8 = 0.00125$ for significance.

6.4   Results

6.4.1   Distribution of Crowdsourced Misogyny Labels

After constructing the labeled dataset of aggressively insulting misogynistic tweets, the distribution seed keywords and category labels are shown in Fig. 6.1 and Table 6.2 respectively. Figure 6.1 immediately shows "bitch" is by far the most common keyword in our sample, consistent with prior work (Hewitt et al. 2016). Regarding **RQ1.1**, Table 6.2 makes it evident that the bulk of diverse usages of potentially misogynistic expletives are perceived to be abusive by a majority of crowdsourced users, accounting for approximately three of every four instances. Non-abusive affectionate and self-effacing usages are the next most common but still rare categories, accounting for a combined percentage less than 15%. Quotes from songs are the rarest but still-present class, with pornographic and non-English labels absent from the set, suggesting Twitter's possibly-sensitive and language inference fields are adequate filters to remove these sample types.

Fig. 6.1 Per-seed keyword in labeled data

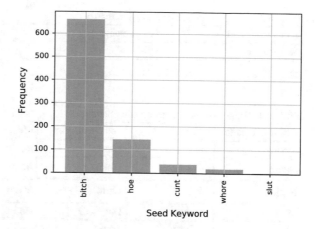

Table 6.2 Per-category distributions in misogyny sample ($n = 849$)

Category	Frequency	Percentage (%)
Abusive remark	661	77.86
Affectionate	65	7.656
Self-identifying	55	6.478
Other	43	5.065
Music lyrics	25	2.945
Pornographic	0	0
Not english	0	0

6.4.2 Automatically Identifying Misogynistic, Harassing, and Hateful Tweets

We now have three datasets of labeled, anti-social Twitter content, which we use to train classifiers and scale up identifying this content from our 2015 English dataset. Before applying these classifiers, however, we first present their performance metrics and most important features. For identifying misogyny, we use a linear SVM, with Table 6.3 showing the 10-fold cross-validation confusion matrix after collapsing labels into "Not Abusive" and "Abusive" classes. This misogyny classifier achieves an AUPRC score of 0.8607. Regarding **RQ1.2**, these results suggest a classifier can generally identify abusive misogynistic instances but is biased toward the abusive category.

To study **RQ1.3** and the most important features across these potentially misogynistic categories, we retrain the linear SVM on each category in a one-versus-rest model. Table 6.4 presents the top ten highest-weighted features in each category with more than 20 positive labels. From this table, we see abusive remarks tend to focus on references to promiscuity, prostitution, and intelligence, with features like "money",

Table 6.3 Misogyny classifier confusion matrix

Predicted/actual	Not abusive	Abusive
Not abusive	55	133
Abusive	80	574

Table 6.4 Highest-weighted features in potentially misogynistic categories

Abusive remark	Affectionate	Self-identifying	Music lyrics	Other
Money	Love	Leave	Better money	Wish
Dumb	🧑	Wanna	Ya	Watch
Bitches	😩	Little	Mean	Called
Mom	Much	I'm	Bad	Remember
Alone	Birthday	Cause	Stay	Dirty
Wit	Bad	Feel	Nicki minaj	Sick
Please	That's	Hoes	Rihanna	Yes
Whore	Friend	🧑	Britney	Lana
Try	Tryna	Never	Girl	Rey
Hate	Happy	Can't	Im	Friend

"dumb", and "whore". Alternately, affectionate tweets tend to include friendly references or well wishes, especially birthdays. Tweets referencing lyrics also likely include mentions of singers, like Nikki Minaj, Rihanna, and Britney Spears, as one may expect given the popularity of Rihanna's song, "Bitch Better Have My Money," and Britney Spears's "Gimme More" (whose first line is "It's Britney Bitch"). The self-identifying category intuitively includes first-person pronouns ("i'm"), but the remaining features and the "Other" category are less easy to interpret.

Applying the abusive misogyny classifier to the datasets provided by Golbeck et al. and Davidson et al. we study **RQ1.4** and the relationship among harassing, hateful, and abusive misogynistic speech in Twitter. Both datasets provide over 20,000 tweet samples against which we apply our classifier. Given the expletive-laden keywords used to generate these datasets and the high density of abusively misogynistic tweets found in our initial misogyny sample, one would expect many of these harassing and hateful tweets to be abusively misogynistic as well. Table 6.5 shows that, for the Golbeck harassment dataset, 66.47% of harassing and 59.04% non-harassing tweets are classified as abusively misogynistic. For the Davidson dataset, 75.24% of hateful tweets, 87.98% of offensive-but-not-hateful tweets, and 58.35% tweets of remaining "unoffensive" tweets are all classified as abusively misogynistic. These results suggest significant overlap between abusive misogynistic speech in online social spaces and harassing and hateful speech.

Table 6.5   Misogynistic content in harassment and hateful datasets

Inferred class	Golbeck et al.	Davidson et al.	
	Harassment	Hateful	Offensive
Abusively misogynistic (%)	66.47	75.24	87.98
Not abusive (%)	33.53	24.76	12.02

Table 6.6   Harassment classifier confusion matrix

Predicted/actual	Not harassment	Harassment
Not harassment	12,429	2,578
Harassment	1,198	13,809

Table 6.7   Highest-weighted features in harassment classifier

Token	Weight
Cunt	0.01513
Fucking nigger	0.00926
Jews	0.00726
Fuck	0.00563
Fucking muslims	0.00463
Cunts	0.00428
Fucking muslim	0.00363
#whitegenocide	0.00340
Like	0.00263
Fucking	0.00258

6.4.2.1   Harassment Classifier

After oversampling the harassment category to achieve class balance and evaluating a series of classifiers, we select a random forest classifier to identify harassing tweets automatically, the confusion matrix for which is shown in Table 6.6. Our best random forest classifier performs with high accuracy (87.42% correct) and achieves an AUPRC of 0.9388 over 10 folds. As with the abusive misogyny dataset, our harassment classifier is also biased towards the positive, harassment class.

As with our misogyny classifier, we likewise identify the most important features contributing to the harassment classification, as shown in Table 6.7. While the seed keywords for the Golbeck dataset included references to feminism, homosexuality, and racism, the primary keywords in our classifier focus on race and ethnicity (e.g., "jews", "muslim", "nigger", and references to white genocide). Additionally, the presence of "cunt" references overlap with our misogyny dataset.

Table 6.8 Hate classifier confusion matrix

Predicted/actual	Not harassment	Harassment
Not harassment	22,870	468
Harassment	835	22,305

Table 6.9 Highest-weighted features in hate classifier

Token	Weight
Faggot	0.05254
Fag	0.03580
Bitch	0.03169
Nigger	0.02195
Bitches	0.02120
Pussy	0.01499
Hoe	0.01204
Like	0.01131
Hoes	0.01097
Fags	0.00962

6.4.2.2 Hate Classifier

We similarly oversample the hate category in the Davidson et al. dataset to balance the hate class with respect to the non-hate classes. Again selecting the random forest classifier for classifying hate tweets, our classifier performs better than the misogyny and harassment classifiers, with high accuracy (97.20% correct) and achieves an AUPRC of 0.9927 over 10 folds. This classifier's confusion matrix for which is shown in Table 6.8. Unlike the abusive misogyny and harassment classifiers, this classifier is slightly biased towards the non-hateful class.

Table 6.9 presents the top ten features in identifying hate speech in the Davidson et al. Twitter dataset. We see these features are more sexually oriented than the harassment dataset, including references to homosexuality and promiscuity in addition to the racial slurs seen above. Also similar to the harassment dataset, one of the high-weight features ("bitches") overlaps with our misogyny dataset.

6.4.2.3 Antisocial Content in Twitter

With these classifiers established, we now apply them to our 739,839,678-tweet 2015 sample from Twitter's public sample stream. After extracting all tweets matching each dataset's seed keywords, our analysis featurizes each tweet and applies the classifier. Table 6.10 shows the number of tweets matching the seed keywords, number of tweets positively classified by the relevant classifier, and the percentage

Table 6.10 Distributions of antisocial content in twitter ($n = 739, 839, 678$)

	Abusive misogyny	Harassment	Hateful
Keyword matches	2,705,586	73,818	112,531
Positive label frequency	2,267,915	4,203	9,008
Twitter percentage (%)	0.3065	0.0006	0.0012

Table 6.11 Inferred gender proportions across datasets ([a]significant at $p < 0.01$)

	Male		Female		χ^2 Test statistic
	Count	Proportion (%)	Count	Proportion (%)	
Twitter 2015 sample	233,941	47.78	255,681	52.22	–
Abusive misogyny[a]	332,823	38.18	538,850	61.82	3.218×10^4
Harassment[a]	1,219	55.94	960	44.06	5.820×10^1
Hate speech[a]	2,293	52.04	2,113	47.96	3.209×10^1

in our Twitter sample. Evident in this table is first the high frequency of abusive, misogynistic insults compared to the harassing and hateful tweets, and second is the overall rarity of this content in Twitter, answering **RQ1.1**. That being said, these distributions should be treated as **floor** estimates on the actual levels of this antisocial content as we purposefully omit instances without expletives or clear racial slurs.

6.4.3   Gender Distributions in Antisocial Tweets

With temporally aligned and large-scale datasets for abusive misogyny, harassment, and hate speech in place, we turn to analyzing the gender differences in these sets. Table 6.11 displays user proportions after applying the gender classifier discussed in Sect. 6.3.2, after keeping only those users whose gender labels were greater than 90% certainty. Apparent from these results is the over-representation of female-labeled users in our abusive misogyny dataset and over-representation of male-labeled users in both the harassment and hateful datasets. To ensure these proportions are significantly different from what one would expect from our random Twitter sample, chi-square tests for equality between our 2015 sample and each dataset show each population proportions differ significantly ($p < 0.01$ after Bonferroni correction).

Given that "bitch" appears in a majority of misogynistic tweets, we also break down gender proportions across the misogynistic expletive keywords we described in Sect. 6.3.3.1. Based on the above results, one would expect gender proportions for

Table 6.12 Inferred gender proportions across misogynistic keywords ([a]significant at $p < 0.01$)

	Male		Female		χ^2 Test statistic
	Count	Proportion (%)	Count	Proportion (%)	
Twitter 2015 sample	233,941	47.78	255,681	52.22	–
"Bitch"[a]	272,569	36.41	475,976	63.59	3.876×10^4
"Slut"[a]	1,555	38.46	2,488	61.54	1.407×10^2
"Whore"[a]	12,007	39.50	18,389	60.50	8.348×10^2
"Hoe"	93,932	47.76	102,731	52.24	2.277×10^{-2}
"Cunt"	22,565	48.17	24,279	51.83	2.864

tweets including "bitch" to be similar to those in the full sample. For the remaining keywords, however, prior research found women primarily find insults about promiscuity the most offensive (Harris 1993), suggesting "slut", "whore", and "hoe" may also overrepresent female-labeled users. Results shown in Table 6.12 are mostly consistent with these expectations: "Bitch", "slut", and "whore" differ significantly from the underlying random sample with a majority of female-labeled users. For "hoe" and "cunt", however, while both subsets include more female-labeled users than male, the proportions do not significantly differ from our random Twitter sample.

6.5 Discussion

6.5.1 Insult or Affection? Disambiguating Uses of Explicit Language

As one may expect, not all uses of explicit language are meant to insult. With common examples of tweets similar to "Happy birthday, bitch", "Karma's a bitch", and "I don't wanna be in a relationship = I wanna be a hoe", one should not naively assume that simple keyword-based filters are sufficient for identifying insults. A similar issue is discussed in Golbeck et al. in which the authors had difficulty finding truly harassing tweets (Golbeck et al. 2017), and the majority of content in the Davidson et al. dataset is labeled only as generically offensive but not hateful (Davidson et al. 2017). We see this effect in our own dataset of labeled tweets, in which a non-trivial 25% of expletive-laden tweets were not seen as abusive by our crowdsourced workers. Despite this less-offensive content's presence, the distributions of affectionate uses or quotes from lyrics is much less prevalent than abusive content, by a factor of three to one. Furthermore, the word "bitch" is of such popularity in Twitter as to warrant special attention in future work.

Additionally, humans have some difficulty in categorizing these sorts of potentially offensive messages without the contextual and cultural awareness that comes from taking part in the conversation, as we see with 9% of our crowdsourced dataset, in which all three labelers disagreed with each other. Both (Hewitt et al. 2016) and (Golbeck et al. 2017) also echo this difficulty. While the features described in Table 6.4 are consistent with our expectations for certain classes (e.g., references to musicians in the Lyrics category and first-person pronouns in the Self-Identifying category), these difficulties imply an automated classifier will have limited efficacy in identifying truly insulting content. For this chapter's purposes, the classifier we construct is purposefully biased towards the abusive class since we are interested in characterizing authors of these potential insults, but a platform for actively filtering such content would need better accuracy (if the tradeoff between information quality and censorship was deemed necessary).

One particularly important class of features for disambiguating intentionally hurtful insults from other uses of this language, however, are emoji. Emoji are a suite of unicode-enabled graphical characters users can embed in their messages similar to emoticons. Since emoji are single characters, text analysis has traditionally filtered them out, and only recently have researchers started to integrate them (Miller et al. 2017; Hu et al. 2017). In this work, we find emojis to be particularly valuable in identifying affectionate uses of otherwise insulting content. For example, many instances of the "happy birthday, [expletive]" and "i love you, [expletive]" patterns include a series of heart-like emoji (e.g., ❤). At the same time, the number of available emoji is increasing, complicating this disambiguation task as new graphical pictographs with different unicode representations but similar meanings are introduced: Over twenty heart-related emoji exist in a recent unicode specification for instance.

6.5.2 Is Twitter Misogynistic, Hateful, or Something Else?

In studying the differences between abusive misogynistic and harassing/hateful content in Twitter, one clear result is that abusive misogyny is significantly more common in our 2015 sample by over two orders of magnitude (Table 6.10). In either case, however, our results suggest a random user is unlikely to encounter such content as all three types of anti-social content account for less than 1% of our 2015 sample. At the same time, a Twitter user is more likely to encounter **overtly** abusively misogynistic content than racist or homophobic content. As discussed in Saleem et al. (2016), however, one should note that keyword-based methods like those used in the three datasets this chapter discusses are likely to underestimate the amount of such content, as more subtle misogynistic, racist, and hateful language does not necessarily include expletives or overtly vulgar words.

In differentiating misogynistic, harassing, and hateful content in Twitter, we also see overlap in the significant features defining our classifiers, with "cunt" appearing in the top-ten hate-related features and "bitch" appearing in both the misogyny and harassment datasets. Likewise, as shown in Table 6.5, a majority of content in both the harassment and hateful datasets are classified as abusive misogyny. These classes of anti-social content therefore seem to have an implicit relationship in their manifestations despite differences in their underlying gender distributions.

While this work implies the sorts of antisocial content studied herein are rare in Twitter, we cannot deny the plethora of stories in which female users on Twitter receive overwhelming volumes of death and rape threats (see #GamerGate and the backlash against Caroline Criado-Perez after circulating a petition to maintain a female image on the British five-pound note (Hardaker and McGlashan 2016)). Related research suggests the disconnect in our findings and anecdotes is driven by a difference in intent and type of language: In this chapter, we define "misogyny" as hurtful, abusive, and intentionally insulting, but this definition excludes threats of sexual violence (e.g., rape and death threats). Instead, threats of sexual violence, while related to misogyny, are more exemplary of *sexist* language, where Manne presents this distinction between "misogyny" and "sexism" as control versus hostility/hatred (Manne 2017). Manne further suggests misogynistic content is more an implicit shaming of women who challenge the male-centric status quo, while other work discusses sexist sexual violence in Twitter as a form of targeted punishment (Cole 2015). Furthermore, as suggested by Hardaker and McGlashan, these targeted sexual threats are also perpetrated primarily by male accounts (Hardaker and McGlashan 2016), further differentiating them from our generally female misogyny dataset.

It may be comforting to see these low incidence rates for abusive misogyny, harassment, and hate. If one challenges existing social norms in Twitter, however, one may become a target of a motivated minority who then inundate the target with misogynistic, hateful, and sexist content. This reactive anti-social behavior provides an avenue for future research both in addressing the paucity of anti-social behavior discussed in Golbeck et al. and Davidson et al. and in designing interventions to reduce such content: creating a digital honeypot for anti-social behavior. Honeypots have seen successful use in cyber security and identifying insiders (Spitzner and Technologies 2003), and here, one could leverage these systems to capture anti-social behavior and identify their sources.

6.5.3 Misogynistic Women and Hateful Men

Digging into the gender differences in the misogynistic, harassing, and hateful datasets, abusively misogynistic accounts receive significantly more female labels, whereas hateful and harassing accounts receive significantly more male labels. In characterizing the types of insults in each set (via the results in top-weighted features), consistencies with communications research on gender-based insults emerge: Misogynistic insults are related to promiscuity and prostitution, which were seen as the most egregious insult for a woman (Harris 1993), whereas insults about homosexuality are more prevalent in the hateful dataset, also seen as one of the worst insults towards a man (Harris 1993; Preston and Stanley 1987). Contrasting with the Preston/Stanely and Harris studies of gender-driven provocation, who found insults of promiscuity were equally likely to come from men and women, we find the authors of abusive references to promiscuity are more likely to be labeled female. The per-keyword study of gender differences in misogyny further support this result, with slurs about promiscuity ("slut" and "whore") having significantly more female-labeled authors. These results are also consistent with the Demos reports (Demos 2016; Barlett et al. 2014).

In reviewing the Golbeck et al. and Davidson et al. datasets, a subtext of racism and white supremacy are present in the most predictive features. While these topics are implicit in a dataset on hate speech like Davidson et al. authors of the Golbeck et al. dataset mention this bias towards white supremacy and justify it as a means to increase the number of harassing samples in their dataset. Our results suggest the sources of racist tweets to be primarily male, which is consistent with studies of online white supremacy (Daniels 2018). Daniels stressed this result does not imply that women are immune to racism, only that the social context surrounding the *online* white supremacy movement is generally male-dominated.

6.6   Limitations and Future Work

Though the studies presented in this chapter strove to be complete, unbiased, and transparent, several key limitations should be addressed and leave open avenues for future work.

Likely the major limitation of this work is its reliance on automated classifiers, of both content and gender. While necessary to operate at the scale of nearly a billion tweets and a year's worth of Twitter data, these classification tools are imperfect, and we did not leverage the most sophisticated algorithms available (e.g., deep learning/neural networks). Furthermore, the labeled dataset on which our abusive misogyny classifier is constructed has two weaknesses in terms of volume and agreement. While the Golbeck et al. and Davidson et al. datasets contained over 20,000 samples each, our dataset has only 1,000. Though our diversity-based sampling process should partly address volume issues, having more and better trained labelers would support a higher-quality dataset. The features associated with three of the four most prevalent classes are consistent with expectations and prior work, but more data would be valuable here.

Constructing these datasets also introduced limitations, as all three datasets relied on keywords as an initial filtering step. As found by Saleem et al. keyword-based methods are insufficient for characterizing online anti-social content, leaving our findings on the prevalence of this content as estimates of their minimums; their true frequencies may be higher and expressed through less overt means. Leveraging similarly aligned anti-social online communities, like anti-feminist/misogynistic or white supremacy community forums, to characterize such antisocial content may present a more robust approach (Saleem et al. 2016). Integrating the social aspects of Twitter and characterizing the *targets* of these classes of anti-social content would also be worthwhile. Additionally, this effort focuses only on misogyny, harassment, and hate speech; sexism and sexual violence (e.g., mentions of rape) were omitted, leaving out a significant class of anti-social behavior.

Beyond limitations in characterizing content, our use of binary gender labels is also fundamentally limited and potentially socially anachronistic. A more nuanced approach to gender should be explored in future work; as it stands, relatively few datasets exist for studying non-binary gender in Twitter.

Finally, this work sought only to characterize authors of anti-social content. Little effort was made to study methods for intervening against or suppressing such content. Future efforts could explore such interventions using the additional understanding presented herein.

6.7   Conclusions

This chapter studies the distributions of three types of anti-social content in Twitter and characterizes the gender makeup therein. Results suggest abusive misogynistic, harassing, and hateful content on Twitter is relatively rare, with our data accounting for less than 1% of the data in a 1% sample of Twitter across the whole of 2015, though these rates are likely only a lower bound on overtly anti-social and insulting content. In characterizing the gender proportions of these anti-social behaviors, results further show abusive misogynistic content has a significantly more female author population than a random sample of Twitter based on automated gender inferences using the author's username, description, and tweet text. Conversely, harassment and hateful content are primarily authored by male-labeled accounts.

References

Barlett J, Norrie R, Patel S, Rumpel R, Wibberley S (2014) Misogyny on twitter. Demos, 1–18 May 2014

Burger JD, Henderson J, Kim G, Zarrella G (2011) Discriminating gender on twitter. In: Proceedings of the conference on empirical methods in natural language processing, EMNLP '11, vol 146. Association for Computational Linguistics, Stroudsburg, PA, USA, pp 1301–1309. http://dl. acm.org/citation.cfm?id=2145432.2145568, http://www.mitre.org/work/tech_papers/2011/11_ 0170/. https://doi.org/10.1007/s00256-005-0933-8

Cole KK (2015) It's like she's eager to be verbally abused: twitter, trolls, and (en)gendering disciplinary rhetoric. Feminist Media Stud 15(2):356–358. https://doi.org/10.1080/14680777.2015. 1008750

Daniels J (2018) Race, civil rights, and hate speech in the digital era. In: The John D. and Catherine T. MacArthur foundation series on digital media and learning, vol 335, pp 129–154. https://doi. org/10.1162/dmal.9780262550673.129

Davidson T, Warmsley D, Macy M, Weber I (2017) Automated hate speech detection and the problem of offensive language. https://aaai.org/ocs/index.php/ICWSM/ICWSM17/paper/view/ 15665/14843

Demos (2016) The use of misogynistic terms on twitter. Technical report, Demos, London. https://www.demos.co.uk/wp-content/uploads/2016/05/Misogyny-online.pdf

Duggan M, Page D, Manager SC (2016) Social Media update 2016. pew research center (November). http://assets.pewresearch.org/wp-content/uploads/sites/14/2016/11/10132827/PI_2016.11.11_Social-Media-Update_FINAL.pdf

Fulper R, Ciampaglia GL, Ferrara E, Menczer F, Ahn Y, Flammini A, Lewis B, Rowe K (2015) Misogynistic Language on Twitter and Sexual Violence. In: Proc. ACM Web Science Workshop on Computational Approaches to Social Modeling (ChASM), 2014, pp. 6–9. https://doi.org/10.6084/m9.figshare.1291081. http://files.figshare.com/1868157/ChASM2014_rfulper.pdf

Golbeck J, Gnanasekaran RK, Gunasekaran RR, Hoffman KM, Hottle J, Jienjitlert V, Khare S, Lau R, Martindale MJ, Naik S, Nixon HL, Ashktorab Z, Ramachandran P, Rogers KM, Rogers L, Sarin MS, Shahane G, Thanki J, Vengataraman P, Wan Z, Wu DM, Banjo RO, Berlinger A, Bhagwan S, Buntain C, Cheakalos P, Geller AA, Gergory Q (2017) A large labeled corpus for online harassment research. In: Proceedings of the 2017 ACM on web science conference—websci '17 pp 229–233. http://dl.acm.org/citation.cfm?doid=3091478.3091509. https://doi.org/10.1145/3091478.3091509

Hardaker C, McGlashan M (2016) Real men don't hate women: twitter rape threats and group identity. J Pragmat 91:80–93. https://doi.org/10.1016/j.pragma.2015.11.005

Harris MB (1993) How provoking! what makes men and women angry? Aggressive Behav 19(3):199–211. https://doi.org/10.1002/1098-2337(1993)19:3<199::AID-AB2480190305>3.0.CO;2-D

Hewitt S, Tiropanis T, Bokhove C (2016) The problem of identifying misogynist language on twitter (and other online social spaces). In: Proceedings of the 8th ACM conference on web science, WebSci '16. ACM, New York, NY, USA, pp 333–335. https://doi.org/10.1145/2908131.2908183

Hu T, Guo H, Sun H, Nguyen TVT, Luo J (2017) Spice up Your Chat: The Intentions and Sentiment Effects of Using Emoji. In: Proceedings of the Eleventh International AAAI Conference on Web and Social Media, Icwsm, pp. 102–111. arXiv:org/abs/1703.02860

Kuznekoff JH, Rose LM (2013) Communication in multiplayer gaming: examining player responses to gender cues. New Media Soc 15(4):541–556. https://doi.org/10.1177/1461444812458271

Liu W, Ruths D (2013) What's in a name? Using first names as features for gender inference in twitter. In: Analyzing microtext: papers from the 2013 AAAI spring symposium, pp 10–16

Manne K (2017) Down girl: the logic of misogyny, 1st edn. Oxford University Press

Miller H, Kluver D, Thebault-Spieker J, Terveen L, Hecht B (2017) Understanding emoji ambiguity in context: the role of text in emoji-related miscommunication. In: Proceedings of the eleventh international AAAI conference on web and social media, Icwsm, pp 152–161. https://www.aaai.org/ocs/index.php/ICWSM/ICWSM17/paper/view/15703

Mislove A, Lehmann S, Ahn YY, Onnela JP, Rosenquist JN (2011) Understanding the demographics of twitter users. Artifi Intell 554–557. http://www.aaai.org/ocs/index.php/ICWSM/ICWSM11/paper/viewFile/2816/3234

Pedregosa F, Varoquaux G, Gramfort A, Michel V, Thirion B, Grisel O, Blondel M, Prettenhofer P, Weiss R, Dubourg V (2011) Others: scikit-learn: machine learning in Python. J Mach Learn Res 12(Oct):2825–2830

Pennacchiotti M, Popescu AM (2011) A machine learning approach to twitter user classification. In: Proceedings of the fifth international AAAI conference on weblogs and social media (ICWSM), pp 281–288. http://www.aaai.org/ocs/index.php/ICWSM/ICWSM11/paper/viewFile/2886/3262

Preston K, Stanley K (1987) What's the worst thing...? Gender-directed insults. Sex Roles 17(3):209–219. https://doi.org/10.1007/BF00287626

Rao D, Yarowsky D, Shreevats A, Gupta M (2010) Classifying latent user attributes in twitter. In: Proceedings of the 2nd international workshop on Search and mining user-generated contents—SMUC '10 p 37. http://portal.acm.org/citation.cfm?doid=1871985.1871993. https://doi.org/10.1145/1871985.1871993

Saleem HM, Dillon KP, Benesch S, Ruths D (2016) A web of hate: tackling hateful speech in online social spaces. In: Text analytics for cybersecurity and online safety. arXiv:org/abs/1709.10159

Spitzner L, Technologies H (2003) Inc: catching the insider threat. In: Acsac (Acsac), pp 170–179. http://dblp.uni-trier.de/db/conf/acsac/acsac2003.html#Spitzner03. https://doi.org/10.1109/CSAC.2003.1254322

Tenuto J (2015) Using machine learning to predict gender. https://www.crowdflower.com/using-machine-learning-to-predict-gender/

Volkova S, Yarowsky D (2014) Improving gender prediction of social media users via weighted annotator rationales. In: NIPS workshop on personalization, pp 1–8

Chapter 7
Stylistic Variation in Twitter Trolling

Isobelle Clarke

Abstract Although Phillips and Milner (The ambivalent internet: mischief, oddity and antagonism online 2017) have emphasised that the term 'troll' and 'trolling' are vague and ethically problematic, due to the fact that they are used as catch-all terms for various behaviours, including more serious and criminal behaviours, resulting in the desensitisation of certain hate crimes, it remains to be understood just what these various behaviours and the numerous styles of trolling are. While we can ethically choose to ignore the word, and avoid adding insult to the injury incurred by troll-victims, it is necessary to explore the various strategies and behaviours that encompass these terms. For example, being able to describe the particular functions and styles of trolling may be more meaningful with respect to understanding where particular behaviours linguistically cross over into more negative and/or criminal behaviours, in addition to understanding what linguistic functions and styles society regards as problematic and transgressive. The present chapter focuses on describing the stylistic variation in a corpus of Twitter trolling using a modified version of Biber's (Variation across speech and writing 1988) Multi-Dimensional Analysis. The analysis reveals 3 main dimensions of linguistic variation, which have been interpreted functionally in the context of trolling. The first main dimension opposes an interactive and involved style with an informationally dense reporting function, the second opposes a dismissive style with a mocking function, and the third dimension opposes an argumentative style with trolling Tweets that forewarn by summarising continuing action. By exploring previous research on trolling and current perceptions of problematic behaviour in society, it is argued that these dimensions predominantly reflect the different styles for promoting misinformation.

I. Clarke (✉)
University of Birmingham, Birmingham, UK
e-mail: Imc789@bham.ac.uk

7.1 Introduction

There is a growing threat of misinformation, abuse and harassment on social network-ing sites (SNS), such as Twitter. Twitter is a social networking microblogging service, which allows users to post messages restricted to 280-characters, called 'Tweets', to a network of associates, called 'Followers'. Over 320 million people have a Twitter account and on average 500 million Tweets are sent per day. While most people use Twitter to post innocuous feelings, opinions, ideas and information to their followers, there are some individuals who exploit the platform to promote a hostile environment and spread false information and propaganda. Although these individuals and their behaviour have been labelled in various ways, they are predominantly called *trolls*, and their behaviour is deemed *trolling*.

Trolling originally referred to the act of posting a message that was exaggerated or false in order to provoke new members to correct the mistake (NetLingo.com 1995–2015). However, despite this original meaning, *trolling* has since been used in numerous ways, and with the influence of the media, it is now operating as an all-encompassing term for most negative and transgressive behaviour online (Hardaker 2010; Phillips 2016), including criminal behaviour, such as hate speech and harass-ment. One notable example was Tanya Gersh and her family, who were targeted by Andrew Anglin and his neo-Nazi troll followers (Beckett 2017). Anglin released personally identifying information of Gersh, such as her address, email address and phone number, as well as the social media accounts of her and her family, and called upon his troll army to harass and abuse Gersh (Beckett 2017). As a result, Gersh received numerous death threats with several targeting her Jewish faith. In this one case study, trolls are shown to exhibit anti-Semitic, harassing, threatening, doxxing and abusive behaviours, which are far beyond the original definition of trolling described above.

Previous academic research also adds to this growing list of behaviours encapsu-lated in the term. Trolls and their posts have been defined as deceptive (Donath 1999), hostile (Hardaker 2010), benign contrarian (Gaus 2012), antagonistic (Herring et al. 2002), inflammatory and abusive (Nicol 2012), malicious (Coles and West 2016), vicious (Morrissey and Yell 2016), provocative (Hardaker 2010, 2013), or of a teasing nature (Mihaylov and Nakov 2016). In addition to the behaviours of trolling, the purpose of trolling has been described. In particular, people troll for amusement (Hardaker 2015), 'for the lulz' (laughing at people's expense) (Phillips 2016), to insult and to disrupt the conversation (Ansong et al. 2013), to obtain a reac-tion (MacKinnon and Zuckerman 2012), to antagonise (Klempka and Stimson 2014), to distract and mislead (Hogan 2012), and to manipulate opinions (Mihaylov et al. 2015). While this paints a gloriously negative and transgressive picture of trolls and trolling, other research has noted its more ambivalent and unproblematic nature. For example, Sanfilippo et al. (2017) conducted focus groups with 10 college students to identify their perceptions of trolling. Importantly, their participants argued that some types of trolling are not problematic and that they should not be responded to or man-aged equally because trolling is a diverse phenomenon. Additionally, Phillips and

Milner (2017) describe a more 'ambivalent' image of trolling[1] in the sense that it can "subsume divergent practices with divergent ends", such as being "[s]imultaneously antagonistic and social, creative and disruptive, humorous and barbed" (2017: 10). While these studies provide various descriptions of trolling behaviours and emphasise the range of possible interpretations of the functions of trolling, there has not yet been an examination into how the structure of language varies for trolling.

All of the research reviewed indicates that trolling varies considerably. Despite this, still relatively little is known about the various styles, communicative functions and linguistic properties of trolling. The aim of this study, therefore, is to use Multi-Dimensional Analysis (Biber 1988) to empirically identify the most important dimensions of stylistic variation in a corpus of trolling Tweets. The findings should lead to more detailed linguistic descriptions of the functional variation in Twitter trolling.

7.2 Methodology

7.2.1 Data

One of the main challenges in analysing the linguistic structure of trolling lies in firstly being able to detect instances of it. There have been four previous methods for collecting trolling, all of which are limited. The first approach defines the behaviours of trolling and then identifies posts that exhibit such behaviour (e.g. Herring et al. 2002). The first problem with this method is that it is circular, as it works off the assumption that trolling only exhibits these pre-defined behaviours, meaning that the results will only confirm this definition. As demonstrated above, *trolling* is used as an all-encapsulating term for several behaviours, thus this approach does not take into account the modern day use of the term. The second problem with this approach is that the researcher's interpretation that this particular post constitutes trolling may differ considerably from the interpretation of the people within the interaction (see O'Sullivan and Flannagin 2003). For example, the poster may not intend it to be a troll and/or the person receiving the post may not interpret it as such.

The second method for collecting trolling overcomes these problems by extracting posts from those individuals that self-identify as trolls (Phillips 2016). While this avoids inflicting the researcher's interpretation on what comprises trolling, previous research indicates that not all trolls self-identify (e.g. Donath 1999). For example, one aspect of some troll's behaviour and its effect (i.e. to cause people to respond)

---

[1] Phillips and Milner (2017) ethically avoid using the generic label 'trolling' due to the fact that individuals often say "I was just trolling", which translates to mean "I was just joking". With 'trolling' being used to label hate speech, regardless of a 'joking' intention or not, this 'joking' sense provides individuals with an escape route for more serious consequences. Phillips and Milner (2017) emphasise that individuals should call out hate speech for what it is and thus avoid using 'trolling' as a behavioral catch-all.

is governed by convincing people of the authenticity and genuineness of their post through hiding their trolling intentions. Phillips and Milner (2017) describe how some individuals provide fake advice, which can have detrimental effects, such as convincing people to delete 'System32' off one's computer in order to speed up processing time. Deleting System32, however, actually turns the computer into a brick. For the 'prank' to work it is essential that the original poster appears genuine and therefore does not self-identify as a troll as this will lead people to doubt the authenticity of the advice. Self-identifying trolls are therefore a sub-culture of trolls (Phillips 2016). Thus, this approach is not appropriate for understanding the different trolling styles on Twitter generally, but rather it is more suited for understanding the stylistic variation in this particular sub-culture of trolls.

The third approach uses particular linguistic markers such as swearing, name-calling, slurs, and specific hashtags known to be populated with trolling and abuse to identify abusive language and trolling (e.g. Cho and Kwon 2015; Synnott et al. 2017). It is not, however, a prerequisite for trolling to contain any of these features. More important, posts that do include such features are not always abusive. For example, profanity can be used to amplify an expression and name-calling and slurs can be discussed amongst acquaintances in a non-targeted way (Clarke and Grieve 2017). Additionally, abuse and trolling can be a lot more subtle and covert than these strategies.

The fourth method is the least problematic for the aims of the present study. It involves using the perceptions of others (Hardaker 2010, 2013, 2015), and then extracts the posts that have been accused of trolling (Mihaylov and Nakov 2016; Synnott et al. 2017). The present study follows this fourth approach, that is, Tweets that were perceived to be and labelled as trolling by other Twitter users were collected for analysis.

This method for data collection was implemented in R using the twitteR package (Gentry 2016) in November 2017. This package requires the researcher to have a Twitter account and API key, which can be obtained by following the instructions on Twitter's developer website (Twitter 2017). Subsequently, the 'searchstring()' function in the twitteR package was used to collect Tweets. This part of the programme extracts Tweets from the public API that include a particular search string ranging from the time of searching up to 6–9 days before. There are specific arguments within this function to collect Tweets to suit one's analysis, including the maximum amount of Tweets to return (n = 25) and the language of the Tweets (lang = en, for English only). For the present analysis, the search string selected was "troll", the language was restricted to only English Tweets, and the maximum amount of Tweets selected was 10,000. Each Tweet containing this search string is returned with various metadata, including whether it was in reply to another user and the screen name of that user, and the ID of the post that it was in reply to. All the post IDs that the Tweets containing "troll" were in reply to were extracted from this file and then using the IDs, these posts were collected using the function 'lookup_statuses()' in the twitteR package. Sometimes the posts were not available, potentially because it was deleted or that particular user has a private or suspended account. In this circumstance, "NA" was returned. These posts were then aligned with their counterpart Tweet containing

Table 7.1 Manual examination of Tweets containing "troll" for an accusation

Potential Accusation containing "troll"	Accusation (yes or no)	Extracted post via statusID that the "troll" Tweet was in reply to
@usrlogin @GoAngelo @seanhannity You better go back to nazi troll school. Your memes are old	Yes	@sparkman92 @GoAngelo @seanhannity https://t.co/K55hzjjspU
@0luwapemi She's a stupid troll, don't give her the attention she is craving	No	A grown woman tweeted this This was after complementing the abuser's penis https://t.co/bnWbccDt6o
@eugenegu @donmoyn @DonaldJTrumpJr @wikileaks You're apparently not a scientist, just a Trump hating troll	Yes	@donmoyn @DonaldJTrumpJr @wikileaks This Wikileaks scandal will go down in history as even bigger than Watergate

the word "troll". The Tweet containing the word "troll" was then manually examined for an accusation that the post was a troll. Table 7.1 illustrates this process. Those Tweets that were responded to with an accusation of being a troll were compiled into one file and repetitions were removed. Overall, the final corpus contains 853 perceived trolling Tweets, totalling 19,186 words.

This method for finding instances of trolling was selected because it accounts for the variation encapsulated within the contemporary use of trolling. This approach also avoids the researcher inflicting their opinion on what is or is not trolling. Perceptions of trolling are inherently personal; what is perceived as trolling by one individual can significantly differ from the next. This is one of the reasons why *trolling* has become a catch-all term. This approach was therefore selected to avoid merely reflecting the researcher's views and to allow for the inclusion of a more varied sample of trolling Tweets. Additionally, using other people's interpretations of trolling to identify trolling was selected because this method gives precedence to the perceptions of others, which is in line with legislation concerning harassment, malicious and abusive communications (e.g. Equality Act 2010: Sect. 26).

While there are several benefits to this approach, using other people's perceptions is limited. First, the person and post receiving the accusation may not actually be trolling and/or the person who is accusing that person may be doing so sarcastically. According to O'Sullivan and Flanagin (2003), it is paramount to know the intension of the speaker to correctly identify a speech act. While the intention of a speaker can be explicitly marked, this is rare, making the correct identification of trolling a complex and time-consuming task. For example, a true instance of trolling could be identified by obtaining confirmation from the poster that the post was intended to be trolling and by having the accuser confirm that the accusation was genuine. Even with 853 examples, this would take a considerable amount of time. Although sarcastic accusations are a potential limitation of the present study, the true meaning of a word is the sum of all that has been said about it. Thus, the accusation of trolling and the post accused, regardless of sarcastic intention, all contribute to the meaning of trolling. Also, it is the perceptions of others (i.e. the accusation) that law enforcement officials consider when they make an arrest (Hardaker 2010). Thus, for the aims of this research, the benefits of using other people's perceptions outweighed the limitations. Overall, accusations of this sort are not preferable. They are however expected. But with the large amount of texts collected, these posts should have relatively little effect on the general results of the analysis.

The second limitation of this method is that certain types of trolling may be more likely to receive accusations, such as highly abusive Tweets. This may mean that the underlying dimensions of linguistic variation may not be fairly representative of all trolling on Twitter. It is important to note that it is not assumed that all occurrences of trolling will have been perceived throughout the data collection period, or that they even will have been responded to with an accusation containing the word "troll". Rather, the final corpus of trolling Tweets and the results of the analysis will reflect those that were perceived and responded to with "troll", as well as those that were not deleted (by either moderators or the original posters).

7.2.2 Short Text Multidimensional Analysis

The approach to examine the stylistic variation in this corpus of Twitter trolling, which is described in more detail in Clarke and Grieve (2017), is a form of Biber's (1988) Multi-Dimensional Analysis (MDA), which has been modified to analyse short texts.

MDA is based on the assumption that texts that share linguistic features are likely to have a similar communicative function (Biber 1988). For example, texts that have the primary function of persuading will likely have similar frequencies and distribution of particular linguistic features. Consequently, MDA is a method used to identify the most common patterns of linguistic variation by subjecting the relative frequencies of numerous grammatical forms in the texts of a corpus to factor analysis. Factor analysis is a multivariate statistical method used to describe the variation amongst multiple observed, correlated variables in terms of a smaller number of latent or unobserved variables, deemed factors.

When applied to the relative frequencies of numerous grammatical features from the texts in a corpus, the factor analysis reveals the most distinct patterns of variation by grouping together the linguistic features that tend to co-occur with each other in the largest amount of texts. With linguistic co-occurrence patterns reflecting a shared communicative function (Biber 1988), these sets of linguistic features (also called dimensions of variation) and the texts that are most strongly associated to them are then interpreted for their functional properties.

Sometimes the dimensions revealed in the factor analysis consist of two sets of correlated linguistic features that are in complementary distribution, which means that the frequent use of one set of features means the infrequent use of the other. As a result, each set is interpreted separately for their functional properties, although together they make up one stylistic dimension of oppositional functions. For example, in Biber's (1988) MDA of spoken and written English texts, it was found that, among others, private verbs, second person pronouns, first person pronouns were in complementary distribution to nouns, attributive adjectives and prepositions. The first set of features that include first and second person pronouns were interpreted as having an involved style as pronouns involve the speaker and hearer into the discourse, whereas on the other side of the dimension, these linguistic features were interpreted as having an informationally dense style because high amounts of information are incorporated into a text through nouns and prepositional phrases.

In addition to spoken and written English, MDA has been applied to numerous languages and specialised discourse domains, including online communication, such as bulletin boards (Collot and Belmore 1996), and blogs (Grieve et al. 2010). These studies have revealed common patterns of stylistic and functional variation, showing how the structure of language varies for different communicative functions. However, the texts used within these studies have all tended to be over a hundred words in length. The reason for this is because the method relies on the relative frequencies of features and the relative frequencies of most forms in short texts tend to be inaccurate and less meaningful than those measured in long texts. Despite the fact that the character limit for Tweets has recently been raised from 140 to 280 characters, Tweets rarely exceed 60 words. As a result, the standard approach to MDA cannot be used reliably on short texts, such as individual Tweets. Therefore, a new form of MDA for short texts is introduced here (Clarke and Grieve 2017), which does not measure the relative frequencies of forms, but instead analyses for the occurrence of features, that is, are they present or absent. This information is then recorded in a binary data matrix and then analysed using Multiple Correspondence Analysis (MCA).

As an extension of Correspondence Analysis, which compares the relationship between two variables, MCA is used to examine the relationship between three or more categorical variables. In this way, MCA is similar to factor analysis used in standard MDA; however, unlike factor analysis, MCA is used for categorical data, such as the present and absent measures returned in this analysis. For the most part, MCA has been used to analyse survey or questionnaire data (Greenacre and Pardo 2006), although it has also been applied within linguistics (e.g. Glynn 2014).

7.2.3 Corpus Analysis

In order to complete this version of MDA, first each Tweet was tagged for part-of-speech information using the Twitter tagger developed by Gimpel et al. (2011). This tagger is a simplified version of the Stanford tagger, but is able to account for the noisiness of Twitter spelling, as well as tag for features specific to Twitter, for example URLs, hashtags and mentioning. Subsequently, the Tweets were then automatically analysed for the presence or absence of 69 grammatical forms, occurring in more than 5 percent of the Tweets by searching for tags, words, and sequences of tags and words. For example, perfect aspect is identified if a form of HAVE (e.g. had, having, has, plus contracted forms) is followed by a past participle verb. The features selected in this analysis are based on the standard feature set used in traditional MDA (Biber 1988), as well as additional features specific to computer-mediated communication. The full list of features can be found in the Appendix. Following automatic detection, this information was recorded in a binary data matrix of Tweets and Features, which was then subjected to Multiple Correspondence Analysis (MCA) in R using the FactoMineR package (Husson et al. 2017).

The MCA identified patterns of co-occurring variables by assigning each category of a variable (e.g. present or absent) a positive or negative coordinate for each dimension as well as a value indicating its contribution to the respective dimension (Le Roux and Rouanet 2010). If the categories' coordinates were of a similar value on a dimension, then this indicated that these variables often co-occur in Tweets. Additionally, the value indicating the categories contribution to the dimension reveals which of the features were most strongly associated to the dimension, and therefore represent the underlying patterns of co-occurrence. The MCA also assigns each individual Tweet a positive or negative coordinate on each dimension with the distance between each individual Tweet reflecting the amount of linguistic features that they do not share. In other words, Tweets that share several features that are associated to the dimension will have coordinates of similar value on that dimension.

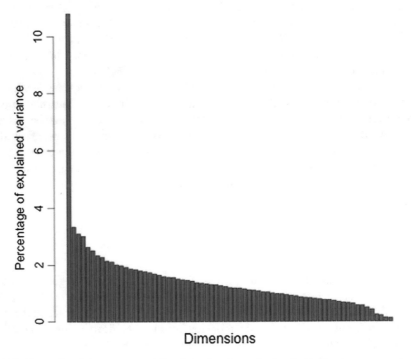

Fig. 7.1 Scree plot of the percentage of explained variance for the dimensions

In order to determine how many dimensions to extract and interpret, the eigenvalues of the dimensions were examined on a scree plot for a regular decrease or 'elbow' (see Fig. 7.1). Figure 7.1 shows a regular decrease in explained variance after Dimension 5, therefore the first four dimensions were extracted. Subsequently, the linguistic features whose contributions exceeded the average contribution for each dimension ($100/(69 \times 2) = 0.7$) (Le Roux and Rouanet 2010), and the Tweets that were most strongly associated to the particular dimensions were interpreted for their underlying functional properties and communicative style. Specifically, the features with positive coordinates that were strongly contributing to each dimension were interpreted separately from the features with negative coordinates, although together they make up one stylistic dimension of oppositional functions. The categories of features and their contributions for these four dimensions are presented in Table 7.2. Note that '_P' and '_A' denotes that the feature is present or absent respectively.

7.3 Dimension 1

Those features strongly contributing to Dimension 1 with positive coordinates are the presence of 37 features and those with negative coordinates are the absence of 15 features, with only the presence of URLs. Apart from URLs, Dimension 1 appears to be opposing the presence of features with the absence of features. This suggests that Dimension 1 is explaining text length as more words tend to mean more features, and thus fewer words can indicate the absence of features.

MCA allows for quantitative and qualitative supplementary variables to be uploaded, which do not contribute to the overall results, but which can be used to investigate whether these variables explain particular dimension patterns (Husson et al. 2017). Consequently, the length of the Tweets were uploaded as a supplementary quantitative variable to check whether Dimension 1 was explaining text length and this revealed that Dimension 1 was strongly positively correlated to text length ($r = 0.897$). An alternative method for checking this correlation is to take the length of the Tweet and correlate that to each Tweets dimension coordinate, which returns the same result.

The reason for Dimension 1 reflecting the length of the Tweet is due to the fact that this version of MDA for short texts does not take the relative frequencies of features like Biber (1988), but rather only analyses whether the feature is present or absent. The relative frequencies of features are taken in traditional MDA as a way to control for texts of different length. Because the relative frequencies of features are not taken in this version of MDA due to the fact that they are less meaningful in short texts, text length is not controlled for. Thus, there is the potential problem that Tweet length will confound the analysis. However, by uploading the Tweet length as a supplementary variable, it was also found that the other dimensions were only weakly correlated (see Table 7.3), suggesting that Tweet length has been controlled for in the results of the MCA, despite the fact that the relative frequencies of features were not measured.

Table 7.2 The features and their contributions for the 4 main dimensions

Dim		Features and contributions
1	+	PERFECT_P (1.2), AUXHAVE_P (1.3), PASSIVE_P (1.2), CONDITIONAL-SUB_P (1), AUXBE_P (2.3), PROQUAN_P (1.3), PROVDO_P (1), RELCLAUSESUBGAP_P (0.7), HAVEMV_P (0.9), CONTRASTIVECONJ_P (1.2), PROGRESSIVE_P (1.1), INFINITIVE (1.7), OBJECTPRO_P (1.1), THIRDPP (2), OTHERSUBORDINATOR__P (0.8), PRIVATEVB_P (1.5), COORDCONJ_P (2.2), PUBLICVB_P (1.5), COPULARVB_P (0.9), BEMV_P (1.6), OTHERADV_P (2.2), NOMINALISATION_P (1.1), VERB-ING_P (1.9), COMMA_P (1.8), PREDADJ_P (1), VERB-S_P (2), PAST_P (2), INDEFINITE-ARTICLE_P (1.5), POSSESSIVE-DET_P (1.3), SUBJECTPRO_P (1.7), DEFINITE_ARTICLE_P (1.6), FIRSTPP_P (1.2), FULLSTOP_P (1.8), ANALYTIC-NEG_P (0.8), PREPOSITION_P (1.6), ATTRIBUTIVEADJ_P (1.2), OTHERVERB_P (1.3)
	–	OTHERNOUN_A (3.1), OTHERVERB_A (3.3), URL_P (1.5), PREPOSITION_A (2.7), FULLSTOP_A (2.2), ATTRIBUTIVEADJ_A (1.7), VERB-S_A (1.5), PAST_A (1.4), OTHERADV_A (1.4), SUBJECTPRO_A (1.3), COORDCONJ_A (1.2), DEFINITE-ARTICLE_A (1.1), COMMA_A (0.8), THIRDPP_A (0.8), FSTPP_A (0.7)
2	+	COPULARVB_P (7.6), PREDADJ (8.3), AUXDO_P (2.4), DEMONSTRATIVEPRO_P (2.4), PRO+CONTRACTVB_P (2.9), STANCEVB_P (1.6), PROGRESSIVE_P (1.1), ANALYTIC-NEG_P (2.9), OTHERNOUN_A (1.3), SUBJECTPRO_P (2.4), PROPERNOUN_A (2.3), PRIVATEVB_P (1.2), SECONDPP_P (1.8), QUESTION_P (0.7), PREPOSITION_A (0.9), ATTRIBUTIVEADJ_A (1), CAPS_A (0.9)
	–	OTHERCONJ_P (1.5), PERFECT_P (7), AUXHAVE_P (6.9), NUMERAL-DET_P (3.9), COLON_P (1.5), HASHTAG_P (1.9), SYNTHETIC-NEG_P (0.9), NUMERAL-NOUN_P (1.4), CAPS_P (2.6), EXCLAM_P (1.2), PROPERNOUN_P (2.2), SUBJECTPRO_A (1.8), FIRSTPP_A (1.5), PREDADJ_A (1.8), SECONDPP_A (1.3), COPULARVB_A (1.3), ATTRIBUTIVEADJ_P (0.7), ANALYTIC-NEG_A (1)
3	+	PERFECT_P (19), AUXHAVE_P (18), SYNTHETIC-NEG_P (2.5), PROVDO_P (3), CONDITIONAL-SUB_P (2.2), PASSIVE_P (2.6), MODALPRED_P (1.6), PRO+CONTRACTVB_P (2.3), OTHERNOUN_A (1.2), FIRSTPP_P (1.7), PREPOSITION_A (1.4), SUBJECTPRO_P (1.5), ATTRIBUTIVEADJ_A (1.2), PROPERNOUN_A (1.6), VERB-ING_A (0.8), DEFINITE-ARTICLE_A (1)
	–	HASTAG_P (2.3), RELCLAUSESUBGAP_P (0.7), PROGRESSIVE_P (1.1), VERB-ING_P (1.3), EXCLAMATION_P (1.1), CAPS_P (2.2), MULTIWORDVB_P (0.9), NOMINALISATION (0.8), DEFINITE-ARTICLE_P (1.6), PROPERNOUN_P (1.5), AUXHAVE_A (1.9), SUBJECTPRO_A (1.1), FIRSTPP_A (1), PERFECT_A (1.6), ATTRIBUTIVEADJ_P (0.9), PREPOSITION_P (0.8)
4	+	RELCLAUSE-SUBJECTGAP_P (1.9), AUXDO_P (2.5), COPULARVB_P (1.6), ELLIPSIS_P (1.5), IMPERATIVE_P (2), NUMERAL-NOUN_P (2), PRIVATEVB_P (2.3), AUXBE_A (4.4), BEMV_P (0.9), VERB-ING_A (4), ANALYTIC-NEG_P (1.2), PROGRESSIVE_A (3.4), PRO+CONTRACTVB_A (0.9)
	–	PROGRESSIVE_P (24), AUXBE_P (18.1), PRO+CONTRACTVB_P (4.3), PASSIVE_P (1.5), VERB-ING_P (7.9), GERUND_P (0.9), HASHTAG_P (0.8)

Table 7.3 Correlation of each dimension to Tweet length

Dimension	Dim 1	Dim 2	Dim 3	Dim 4
Correlation to Tweet length	0.897	−0.108	−0.06	0.083

It is important to discuss the presence of URLs amongst the absence of features on the negative side of the Dimension. By examining the Tweets most strongly associated to negative Dimension 1, these Tweets only contain URLs. URLs can be, among others, images, gifs, links to other websites and content, videos and memes. Memes come in various forms, but most often, they are well-known images with some text that follows a particular stylistic pattern (Leaver 2013). Memes are a core feature of 4chan, the anonymous imageboard, and trolling culture (Phillips 2016). Memes are constantly being created, remixed and reposted as a way to express political emotions (e.g. Obama trolling, see Burroughs 2013), as well as to assert one's own knowledge of trolling culture (Phillips and Milner 2017). For example, Phillips (2016) describes how memes that contain the phrase "an hero" among other text indicate trolling cultural knowledge. The reference originated from a spelling mistake on a post on the MySpace memorial page of Mitchell Henderson, who committed suicide (KnowYourMeme.com 2017). The post stood out with the mistake "an hero", as opposed to "a hero", and with the implication that committing suicide is a heroic act. It has since been used in various memes and in trolling interactions to mean "kill yourself" (KnowYourMeme.com 2017). Memes and images can therefore be seen as inextricably linked to trolling.

Additionally, URLs can also be used to direct the readers to sources and other web content. Alongside trolling, 'fake news' and misinformation has been a growing concern in recent years. As a result, information seekers have been led to sift through numerous reports of the same story from different sources to distinguish the facts from the bias and lies. When exploring accusations of trolling during data collection, it was hard to miss the large proportion of requests for sources. Requests for sources of informed opinions or information are increasing and this has led to an explosion of the term 'post-truth' in public discourse. Lewandowsky et al. (2017) suggest that in this post-truth era expert knowledge may eventually become secondary to the opinions of those who are most vocal and influential on social media, such as celebrities, big corporation and botnet puppeteers. They note that trolls and bots played a huge part in the spread of misinformation during the 2016 presidential campaign. The URLs may therefore be connected to the spread of misinformation and propaganda.

Overall, while Dimension 1 for the most part explains text length, it could also be opposing trolling Tweets that are completely textual with trolling Tweets that are image-based, for example, memes or those that spread misinformation through links to other websites and sources, both of which are known trolling strategies.

7.4 Dimension 2: Interactive Versus Informationally Dense Reporting

The features with positive coordinates that are strongly contributing to Dimension 2 have an interactive and single addressee style. The presence of subject pronouns and second person pronouns indicates that the writer is addressing a particular person and involving them into the discourse. Additionally, the presence of question marks indicates a request for information, which encourages further interaction. Demonstrative pronouns (e.g. that's) imply an involved function because there is an assumption that the reader will understand what the pronoun is referring to. Pronouns with the verb contracted (e.g. you're, youre) are characteristic of a more reduced verbal style. Private verbs (e.g. know, think) and stance verbs (e.g. like, need, wanna) are used to express private attitudes, thoughts and feelings and have been shown to be used more frequently in texts with an involved and interactive function (e.g. Biber 1988). Copular verbs and predicative adjectives (e.g. the trailers looked decent) are used to modify a subject noun phrase in a less integrated way, suggesting a fragmented production of text, for example *the boy is young* (predicative) versus *the young boy* (attributive). This interpretation is supported by the Tweets most strongly associated to this Dimension, which are all interacting with a particular addressee and reflect a more oral style.

1. @RedPandasDaily i dont think youre getting my point, you can have any views you like and its totally okay, but dont be vocal about it, like tweeting about "blocking nazis" and such its unprofessional after all, and im sure we can both agree that the red pandas are more important than any of this.
2. @AlwaysThinkHow @huckfinn22 @peterdaou No, you are divisive and that's exactly what you're trying to do. All of your rhetorical nonsense is just lies. Do you even know why you don't like him?
3. @iamfogo @MichaelRapaport I didn't wanna get into all this, but I do not like it when somebody misinterprets me. I am sorry if I came off as rude.
4. @bigbro8605 No.Don't need to know art history.It's a movie, not an art show. I don't care about history. Regardless, they're holding back reviews until the last day, so chances are the movie isn't any good anyway. The trailers looked decent (at least the recent ones), but that's not good.
5. @JimmyMatho @docamitay @FaithGoldy @jordanbpeterson @GadSaad @FreeAdvocate Calling him out for being condescending is rude? How about this for rudeness: I think you are a spineless sycophant who doesn't even have the intellectual capability of appropriately analyzing the conversation you're commenting on.

While features with positive coordinates indicate a more fragmented production of text, those features with negative coordinates that are strongly contributing to Dimension 2 are used to report on and integrate information into a text in an efficient and concise manner. For example, attributive adjectives (e.g. encrypted message, sexual advances, funniest thing) add detail to nominal forms in fewer words and structures than its predicative alternative (Biber 1988). The presence of several nominal forms, including proper nouns (e.g. Hillary, Feinstein, Subway, Sean Hannity, Moore's) and numeral nouns (e.g. 2008) indicates that the texts are informationally dense as nominal forms refer to particular things, people and places and thus the co-occurrence of these forms suggests that there are numerous referents in a single tweet. Not only are numeral nouns associated to this dimension, but also numeral determiners (e.g. *five* companies, *three* divorces), suggesting a precise presentation of information. Perfect aspect is used for describing past and completed events (e.g. have now pulled, I've read, has intercepted, have confessed). Although hashtags are multifunctional, the co-occurrence of hashtags with these features suggests that they are functioning to orient to a particular topic and integrate additional information to the feed. This interpretation is supported by the Tweets most strongly associated to negative Dimension 2. All of the Tweets are reporting on an event or previous action and are informationally dense, containing several referents in the form of proper nouns and numerals.

6. Our enigma team has intercepted an encrypted message revealing plans for a RARE Cyber Monday item: Cyber Dual Unarmed, which will require membership, cost 5,000 ACs, be color-custom, and give a +60% damage boost, but only on Wednesdays.

7. At least five companies have now pulled their ads from Sean Hannity's show following his Roy Moore coverage: —@Keurig—@realtordotcom—@23andMe—@ELOQUII—@NaturesBounty https://t.co/fsMpagpG5g

8. Purportedly Moore's main accuser Leigh Corfman has had three divorces, filed for bankruptcy three times, and has been charged with multiple misdemeanors. Posts on Moore's FB page indicate that Corfman, has claimed several pastors at various churches made sexual advances at her.

9. @cinemaven @Demvoter @Viktor_DoKaren @lynchem1 @WilDonnelly That is the funniest thing I've read all day!□□□□ Actually, I supported Hillary for Senator in 2000, then supported her for Pres in 2008. Very disappointed in the cheating and corporatism of the Dem Party in 2016. Voted Dem since Dukakis but I've #Demexited. HRC gave us Trump.

10. @SLandinSoCal @realDonaldTrump There was NO Russian hacking or collusion. Feinstein and Clapper have confessed there is absolutely no evidence of Trump-Russia collusion. Regardless of the Papadopoulos meetings or lies. CIA routinely use Russian and Chinese code to cover their tracks.

Overall, Dimension 2 is therefore interpreted as opposing Tweets that have a more interactive and oral style with those Tweets that reflect a reporting and informationally dense style. In Biber (2014), it was acknowledged that a dimension contrasting a more oral style with a more literate form has been observed in nearly all studies using MDA, even in studies specifically examining texts that are just spoken or only written, suggesting that this could be a universal dimension. The fact that this has been observed in Twitter trolling lends additional support to Biber's (2014) theory. Additionally, this Dimension also demonstrates that trolling can be addressee-

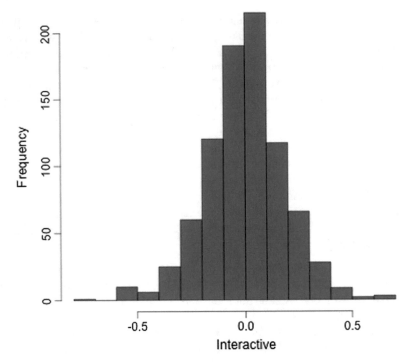

Fig. 7.2 Histogram of each Tweet's Dimension 2 coordinate

focused and thus interact with a particular person or that it can take the form of reporting events in an informationally dense style. Previous research on trolling has shown that trolls can interact with and target particular individuals (Morrissey and Yell 2016). Additionally, in recent years, the notion of fake news has become more apparent and inextricably linked with trolling. In particular, Russian troll armies or bot puppeteers have attempted to influence public perceptions and debates by spreading misinformation in massive quantities to make it appear real (Lewandowsky et al. 2017). Press reportage (regardless of fake or real) is characterised by past tense, nouns, proper nouns and attributive adjectives (Biber 1988). While determining whether the trolling Tweets constitute the spread of misinformation is beyond this analysis, it can be argued that this informationally dense reporting style can facilitate the spread of misinformation, which is a known trolling strategy.

Following interpretation, each Tweet's Dimension 2 coordinate was plotted on a histogram to observe the distribution of Tweets with respect to this dimension. Figure 7.2 reflects a normal distribution, which suggests that there is not a binary distinction between trolling Tweets exhibiting an interactive style with trolling Tweets reflecting an informationally dense style. Instead, the bell curve shows that the majority of Tweets draw on both an interactive and informationally dense style.

7.5 Dimension 3: Dismissive Versus Mocking

Those features with positive coordinates that are strongly contributing to Dimension 3 appear to have the function of introducing real or imagined events. Perfect aspect is used to refer to completed action (e.g. you've *tweeted* me twice already, it must *have been*, what you've *done*), but this co-occurring with conditional subordinators (e.g. *if* he ever does, *if* she did that to my stuff) and modals of prediction (e.g. I *would* have taken that same hammer, That *would* be about 500 or so people, you realize?) indicates that the consequences of an imagined scenario are being described. Other features strongly contributing to this dimension suggest an emphatic function, for example synthetic negation (e.g. *no* defence, *no* way, *no* link) is indicative of a more emphatic style, than analytic negation (Tottie 1983), and is used to negate a particular entity or action. There are features that can be categorised as forms of reduction, including pro-verb do (e.g. if he ever *does*, if she *did* that to my stuff, I can't condone what you've *done*, everyone knows exactly what Moore *did* to this girl), and pronouns with contracted verbs (e.g. we're, I'd, you've), which could suggest an impulsive production of text.

While the function of describing real or imagined events in an impulsive and emphatic way appears to connect these linguistic co-occurrence patterns, from a closer examination of the Tweets most strongly associated to this dimension, and thus in the context of trolling, it can be suggested that the co-occurrence of these features have the underlying function of dismissing a previous statement, assumption or action. Examples 11 and 12 use conditional subordinators and modals of prediction to describe the consequences of an imagined event. In particular, Example 11 reveals these consequences as implausible as a way to dismiss the veracity of a previous post. In Example 12, the author describes what they would have done if some action had happened to them as a way to dismiss the acceptability of such action. The perfect aspect and subject pronouns are used in Example 13 to describe the action of the previous poster as a way to imply a lack of belief that they have a link to a particular fact, and therefore dismiss their previous post, whereas these same features are used in Example 14 to describe the action of someone in order to reject it. Example 15 implies that other people's assumptions or statements about an event are implausible by indicating the consequences of an imagined event, that is, if all their statements were true.

11. @RyanRational1 @FoxNews @chelseahandler Really Ryan? Exactly which "half" of my President's campaign team has been indicted? That would be about 500 or so people, you realize? President Trump needs no defense. But if he ever does, we're here for him—65+ million of us and growing.
12. @DrPhil I would have taken that same hammer and whooped Brandi's ass if she did that to my stuff! You ain't gonna break my expensive shit and get away with it, no way! Woman or not, I'd beat that ass for breaking my items. She asked for it.
13. @JustGoree you've tweeted me twice already and there's still no link

14. @MooreSenate I'm a Christian conservative but I can't condone what you've done. Please step aside.
15. @Amber_Addison_ @MooreSenate @SenateMajLdr I love how everyone knows exactly what Moore did to this girl. Were you there too? It must have been very crowded in that room.

Alternatively, those features with negative coordinates that are strongly contributing to Dimension 3 are less about dismissing the actions or statements of somebody else; instead, they are more about showing and identifying particular referents. The features are similar to those described by Biber (1988) as having an explicit and elaborated function. For example, relative clauses on the subject position (e.g. the Nazis were German Leftists *that didn't want to be under Russian USSR control*) allow for explicit and elaborated descriptions of the referent (Biber 1988). There are features that indicate a high degree of specificity, such as nominalisations (e.g. abbreviation, information), proper nouns (e.g. Nazi, Democratic Party) and definite articles (e.g. *the* Nazi Party, *the* biggest shock, *the* street, *the* impotent rage). The presence of hashtags (e.g. #MAGA, #sfnbanter17, #MadOnline) co-occurring with these features suggests a topic-focused style. Capitalisation and exclamation marks (e.g. JUST WAIT!, LOCK HIM UP!) co-occurring with features indicating a more explicit and elaborated style suggest that they are employed to make a point clear and imply shouting.

Although the features are associated with an explicit and elaborated style, from a closer examination of the Tweets most strongly associated to the dimension, it appears that this style is employed in order to mock others. Example 16 mocks those on the left of the political spectrum by drawing a comparison between them and Nazis. Example 16 also encourages other people online to provoke 'leftists' by reminding them of this. Additionally, Example 17 appears to be mocking a particular group of people about the effect that Trump's new tax reform will have on them, and Example 18 seems to be mocking the democrats for their reaction towards Donald Trump Junior's communication with Wikileaks. Example 20 is explicitly mocking a particular individual to the extent that they even quote that individual's Tweet to point out the absurdity.

16. Trigger a leftist by always reminding them what the official name of the Nazi Party is: "Socialist Workers Party of Germany" Nazi is just an abbreviation the Nazis were German Leftists that didn't want to be under Russian USSR control Pic: Nazi 1932 election poster.
17. @schlichting1103 @seanhannity @SaraCarterDC @GreggJarrett Speaking of money my good hannity people U R going to be in for the biggest shock of your life when U get yr new tax bill! JUST WAIT! #MAGA!
18. @DonaldJTrumpJr @wikileaks Wikileaks: *Releases enough information to put the whole Democratic Party in jail* Dems:"Meh" *Trump Jr. responds to a DM from Wikileaks after 2 days* Dems: "LOCK HIM UP! TREASON".
19. anyone still at #sfnbanter17: there is a place directly across the street that sells warm cookies until 3am.

20. So #MadOnline Laugh at the impotent rage Enjoy their death rattle This pathetic
     farce is their best show Peak MAGA is defending child rape This? This here?
     Is as good as it gets for them All. Downhill. From here. https://twitter.com/
     PhxGOP/status/930270372989100032 ...

Overall, Dimension 3 is therefore interpreted as opposing Tweets, which have a
dismissive style with Tweets that function to mock others through an explicit and
elaborated style. Previous research has revealed that trolls can take the opposing
view in a debate even if they do not believe it themselves and will argue until they
win or their opponent gives up and stops responding (Phillips 2016). One strategy
for winning a debate can be to show that the comment or action of one's opponent
is not worthy of consideration. For example, Aro (2016) describes how the Russian
trolls targeted her investigations and reports and attempted to make her work seem
unreliable in order to discredit her argument. Thus, the dismissive style found in the
Tweets strongly associated to positive Dimension 3 demonstrates a particular stylistic strategy employed by trolls to win a debate and subsequently fulfil their trollish
nature, as described by Phillips (2016). Additionally, previous research has emphasised that some trolls troll "for the lulz", which is an aggressive kind of laughter that
results from another person's misfortune (Phillips 2016). Mocking is similar to 'lulz'
as it can also involve laughing at others in an aggressive manner. Thus, the explicit
and elaborated descriptions of referents, which are used in the context of trolling to
mock others corresponds to previous descriptions of trolling, and demonstrates the
particular linguistic features which realise this communicative function.

By plotting each Tweets Dimension 3 coordinates (see Fig. 7.3), it can be seen
that the majority of Tweets fall in the middle, which indicates that there is not a
binary distinction between trolling Tweets that exhibit either a dismissive style or
a mocking style, but rather it shows that the majority of the Tweets draw on both
styles.

7.6   Dimension 4: Argumentative Versus Forewarning

Those features with positive coordinates that are strongly contributing to Dimension
4 have an argumentative style. The co-occurrence of auxiliary do and analytic negation indicates that an event or premise is being negated and thus is being disputed
(e.g. you *don't* dictate terms, MCCONNEL *DOES NOT* WANT JUDGE MOORE,
Don't let Jim clarify, and 99% not, you are *not* one). Several forms are concerned with
being and existence, suggesting a certain and definitive presentation of information.
For example, copular verbs are used to describe a particular attribute or characteristic
of a subject noun phrase (e.g. THEY *ARE AFRAID*, Just decide your interpretation
is correct), and BE as a main verb (e.g. You *are* not one, You *are* the reason I left)
is used to describe the identity of the referent. Relative clauses on subject position
(e.g. an alleged rapist *who actively destroyed his accusers*, any questions *that may
clarify*, the republican actors *that have been in trouble*, philosophical background

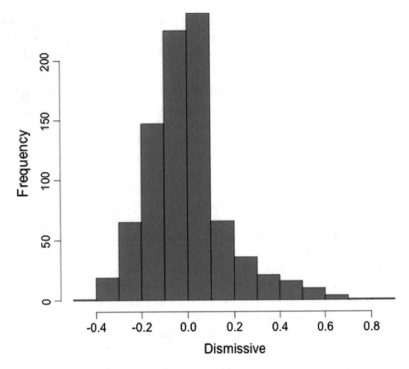

Fig. 7.3 Histogram of each Tweet's Dimension 3 coordinate

that would warrant attention as a serious scientist) also allow for the precise presentation of information as they can be used to be more explicit about the particular referent. Imperatives (e.g. Get bent, Don't ask questions that may clarify, VOTE MOORE FOR SENATE) are used to make orders or demands and are common in argumentative discourse as a way to either encourage people to do something, or to insult them. Private verbs (e.g. we should *believe*, DOES NOT *WANT*, Just *decide* your interpretation, Just like when you assclowns always *hope* a mass shooting, I *know* scientists) are used to introduce attitudes, thoughts and feelings (Biber 1988). Arguments often derive from a difference in opinion, belief, or attitude. Thus private verbs, which allow for the expression of opinions and feelings can be at the centre of an argumentative style. This interpretation is supported in the Tweets most strongly associated to this Dimension. All of the Tweets have an argumentative style, which appear to be aggressive.

21.   @djsiilver @CNN Sorry, you don't dictate terms. You supported the wife of an alleged rapist who actively destroyed his accusers … but said we should believe everyone ELSE. Get bent.

22.   □□□†□THEY ARE AFRAID OF A MAN WITH GODLY PRINCIPLES THAT THEY CAN NOT CONTROL…!THEIR PLAN IS TO DESTROY HIM LIKE THEY TRIED TO DO TO PRESIDENT TRUMP! MITCH

MCCONNELL DOES NOT WANT JUDGE MOORE TO STAND IN HIS WAY AND STOP □ HIS CORRUPT USA SENATE!!!VOTE MOORE FOR SENATE

23. @Wonderymore @RStarovich @brucewolf @AmyJacobson Don't let Jim clarify his position. Don't ask any questions that may clarify. Just decide your interpretation is correct and then REACT.

24. @LorddeVelville @kimwim @kylegriffin1 Just like all of the republican actors that have been in trouble…oh wait you ignorant jackass! Just like when you assclowns always hope a mass shooting is a conservative and 99% not. You are the reason I left the democrat party. #maga #metoo

25. @godFreeWorld @A_3rdWay @CanAgnosAtheist @edthegodless "We scientists". LOL. Sure. I know scientists. You are not one. Or perhaps you emulate a scientist, but don't have the logical and philosophical background that would warrant attention as a serious scientist.

By contrast, those features with negative coordinates that are strongly contributing to Dimension 4 have a style of summarising current and continuing action. Pronouns with contracted verb and the progressive is used to describe continuing action of the subject pronoun (e.g. *I'm voting* for Roy Moore, *You're repeating*, *You're accusing*). The gerunds automatically identified by the tagger are those verb phrases functioning as prepositional complements (e.g. You're accusing someone *of being* a child molester). Prepositional complements like these complete the meaning of the verb phrase. The fact that gerunds are co-occurring with progressive tense suggests a strong focus on describing the action. Agentless-passive constructions (e.g. Investigations are *being opened*, a part of what's *being resisted,* you could *get sued*) are used to remove the agent and thus again add to this strong focus on describing the action. By examining the trolling Tweets most strongly associated to negative Dimension 4, it appears that the underlying function for summarising continuing action is to forewarn. Example 26 is warning the addressee that they are going to be muted due to their actions. Example 27 is giving notice about current investigations and forewarning people that this information will be covered on a television programme. Example 28 is warning people that they are the ones who are being resisted if they are not resisting establishment democrats. Example 29 is notifying their audience in advance about their voting intentions. And finally, Example 30 is giving an advance warning to an individual of the possibility of being sued for accusing another person.

26. @PizzaPie1018 @TurnTNBlue @Rightwingmadman @DonaldJTrumpJr @wikileaks Regardless. Its quite apparent you're a mindless drone. You're repeating what you're told and spamming the same shit over and over again while never adding anything, only contradicting yourself. Muted.

27. @PrisonPlanet @Cryogenik28 Investigations are being opened regarding the transfer of USA's NUKE making materials to Russia under Obama admin/Hillary SOS tick tock watch #Hannity tonight

28. If you are not resisting #establishment Dems, you are NOT a part of #TheResistance but a part of what's being resisted. #OurRevolution

29. .@RepMoBrooks: "Roy Moore will vote right, that's why i'm voting for Roy
     Moore." #ALSEN
30. @RobertJMolnar @RealMattCouch You're accusing someone of being a child
     molester? U better have solid proof Son or u could get sued.

Dimension 4 is therefore interpreted as opposing Tweets that have an explicitly
argumentative or disputing style with Tweets that function to forewarn by summarising continuing action. This argumentative style found in this corpus has also been
described in previous research on trolling. In particular, Hardaker (2010) and Phillips
(2016) both describe that trolls are argumentative and hostile.

Interestingly, some of the examples strongly associated to negative Dimension 4
seem to be summarising the actions of others in a negative way in order to rebuke it
(e.g. Example 26, 28, 30), whereas Example 27 and 29 appear to be more positive
and are, to an extent, commending the actions that are being summarised. This
reveals that Tweets summarising action with a positive sentiment are not regarded
as less trolling than those that have a negative sentiment. Nevertheless, the trolling
Tweets that are forewarning with negative sentiment appear to be taking on a more
threatening form of forewarning than those that are more neutral or positive. Previous
cases of trolling, such as Tanya Gersh described previously, have demonstrated that
trolling can take the form of threats. While Gersh received threats concerning her
safety, the threats presented here (e.g. Example 26, 28 and 30) appear to be more
ideologically motivated. In other words, it appears that the trolls in these examples
are threatening the beliefs of individuals in order to encourage them to change their
point of view.

Figure 7.4 is a histogram of each Tweet's Dimension 4 coordinates. Similar to the
other histograms, Fig. 7.4 reflects a bell curve with the majority of the Tweets falling
in the middle.

7.7   Conclusion

While it is generally acknowledged that the term 'trolling' encompasses a wide-range
of behaviours and styles, the present analysis sought to explore empirically how the
structure of language varies within trolling on Twitter in order to identify its different styles and functions. By following Miyahlov and Nakov's (2016) approach, 853
instances of trolling were collected. Subsequently, these trolling Tweets were analysed using a novel form of categorical multidimensional analysis (Clarke and Grieve
2017). After controlling for text length in the first dimension, the present analysis
found 3 subsequent main dimensions of stylistic variation, which have been assigned
the interpretative labels: interactive versus informationally dense reporting, dismissive versus mocking through an explicit and elaborated style, and argumentative
versus forewarning through summarising continuing action.

The interactive versus informationally dense stylistic dimension reflects the findings of previous research employing MDA, which opposes an oral style with a

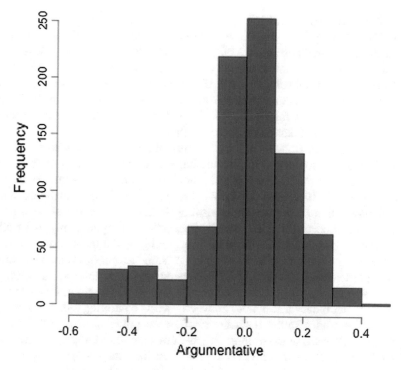

Fig. 7.4 Histogram of each Tweet's Dimension 4 coordinate

literate form (Biber 1988, 2014). It also demonstrates that some instances of trolling can have a more interactive nature by directly addressing or responding to people or individuals, whereas other instances of trolling are less interactive and have a more informationally dense and reporting style. Previous research on trolling supports this finding. For example, Morrissey and Yell (2016) describe case studies of three individuals who were targeted by trolls. Several of the examples that they provide illustrate this interactive style by directly addressing the targeted individuals through the second person pronoun and asking particularly personal and crude questions. Additionally, previous research has shown that some trolling is less explicitly interactive and displays a more informationally dense and reporting style. Whether this style is used to communicate false (Donath 1999), exaggerated (Netlingo.com, 1995–2015), provocative (Herring et al. 2002), or some other type of information is beyond the interpretation of this dimension, rather the overarching dense reporting style is reflected here in the co-occurrence of nominal forms, perfect aspect and so on.

The next main dimension contrasts trolling Tweets that exhibit a dismissive style with trolling Tweets that function to mock others. The dismissive style found here reflects a particular strategy when debating, which is to show that a particular comment or action is not worthy of consideration by dismissing its appropriateness, plausibility or accuracy, which has been described as a trolling strategy by Aro (2016). The mocking style revealed on the opposite side of this dimension through explicit and elaborated descriptions of the referent achieves another typical trolling strategy, which has been noted in much of the literature (e.g. Phillips 2016; Phillips and Milner 2017). Specifically, one of the functions of trolling is "for the lulz", which is an aggressive, mocking kind of laughter. Thus, these particular linguistic features have been shown to allow for explicit and elaborate descriptions, which in the context of trolling provide the function of mocking others.

The final dimension opposes trolling Tweets that have an argumentative style with trolling Tweets that forewarn by summarising the continuing action of others. The argumentative style reflects research, which notes that trolls can be argumentative and hostile (Hardaker 2010; Phillips 2016). What is most interesting about the summaries of continuing action in the context of trolling is that the summaries need not be negative to constitute trolling. However, it appears that the explicitly negative trolling Tweets take a more threatening form of forewarning, while the neutral or positive summaries tend to be giving advance notice of some action or event. This finding may have particular applications for studies using sentiment analysis on trolling.

By plotting each Tweet's dimension coordinates on a histogram, it was revealed that there are not binary distinctions between Tweets exhibiting either of the styles on a single dimension. Rather, the majority of Tweets fall respectively in the middle, suggesting that several of the trolling Tweets draw on multiple strategies and styles.

Overall, however, the findings reflect the most important dimensions of stylistic variation found in this corpus of trolling. It is hard to ignore the political focus of several of the Tweets that are most strongly associated to the dimensions. Notably, it appears that the trolls that populate the corpus are those expressing anti-Democratic party, pro-Trump and/or pro-Moore[2] sentiment. As mentioned previously, Lewandowsky et al. (2017) note that trolls and bots have played a huge role within the political sphere, and to an extent have influenced public opinion. Additionally, Nagle (2017) describes that much of trolling defines itself as opposing the liberal establishment. The dominance of the right wing and pro-Republican views and information found in this corpus of trolling can therefore be said mirror the anti-liberal establishment and values expressed by many trolls.

It is impossible to know how many instances of trolling occurred during data collection but were not actually collected either as a result of restrictions on the public API, deleted Tweets, or perhaps trolling Tweets that were not responded to with 'troll'. Nevertheless, it can be argued that the following main dimensions of stylistic variation found in this study reflect what is currently perceived as problematic in society. Phillips (2016) describes that trolls are often regarded as transgressive in the sense that they go against what society perceives to be good and appropriate. Current media reports, academic research, big organisations, and politicians are emphasising the threat of Russian trolls and the spread of propaganda and misinformation (e.g. Lewandowsky et al. 2017; Aro 2016). Being accurately informed is therefore

---

[2] In November 2017 during the special election for the U.S. Senate, 9 women accused the Republican candidate and at the time Judge Roy Moore for sexual misconduct.

something that is highly valued in society and thus those who attempt to prevent this process and spread misinformation are likely to be regarded as deviant or as trolls.

While the main stylistic dimensions found in this corpus may be reflecting other things that society views as problematic, it may be argued that several of the main styles allow for misinformation to be presented, responded to and/or managed. A piece of misinformation may be communicated in an interactive style, or a person/troll may interact with and respond to a particular piece of propaganda, such as Example 2. Alternatively, misinformation can be communicated and rejected through an informationally dense style. Example 10 is an informationally dense Tweet, which rejects a specific story and presents an alternative narrative in a factual way, despite the fact that the information within this narrative has not yet been proven right or wrong.

Additionally, a dismissing style can be employed to further another type of misinformation, or to demonstrate that it is in fact misinformation. For example, in Example 13, it is possible to assume that the poster has previously demanded a link to a source for a particular piece of information. However, it has not been provided, despite the fact that this other individual has tweeted twice. By commenting on the fact that the individual has not provided a link, the poster sheds doubt on the veracity of the statement and ultimately dismisses it as not worthy of consideration. Aro (2016) described this dismissive strategy of trolls, highlighting that the trolls who targeted her attempted to discredit her work as a way to promote their own ideology.

Furthermore, information and knowledge is something that sparks critical debate and arguments, especially if that information is notably biased. An argumentative style can be used to counteract a particular piece of information to restore order and truth, or to argue against accurate information and essentially promote misinformation.

Finally, giving advance warning about particular events or consequences of action can be ideologically motivated. Example 30, for instance, firstly summarises the accusations made by the addressee and then forewarns of the consequences of this without any proof. It may be suggested that the aim of doing so is to encourage the addressee to retract their accusation and change their way of thinking. This particular example shows that forewarning can be employed to counter (mis)information and simultaneously promote an alternative narrative, which may be (mis)information.

Despite the dominance of trolling Tweets expressing right wing and Republican sentiment, however, the results show that even within this particular corpus of trolls several strategies and linguistic styles are drawn upon. Overall, the findings from this research show that trolling is a multifunctional phenomenon, which varies considerably in terms of its linguistic structure.

Appendix: The Feature Set

Feature	Definition	Example
AMPLIFIER	Refers to adverbs used to intensify the verb/adjective	very, absolutely, so
ANALNEG	Refers to 'not' plus contracted forms	can't, cannot, not
ATTRIBADJ	Attributive Adjectives: Adjectives that come before the noun and any other adjective not tagged as predicative	The big cat
AUXBE	Auxiliary be	She was killed
AUXDO	Auxiliary do	I don't like your attitude
AUXHAVE	Auxiliary have	She has spent it all
BEMV	BE as a main verb	She was a beautiful girl
BRACKET	Brackets	()
CAPS	Capitalisation—two or more capital letters that is not tagged as an acronym	MAKE AMERICA GREAT AGAIN
CCONJ	Coordinating conjunctions	and, &
CNTRSTCONJ	Contrastive conjunctions	but, by contrast
COLON	Colon	:
COMMA	Comma	,
CONDISUB	Conditional subordinator	If you ever speak to me like that again, unless you have all the money in the world
COPVB	Copular verbs: verbs that are followed by predicative	She looked beautiful, She was beautiful
DEFART	Definite article	the
DEMDET	Demonstrative determiner	this house, that house, those houses
DEMPRO	Demonstrative pronoun	that was the best day, this is the life
DETQUAN	Quantifiers used as determiners	She ate several sandwiches
ELIPS	Ellipsis	...
EXCLAM	Exclamation mark	!
FSTPP	First person	I, We, us
FULSTOP	Full stop	.

Feature	Definition	Example
GERUND	Prepositional complement	Sarah talked about leaving her job
HASHTAG	Hashtag	#
HAVEMV	HAVE as main verb	He had a wonderful smile
IMPERATIVE	Clauses in imperative mood	Go away!, Don't be foolish!
INDEFART	Indefinite article	A, an
INFINITIVE	Infinitive	to be, to go, to have, to say
ING	Verb in -ing form	Having, going, seeing
IT	The pronoun IT plus contractions	It, it's
MDPOSS	Possibility modals	can, may, mightn't
MDPRED	Prediction modals	will, shall, I'll
MULTIWVB	Multi-word verb: particle verbs and prepositional verbs	look up, look forward
NOMIN	Nominalisations	action, statement
NUMDET	Numerals used as determiners	3 mice, four children
NUMNOUN	Numerals used as nouns	He gave me seven.
OBJPRO	Object pronouns	them, him, us
OTHERADV	Other adverbs that are not tagged as amplifiers, downtoners, time and place adverbials, etc.	She danced beautifully
OTHERCONJ	Other conjunctions not tagged as either contrastive or coordinating	Consequently, therefore, moreover
OTHRINTJ	Other interjections that are not tagged as laughter, positive interjection 'Yes', negative interjections 'No'	Wow, OMG, Congrats!, well
OTHERNOUN	Other nouns that are not tagged as numeral, quantifiers, nominalisations, ordinals	tea, book
OTHRSUB	Other subordinators that are not tagged as time, place, cause, concessive, and conditional subordinators	whereas, like
OTHRVERB	Other verbs that are not tagged as private verbs, public verbs, verb-ing, past tense verbs, participle verbs, third person singular, suasive verbs, perception verbs, copular verbs, BE as main verb, auxiliary be, auxiliary have, pro-verb do, auxiliary do, stance verb	

Feature	Definition	Example
PASSIVE	Agentless-passive constructions	Sally was prosecuted
PAST	Past tense verbs	went, saved, held
PERCEPTVB	Verbs of perception	hear, smell, taste
PERFECT	Perfect aspect	She had been to the shops already.
POSSDET	Possessive determiner	my cat, his dog, her lips, their sandwiches
PREDADJ	Predicative adjectives: Adjectives that come after copular verbs	She was ugly, She looked stressed
PREP	Preposition	down the road, in your car
PROCONTRACT	Pronoun with a verb contracted	You're, I'm, He'd
PROGRESSIVE	Progressive aspect	I am going, she was talking, he is thinking
PROQUAN	Quantitative pronoun	Everyone, everything, anyone, anything
PROVDO	Pro-verb do.	He had done it also, She did it better.
PRPN	Proper nouns	Donald Trump, London, New York
PRVV	Private verbs	think, wonder, anticipate
PUBV	Public verbs	stated, said, shouted
QUES	Question mark	?
RELCLAUSESUBGAP	Relative clause on subject position	A girl that likes cheese, the house that was haunted
SINFLECT	Third person singular verbs	talks, likes, thinks
SNDPP	Second person	you, you're, your
STANCEVB	Stance verbs	want, seem, appear, need
SUBJPRO	Subject pronoun	I, he, she, we, they
SYNNEG	Synthetic negation	No, neither, nor, no more
THRDPP	Third person pronoun	he, she, they
TIMEADV	Time adverbial	last night, yesterday, again
TIMESUB	Time subordinator	Before he went to the shops, he watched the telly
URL	URLs—can be images, videos, gifs, links…	
WHW	WH-words that are not tagged as adverbs/subordinators	who, how, what, when

References

"troll" NetLingo® The Internet Dictionary (1995–2015). http://www.netlingo.com/word/troll.php. Accessed 31 Oct 2015

Ansong ED, Takyi T, Damoah D, Ampomah EA, Larkotey W (2013) Internet trolling in Ghana. Int J Emerg Sci Eng 2(1):42–43

Aro J (2016) The cyberspace war: propaganda and trolling as warfare tools. Eur View 15:121–132

Beckett L (2017) I was the target of a neo-Nazi 'troll storm' The Guardian. Thursday 20 April 2017. https://www.theguardian.com/us-news/2017/apr/20/tanya-gersh-daily-stormer-richard-spencer-whitefish-montana. Accessed 29 Dec 2017

Biber D (1988) Variation across speech and writing. Cambridge University Press, Cambridge

Biber D (2014) Multi-dimensional analysis: a personal history. In: Sardinha TB, Pinto MV (eds) Multi dimensional analysis, 25 years on: a tribute to Douglas Biber. John Benjamins Publishing Company, Amsterdam, pp xxvi–xxxviii

Burroughs B (2013) Obama trolling: memes, salutes and an agonistic politics in the 2012 presidential election. Fibreculture J 22:258–277

Cho D, Kwon KH (2015) The impacts of identity verification and disclosure of social cues on flaming in online user comments. Comput Hum Behav 51:363–372

Clarke I, Grieve J (2017) Dimensions of abusive language on Twitter. In: Proceedings of the first workshop on abusive language online 1–10. Vancouver, Canada: ACL, 4 Aug 2017

Coles BA, West M (2016) Weaving the internet together: imagined communities in newspaper comment threads. Comput Hum Behav 60:44–53

Collot M, Belmore N (1996) Electronic language: A new variety of English. In: Herring SC (ed) Computer-mediated communication: linguistic, social and cross-cultural perspectives. Benjamins, Amsterdam, pp 13–28

Communications act (2003) http://www.legislation.gov.uk/ukpga/2003/21/contents. Accessed 8 Aug 2017

Donath JS (1999) Identity and deception in the virtual community. In: Kollock P, Smith MA (eds) Communities in cyberspace. Routledge, London, pp 27–59

Equality Act (2010) Section 26. https://www.legislation.gov.uk/ukpga/2010/15/section/26. Accessed 29 Dec 2017

Gaus A (2012) Trolling attacks and the need for new approaches to privacy torts. Univ San Franc Law Rev 47:353–376

Gentry J (2016) 'twitteR' package. https://cran.r-project.org/web/packages/twitteR/twitteR.pdf. Accessed 21 Nov 2017

Gimpel K, Schneider N, O'Connor B, Das D, Mills D, Eisenstein J, Heilman M, Yogatama D, Flanigan J, Smith NA (2011) Part-of-speech tagging for twitter: annotation, features, and experiments. In: Proceedings of the 49th annual meeting of the association for computational linguistics: short papers 19–24. ACL, Portland, Oregon, 19–24 June 2011

Glynn D (2014) Correspondence analysis: Exploring data and identifying patterns. In: Glynn D, Robinson JA (eds) Corpus methods for semantics: quantitative studies in polysemy and synonymy. John Benjamins, Amsterdam, pp 443–485

Greenacre M, Pardo R (2006) Multiple correspondence analysis of a subset of response categories. In: Greenacre M, Blasius J (eds) Multiple correspondence analysis and related methods. Hall/CRC Press, Boca Raton, FL, Chapman, pp 197–217

Grieve J, Biber D, Friginal E, Nekrasova T (2010) Variation among blogs: A multidimensional analysis. In: Mehler A, Sharoff S, Santini M (eds) Genres on the web: computational models and empirical studies. Springer, New York, pp 303–322

Hardaker C (2010) Trolling in asynchronous computer-mediated communication: From user discussions to academic definitions. J Politeness Res. 6(2):215–242

Hardaker C (2013) Uh not to be nitpicky, but...the past tense of drag is dragged, not drug. An overview of trolling strategies. J Lang Aggress Confl 1(1):58–86

Hardaker C (2015) I refuse to respond to this obvious troll: an overview of responses to (perceived) trolling. Corpora 10(2):201–229

Herring SC, Job-Sluder K, Scheckler R, Barab S (2002) Searching for safety online: managing "trolling" in a feminist forum. Inf Soc 18:371–384

Hogan B (2012) Pseudonyms and the rise of the real-name web. In Hartley J, Burgess J, Bruns A (eds) A companion to new media dynamics. Blackwell Publishing Ltd, Chichester, pp 290–308 https://dev.twitter.com/oauth/overview/application-owner-access-tokens

Husson F, Josse J, Le S, Mazet J (2017) Package 'FactoMineR'. http://factominer.free.fr. Accessed 30 June 2017

Klempka A, Stimson A (2014) Anonymous communication on the internet and trolling. Concordia J Commun Res 1–14

KnowYourMeme.com (2017) An hero. http://knowyourmeme.com/memes/an-hero. Accessed 29 Dec 2017

Le Roux B, Rouanet H (2010) Multiple correspondence analysis. SAGE Publications Inc, California

Leaver T (2013) Olympic trolls: mainstream memes and digital discord? Fibreculture J 22:216–233

Lewandowsky S, Ecker UKH, Cook J (2017) Beyond misinformation: understanding and coping with the post-truth era. J Appl Res Mem Cognit 6(4):353–369

MacKinnon R, Zuckerman E (2012) Don't feed the trolls. Index Censorsh 41(4):14–24

Mihaylov T, Nakov P (2016) Hunting for troll comments in news community forums. In: Proceedings of the 54th annual meeting of the association for computational linguistics. ACL, Berlin, Germany, 7–12 Aug 2016, pp 399–405

Mihaylov T, Georgiev GD, Nakov P (2015) Finding opinion manipulation trolls in news community forums. In: Proceedings of the 19th Conference on Computational Language Learning. ACL, Beijing, China, 30–31 July 2015, pp 310–314

Morrissey B, Yell S (2016) Performative trolling: Szubanski, Gillard, Dawson and the nature of the utterance. Pers Stud 2(1):27–40

Nagle A (2017) Kill all normies: online culture wars from 4chan and Tumblr to Trump and the alt-right. Zero Books, Hants

Nicol S (2012) Cyber-bullying and trolling. Youth Stud Aust 31(4):3–4

O'Sullivan PB, Flanagin AJ (2003) Reconceptualizing flaming and other problematic messages. New Media and Society 5(1):69–94

Phillips W (2016) This is why we can't have nice things: mapping the relationship between online trolling and mainstream culture. The MIT Press, Cambridge, MA

Phillips W, Milner RM (2017) The ambivalent internet: mischief, oddity and antagonism online. Polity Press, Malden, MA

Sanfilippo MR, Yang S, Fichman P (2017) Managing online trolling: From deviant to social and political trolls. In: Proceedings of the 50th Hawaii international conference on system sciences, Waikoloa, HI, 4–7 Jan 2017

Synnott J, Coulias A, Ioannou M (2017) Online trolling: The case of Madeleine McCann. Comput Hum Behav 71:70–78

Tottie G (1983) Much about not and nothing: a study of the variation between analytic and synthetic negation in contemporary American English. CWK Gleerup, Lund

Twitter (2017) Authentication, 6 Dec 2016

Woolf N (2016) Lesley Jones bombarded with racist tweets after Ghostbusters opens. The Guardian. https://www.theguardian.com/culture/2016/jul/18/leslie-jones-racist-tweets-ghostbusters. Accessed 6 Sept 2017

Chapter 8
GamerGate: A Case Study in Online Harassment

Sarah A. Aghazadeh, Alison Burns, Jun Chu, Hazel Feigenblatt,
Elizabeth Laribee, Lucy Maynard, Amy L. M. Meyers, Jessica L. O'Brien
and Leah Rufus

Abstract In 2013, an online movement called GamerGate gained notoriety and
would reflect the reach, scope, and severity of harassment in social media. This
chapter looks at a timeline of Gamergate, platforms where it flourished, characteristics of the movement, and connections to scholarly work on gaming culture and
feminism.

8.1 Timeline of GamerGate

Trouble emerged that February following the release of an independent video game
called Depression Quest. Created by a female developer, Zoe Quinn, the game's goal
is to spread awareness about depression and provide support for those suffering from
the disorder through a narrative fiction interface. Steam, a popular online gaming
platform, added the game to their collection in August 2014. Increased exposure led
to positive reviews in popular gaming media, along with a plethora of disparaging
online comments. Many gamers felt Depression Quest was lauded with awards,
not because of excellent game design and execution, but because it symbolized
the gaming world's movement to be more inclusive and progressive. These gamers
resented the perceived manipulation of reviews for the purposes of pushing their own
social and political agenda.

Individually driven harassment coalesced into an organized movement after
Quinn's ex-boyfriend, Eron Gjoni, published a blog dedicated to disparaging Quinn.
In the "Zoe Post" Gjoni accused Quinn of having an affair with Nathan Grayson, a
video game journalist. Gjoni then linked the Zoe Post to the highly trafficked online
imageboard 4chan. Likeminded users gathered on 4chan to coordinate attacks on
Quinn and used the Zoe Post to justify accusations of sexual manipulation for positive reviews. Following Gjoni's release of the Zoe Post, a subsection of gamers
claimed to be advocating for ethics in gaming journalism. However, the outrage

S. A. Aghazadeh · A. Burns · J. Chu · H. Feigenblatt · E. Laribee
L. Maynard · A. L. M. Meyers · J. L. O'Brien · L. Rufus (✉)
University of Maryland, College Park, USA
e-mail: lrufus@umd.edu

© Springer International Publishing AG, part of Springer Nature 2018
J. Golbeck (ed.), *Online Harassment*, Human–Computer Interaction Series,
https://doi.org/10.1007/978-3-319-78583-7_8

against journalists often took the form of misogynistic tweets, and outright threats to Quinn and her supporters. These became especially aggressive when doxing- exposure of personally identifiable information online including elements like address or social security number- created a real threat to Quinn's safety.

By the end of August, gaming journalists seemed to be supporting Quinn and other professional female game developers who had received online threats. One of the first targets was popular feminist blogger Anita Sarkeesian. In 2009 Sarkeesian launched Feminist Frequency, a blog dedicated to addressing feminist issues through a cultural lens. Following the success of Feminist Frequency, Sarkeesian raised funds to create Tropes and Vs. Women In Video Games. This online video series focused on the sexism prevalent in the gaming industry, concentrating on topics such as racist stereotypes, lack female characters' body diversity, and women being used as a reward. As Sarkeesian gained more and more notoriety for making feminism accessible among pop culture fans, she received a barrage of online harassment and threats. With her public denouncement of the GamerGate movement, the threats increased and intensified, eventually forcing Sarkeesian her home on August 24, 2014. A bomb threat followed in October, forcing Sarkeesian to cancel a scheduled lecture at Utah State University. This threat, which claimed it would be "the deadliest school shooting in American history" led to an FBI investigation. With federal agents involved, mainstream media began covering what would be called "GamerGate."

Previously referred to by early proponents as "quinnspiracy," the Twitter hashtag "GamerGate" gained traction after actor Adam Baldwin used the term in a tweet on August 27, 2014 to pledge his support to those claiming female game developers received better reviews due to their sex. A few days later the far-right news website, Breitbart, published an opinion article supporting the GamerGate movement. The article led non-gaming, right-wing internet users to join the movement. No longer confined to questioning video game journalism and misogyny in popular cultural, GamerGate is seen to stand fundamentally against political correctness and the liberal-progressive agenda.

With reinforcements from the right-wing leaning internet, harassment continued to expand across social media platforms. By mid September, the amount of doxing and threats reached a point where 4chan's founder, Christopher Poole, instituted a ban on GamerGate. Organizers quickly moved to 8chan, known for espousing the importance of free speech on the internet. Soon the GamerGate discussion board became the second most popular board.

As GamerGate increasingly dominated conversations on Twitter and imageboards like 8chan, more users began to speak out against the misogyny of many GamerGate advocates. Brianna Wu, a female videogame developer, was one such user. In mid October, Wu tweeted out a joke mocking GamerGate for exaggerating the effects of women in the video game world. Harassment and threats began pouring in immediately. When her personal information was leaked online, Wu left her home, fearing for her safety. Eventually, Wu would hold meetings with the FBI and Homeland Security. Combined with the threats to Quinn, Sarkeesian, and Utah State University, the FBI would confirm in December of 2014 that there were records being compiled against GamerGate harassers.

Celebrities like Felicia Day, Seth Rogen, Patton Oswalt, and Chris Kluwe began speaking out against GamerGate in October. With this increase in exposure, anti-GamerGate users started using the hashtag stopgamergate2014. This hashtag trended worldwide for days after its creation, symbolizing a concentrated attack against GamerGate.

Serious threats also occurred to GamerGate proponents; in May 2015 a bomb threat at a restaurant hosting a GamerGate group led to a police evacuation.

After repeated requests for access, the FBI released its GamerGate records in 2017. The heavily redacted files contain several instances in which harassment and physical threats were admitted to, but police decided against pursuing a criminal case. Many of the GamerGate harassers turned out to be minors, and they received only warnings from authorities. In other instances, the FBI was unable to identify the people behind death and rape threats, and were unable to pursue the matter further.

8.2   Platforms and Hashtags

Media researchers have declared GamerGate a "born-digital" controversy (Burgess 2016). The users of message boards that launched the toxic campaign have been described as "trolls in the Internet's basement" (Stuart 2014), yet their power and presence grew significantly throughout GamerGate, mediated by the growth of mainstream and lesser-known social media platforms. What follows is a brief review of the online platforms and platforms that launched and fueled the attacks.

8.2.1   4chan

According to the Encyclopedia of Cyber Warfare, 4chan was created by a Google employee Christopher Poole when he was in high school as a board for trading images of Japanese manga and anime. The "hacktivist" group Anonymous exploited a 4chan feature that allows users to post without registering on the site as it carried out some its online campaigns (Springer, p. 112).

In *The #GamerGate Files*, researchers say one of the first public battles between gamer Zoe Quinn and a group called the Fine Young Capitalists unfolded on 4chan message boards /pol/ and /v/ (Kidd and Turner 2016, p. 126). Quinn's own review of 4chan discussion logs revealed the campaign of threats and intimidation that eventually became known as #GamerGate originated from a small group of users on 4chan (Johnston 2014). Discussions of Quinn and #GamerGate were banned from 4chan in late September 2014 (Massanari 2017).

8.2.2   Reddit

The online social forum Reddit is often referred to as the "front page of the Internet" (Molina 2017). It boasts on its website that it's the seventh largest website in the United States, with more than 250 million users worldwide.

In 2015, researchers declared Reddit had become a hub for anti-feminist activism (Massanari 2017). The platform allows users, who often use pseudonyms, to create their own communities referred to as "subreddits." These communities allow people with similar interests to find each other and share opinions and information. Massanari argues that Reddit allows a masculine "geek culture" and "toxic techno-culture" to thrive, and this environment provided a supportive home for communities like Reddit's /r/KotakuInAction (KIA) and /r/TumblrInAction (TIA) to launch their #GamerGate attacks (Massanari 2017).

8.2.3   Twitter

According to the social networking site's information page, Twitter is the "place to find out about what's happening in the world right now." Critics say it's also the best place to "hurl abuse and get noticed for it". In the case of the #GamerGate controversy, Twitter served as a platform for propagating public harassment against Quinn and anyone who dared weigh in (in less than 140 characters) on either side, including a professor who supported #GamerGate and was subjected to obscene physical threats.

Newsweek hired the media analytics firm Brand Watch to analyze 500,000 of more than two million tweets related to #GamerGate from September 1, 2014 through October 23, 2014. It found most of the tweets using the hashtag #GamerGate were aimed at harassing women in the gaming world (Wofford 2014).

8.2.4   8chan

When GamerGate posts were removed from 4chan in late 2014, supporters of the movement reunited on 8chan, a message and image board site "for those looking to really push free speech to its outer limits" (Tunison 2017). "Thousands of angry users fled to 8chan" and it quickly became the second most popular image board site on the web (Dewey 2018). It also became the hub for GamerGate related threats and attacks against journalists and women gamers, including death and rape threats and the release of personal information about them.

Both 4chan and 8chan are inspired by the Japanese image board site 2chan, but 8chan is the most controversial because it's also become a "hive for pedophilia discussion" (Tunison 2017). Google removed 8chan from its search results in 2015 because of content related to suspected child abuse. As of September 2017, The Daily Dot reported 8chan is still "active and apparently building" (Tunison 2017).

8.2.5 YouTube

YouTube, owned by Google, is considered the most popular video sharing and viewing site on the Internet (Boswell 2017). It has millions of subscribers all over the world who create, watch and share videos on an extraordinary range of topics. Much of the GamerGate saga has played out on YouTube when commentators created, posted and shared videos that stoked anger on all sides of the controversy.

Researchers of the GamerGate media ecology found that YouTube was the second most used domain of those who used the hashtag #GamerGate on Twitter (Twitter was the first). They found distinct "clusters of controversy" on YouTube made up mostly of YouTubers trying to explain and defend GamerGate; others specifically criticizing GamerGate as a misogynist movement; and a cluster dedicated to GamerGate target and cultural critic Anita Sarkeesian (Burgess 2016). One of those Twitter and YouTube users, actor Adam Baldwin, is credited with creating the hashtag #GamerGate (Kidd and Turner 2016).

8.2.6 Hashtags

The idea of the hashtag, signified by the pound sign, was introduced for Twitter in 2007 as a way of creating "ad hoc channels." The # symbol had been used in Internet Relay Chat (IRC) communities, and the intent was to use such "channel tags" to allow users to follow conversations or topics of interest (Bruns 2011). In GamerGate, the hashtag became the agent that spread the contagion of controversy. Writer Casey Johnston describes the entire drama as a "hashtag campaign" (Johnston 2014).

The attacks on Depression Quest creator Zoe Quinn began using the hashtag #Quinnspiracy. When actor Adam Baldwin jumped into the fray, he introduced #GamerGate, which became the dominant tag for the movement. A Newsweek analysis found most of the Tweets using #GamerGate were aimed at gamer Brianna Wu and feminist critic Anita Sarkeesian (Wofford 2014).

Soon another hashtag appeared relating to the controversy. According to Johnston, #notyourshield was created by supporters of #GamerGate who wanted to focus the debate on ethics in gaming journalism and did not want to be connected with posts harassing women. She reported that #notyourshield first appeared on the /v/ video games board on 4chan "as a suggestion for responding to 'social justice warriors' who claimed the #GamerGate campaign was misogynistic" (Johnston 2014).

Critics of #GamerGate created a series of hashtags to try to shut down the movement, among them #StopGamergate2014 and #GamersAgainstGamergate. Researcher Libby Hemphill analyzed the tags for a week in October of 2014 and found that #GamerGate was used by more than 33,000 Twitter users more than 279,000 times, while #StopGamergate2014 was used by just over 6,000 users in 16,000 tweets (Hemphill 2014).

In October, 2014 Bustle.com reported "the Internet is blowing up" with another hashtag in response to "sexist BS" of the #GamerGate movement (Anwar 2014). The #INeedDiverseGames campaign argued gamers were no longer overwhelmingly white, heterosexual men. It called for video game creators to make games that reflect a more diverse community.

8.3 Characteristics of Harassment

8.3.1 Extremely Offensive and Derogatory

Harassment from GamerGate supporters often filled the inboxes or Twitter feeds of anyone who was targeted with derogatory and offensive messages. Female gamers and feminist supporters were referred to as "bitch," "cunt," "whore" and "skank", and other offensive terms which represent adultery or infidelity. Other offensive messages included describing the quality of someone's work with profanities ("shitty game"), calling someone ugly, and calling out minorities with derogatory stereotypes.

8.3.2 Extremely Violent

Harassment messages and posts usually included violent language and specific violent actions. Two types of violent messages can be found in GamerGate messaging: general violence and female-specific violence. Generally violent messages can be applied to both male and female users, and messages can be both vague and extremely detailed. Generally violent threats used verbs like "beating", "hurting," "choking," and "killing." Detailed threats included specific plans, weapons of choice, times and locations, and even plans of disposing corpses. Female-specific violence mainly consisted of specific sexual attacks. Threats ranged from general rape threats to detailed rape plans. Certain threats were also attached to women's children.

8.3.3 Extremely Revealing

A major part of the harassment campaign was to reveal personal information about targeted individuals to the public so that more people could be involved, and so that threats could be more realistic. This included publishing the victims' personal information, such as home addresses and relatives' home addresses, phone numbers, email addresses, passwords to various social media accounts, and file storage accounts. After personal information had been released, verbal threats made over the internet became more planned and detailed. For example, Brianna Wu—a female game designer- called police after specific threats of rape and murder toward her and her family were posted online along with her home address.

8.3.4 Suggestive

Most of the examples of harassment were violent and scary and some explicitly suggested that targeted individuals change a particular behavior. Suggestions included asking the individual to stop supporting female gamers, or asking female gamers to stop playing and making games. More extreme suggestions involved people suggesting female gamers commit suicide. Some suggestions indicated consequences if requirements were not met. One example would be a threat sent to Utah State University asking Anita Sarkeesian, a female media critic, to cancel her talk, or else "a Montreal Massacre style attack will be carried out against the attendees".

8.3.5 All-Inclusive Attack

GamerGate is often compared to the 2016 presidential election in terms of its focus on attacking liberalism, with a focus on racial and gender equality. While other harassment campaigns focused their attacks on one specific group or person, GamerGate supporters expanded their attacks. Harassment evolved from personal attacks against Zoe Quinn to general attacks against feminism, minority gamers, and the overall idea of inclusion.

8.4 Connections with Other Harassment Movements

GamerGate was a turning point in the consolidation of online harassment movements, both in terms of building networks and of perfecting and normalizing harassment tactics. During GamerGate, trolls learned that they could use the web with impunity to quickly connect and organize mobs of like-minded individuals to attack anyone they saw as a threat. The fact that bombing, revenge porn, rape, and assassination threats could be effectively used to achieve online and offline objectives was noticed by a collection of incipient online communities that soon adopted mob harassment as a modus operandi to lift their profiles (Sheer 2017; Romano 2017).

These communities revolved around different issues but had one thing in common: the hatred of women. In addition to gamers, the list below includes some of these communities with the clarification that they are not necessarily formally-defined, are in constant flux, and some may overlap, depending on certain topics and forums:

- Coders
- White supremacists
- PUAs ("Pick up artists," focused on the theory and practice of strategies to "bed" women, including everything from sexual assault to lowering women's self-esteem)
- Men's rights movement (slightly more organized groups dedicated to fighting what they consider the oppression and discrimination of men by women)
- Incels (men who claim to be involuntarily celibate because women reject them)
- MGTOW (Men Going Their Own Way, a group that seeks to avoid any type of contact with women)
- Far-right militants (this a loosely connected block that may include some or all of the above and tend to take a more political approach)
- Others

These communities began to coalesce and cross-pollinate in online spaces such as Reddit, where forums like RedPill, 4Chan and Daily Stormer became widely known. They have come to be known as the "manosphere," which is in essence a network of forums, blogs, and websites focused on the defense of their version of masculinity from the advances of feminism (Marche 2016; Crecente 2017; Ratchford 2017).

Organizers of some of these spaces have sometimes claimed their main objective is to provide men with support to navigate masculinity issues in current times rather than promoting misogyny.

However, "In many alt-right communities, men are encouraged to view women as sexual and/or political targets that men must dominate" (Romano 2017). In these communities men think of themselves not as sexist aggressors, but as victims fighting against their "emasculation and sexual repression" by feminists and society at large. At their core, these communities cultivate a distrust of women and the narrative that the equality of women "necessarily disempowers men."

Hatred of women occupies a lot of these spaces. Common blog posts and discussions include things such as "99% of all the problems in the world today come from the fact that men in America and western Europe don't smack their women. FACT!" (Daily Stormer 2017), "Treating women badly, because they deserve it" (Reddit/RedPill.com 2016), or calls to make rape legal (Roosh 2015). It is also possible to observe that misogynistic killers like Elliot Rodgers was celebrated as a "hero" in manosphere forums, after he killed six people and injured several more in a shooting spree in California in 2014 as revenge for women not being willing to have sex with him (Valenti 2014; McGuire 2014).

"What turns them into larger groups is a process described by researchers as small-network theory. Here's how it works: Groups of people come together over shared interests, such as local football teams. Each group may be brought together as fans of different teams, but these people may have a shared resentment, such as distaste for a particularly divisive team like the New England Patriots. When a big event happens, such as a cheating scandal or Super Bowl victory, those different team's fan groups begin to cross-connect, working together and ultimately creating a larger force" (Sheer 2017).

As these groups began to find each other and echo each other's views, they started to feel more comfortable adopting GamerGate harassment tactics as part of their online routine. The result is that today, online harassment to silence minorities and especially women is no longer an odd episode, as was initially the case with GamerGate, but has become a "normal" part of the Internet. Harassment has been normalized. According to a 2017 Pew study, 41% of Americans have experienced online harassment, which the study defined as "offensive name-calling, purposeful embarrassment, physical threats, stalking, sexual harassment, or harassment over a sustained period of time" (Duggan 2017).

The study suggests men report slightly more harassment than men. However, women seem to face more gendered, sexualized and violent forms of harassment. "Men are somewhat more likely than women to have been called offensive names online (30% vs. 23%) or to have received physical threats (12% vs. 8%). By contrast, women – and especially young women – receive sexualized forms of online abuse at much higher rates than men. Some 21% of women ages 18 to 29 have been sexually harassed online, a figure that is more than double that of men in the same age group (9%) (…) Overall, 11% of women have specifically been harassed because of their gender, compared with 5% of men" (Duggan 2017).

Social media companies' permissive tools and policies largely contribute to the problem. For example, in 2017 it was documented that Facebook was banning user accounts for posting "men are scum," but did not ban user accounts for posting "women are scum." The result is that women receive threats and hateful comments that, even when reviewed by Facebook, were not considered in violation of their policy. However, when the harassed women defended themselves, in some cases using terms as innocuous as "ugly," they got banned. For example, comedian Marcia Belski reported on Twitter: "Kill yourself n*******" reviewed & found not to violate standards. "All men are allegedly ugly?" removed and the woman banned within hours" (Gibbs 2017).

It is important to understand that GamerGate did not "start" online harassment. Some of these misogynist communities have been documented as conducting online harassment very well before GamerGate, usually targeting women with strong voices with the specific objective of silencing them has been documented. Female journalists and bloggers have often been the target.

For instance, in 2007, technology writer Kathy Sierra was the target of death and rape threats—including images of her with a noose—that eventually led her to cancel her blog and a keynote speech she was meant to give at ETech conference in San Diego that year. Much of the blogosphere expressed her support when she publicly spoke up about the harassment. For instance, Robert Scoble, of then popular technology blog Scobleizer, acknowledged what at the time seemed an increasing trend of online attacks against women. "It's this culture of attacking women that has especially got to stop. I really don't care if you attack me. I take those attacks in my stride. But, whenever I post a video of a female technologist there invariably are snide remarks about body parts and other things that simply wouldn't happen if the interviewee were a man" (BBC News 2007).

In 2013, feminist reporter Sara Alcid narrated some of the harassment she had routinely received over the years for doing her work. "The harassment I've experienced online has ranged from being told by Twitter egg avatars that I'm possessed by the devil for supporting abortion access, to a group of *"men's rights activists"* rounding up as much of my personal information as possible, including things like my mother's obituary, and writing a series of blog posts about me that were meant to do one thing. This one thing, the thing all online harassment of women stems from, is the desire to stop women from sharing their opinions and thoughts on the Internet—to chip away at our power and presence in an increasingly important space" (Alcid 2013).

As documented throughout this chapter, the trend has generalized and, after GamerGate, misogynist communities have only intensified their routine use of online harassment as their method of choice to pursue their agendas. Along the way, they are helping set the standard of what is culturally acceptable (Perry 2017; Allen 2014; Carson 2017).

This is not to say that all misogynist harassment that takes place on the Internet is or can be directly linked back only to these specific U.S. communities. International studies show gendered, misogynist harassment of women is normalizing globally (Hunt 2016; Al Jazeera News 2017). Many cases have also been reported around the world. For example, in 2013, when Carolyn Criado-Perez made a campaign that convinced the Bank of England to make Jane Austen the new face of the £10 note, she received intense online harassment characterized by death and rape threats (Philipson 2013).

A report about online abuse of female journalists by the Organization for Security and Cooperation in Europe (OSCE) documents cases in several countries. It also finds that many women who have experienced online harassment were not feminists or were promoting feminist causes when they were attacked. "They weren't espousing feminist views – in fact, they weren't making any kind of political argument at all. They were simply women with a public voice. More than this, they were women exercising (or rumoured to be about to begin exercising) their public voices in arenas – technology and cars – which have traditionally been considered to be male territory. The 'Girls: Keep Out' sign on the tree house all grown up and with a nasty temper".

One of the reasons harassment has become so popular for these groups—in addition to giving them an opportunity to exercise the kind of masculinity they promote—is that it yields results.

One of the most dramatic examples took place during the 2016 U.S. presidential campaign, when white supremacist and alt-right groups trolls deployed tactics from sending "vicious and often anti-Semitic messages to journalists covering Trump, accusing them of biased coverage and threatening their safety" to conspiracy theories such as "pizzagate," the infamous conspiracy theory about an alleged child-trafficking ring at a Washington, DC, pizzeria that "led a man to enter the shop with a gun, demanding to 'investigate' the supposed threat" (Crecente 2017; Harveston 2017; Stone 2014; Maiberg 2017; Nussbaum 2017; Marantz 2016).

Not all white supremacist and conspiracy theories' promoters during (and after) the campaign were anonymous. Mike Cernovich, who claims to be a journalist, has been linked to the creation and propagation of "pizzagate" and regularly creates misogynist content, such as a video celebrating his "love of choking women and being arrested for rape" (Berger 2017).

Cernovich is a good example of an individual who "discovered" the power of reframing rhetoric to appeal to the language of the internet. He once shared a meme that paired an image of able-bodied male Syrian refugees playing soccer outside their camp in a Hungarian train station with the caption "There is no oppression. The media lied." After seeing it shared over 5,000 times in what would be his first viral post, "Cernovich realized that a meme could reach more people than a newspaper story, without having to cross an editor's desk" (Marantz 2016).

Recently, in October of 2016, Cernovich released "MAGA Mindset", a book about Trump's "unapologetically masculine" persona, the bio section reminding readers that Cernovich has "been banned from television for telling it like it is" (Marantz 2016). There is a direct connection visible between what fueled GamerGate in 2014 and the rise of alt-right branding that also touted a Pro-Trump agenda during the 2016 election cycle. In each campaign, the main rhetoric centered on an expressed distrust of women and a shared imperative to limit feminist participation in public spaces.

Another visible figure in the shift towards harassment is former Breitbart editor Milo Yiannopoulos, who had previously written missives about gamers being an embarrassing group of people, but subsequently used GamerGate as a spark for new energy behind internet attacks on women. His dismissiveness of gamer culture was forgotten in light of an unlikely new ally against feminists, as an opinion he wrote in Breitbart about GamerGate shows:

> It's easy to mock video gamers as dorky loners in yellowing underpants. Indeed, in previous columns, I've done it myself. Occasionally at length. But, the more you learn about the latest scandal in the games industry, the more you start to sympathise with the frustrated male stereotype. Because an army of sociopathic feminist programmers and campaigners, abetted by achingly politically correct American tech bloggers, are terrorising the entire community – lying, bullying and manipulating their way around the internet for profit and attention (Yiannopoulos 2014).

An analysis about GamerGate by journalist Matt Lees suggests that "this hashtag was the canary in the coal mine, and we ignored it" (2016). Lees connects the events of GamerGate to the foundation of language, focus, and tactics for a new and growing alt-right community on the internet, tactics, he says, that obscure "dissenting voices" by claiming fire on both sides. He says, "even when abuse was proven, the usual response was that people on their side were being abused too. These techniques, forged in GamerGate, have become the standard toolset of far-right voices online" (Lees 2016).

It should be noted that an important tool for online harassment is humor: the packaging of violent messaging within jokes mirroring the quippy self-aware cadence of millennial humor, internet memes employing the likeness of a cartoon frog, Willy Wonka, and other otherwise benign figures. Use of humorous subversion in order to convey a particular point is an established practice on the internet, and by incorporating the method into the messaging of hate and violence, the form serves to provide a shortcut to find readers that would sympathize.

But it also serves another purpose: plausible deniability. By asserting that an internet post is to be read as irony or a joke, the implied onus then falls to the audience to respond well to it. The theory goes that if it's not a serious claim, the source of the content can't be held liable for the reaction it may cause. "The claim of a joke provides an arm's length from responsibility over the content of the post, however shocking or offensive. It [becomes] a distinction without a difference. The joke [protects] the non-joke" (Nussbaum 2017).

Sometimes, this line is blurred by a dual endorsement and rejection of the premise of the joke, as in the case of a September 2016 Twitter post by Donald Trump Jr. The president's eldest son shared a meme popular among white supremacists which shows Donald Trump Sr. surrounded by an assortment of close campaign affiliates, stamped with the term The Deplorables, and styled in an homage to Sylvester Stallone's action film *The Expendables*. Trump Jr. captioned the post with "All kidding aside I am honored to be grouped with the hard working men and women of this great nation that have supported@realdonaldtrump *[sic]* and know that he can fix the mess created by politicians in Washington."

The assorted crew includes, among political colleagues Mike Pence and Ben Carson, Trump's two sons standing with *InfoWars'* conspiracy theorist Alex Jones, Yiannopoulos (who has been banned from Twitter for employing hateful rhetoric), and a Trump-hairstyle-wearing Pepe the Frog. It's the inclusion of Pepe that is perhaps most striking in the image: though popular since its 2005 creation by artist Matt Furie, the meaning of the character has evolved dramatically and has in more recent years become a recognizable symbol of the alt-right. Its metamorphosis sparked on the 4chan message board in 2014, the same year that GamerGate began escalating, and is now widely considered to be associated with neo-Nazi internet narratives.

Shortly after Trump Jr.'s post, Ku Klux Klan leader David Duke shared his own version of the meme via Twitter and included two things: the tagline "Anti-Racist is a code word for anti-white" and "November 8", the date of the 2016 election. Just two weeks after Trump Jr. shared the Deplorables meme on Twitter, the Anti-Defamation League officially designated Pepe the Frog as a hate symbol.

While it has now been documented that many trolls and bots were not "organic," as they originated in Russian troll farms, it has also been documented that the misogynist network that followed GamerGate had a symbiotic relationship with outlets from the extreme right such as Breitbart and their editors, whose narratives candidate Trump would often and purposefully adopt. That allowed them to make a place for themselves within the Republican party. It also allowed them to use misogyny to "lure" men from non-cohesive interests and communities and use them as critical mass to populate radicalized political action (Harveston 2017; Stone 2014; Maiberg 2017). This is recognized even by Breitbart itself, as seen in the 2017 article "Leftists Think GamerGate Caused Donald Trump; Maybe They're Right." Pieces like this one emphasize a narrative by deceitful, misinformed troll GamerGaters, Trump supporters, and men. The author asserts that "the mythology of GamerGate as a major political turning point of our age acquires some grounding in reality" (Bokhari 2017).

The impunity that covers online harassment by these groups has created a permissive environment that has emboldened offline harassment too.

An example took place after the death of Heather Heyer in a white supremacy rally in Charlottesville in 2017, when one of the white supremacists drove his car into the crowd. Supremacist propaganda site Daily Stormer celebrated her death and asserted that she had "no value" to society since she was a woman who had not procreated. The website's founder, Andrew Auernheimer, went on to ask readers to find out where her funeral would take place. "What's the location of the fat skank's funeral … get on it, e-sleuths. I'd do it myself but slammed with current logistical issues. I want to get people on the ground there" (Worley 2017; Buncombe 2017). Her body was subsequently buried in a secret grave to protect it from attacks.

While harassment movements have been discussed here mainly in the context of GamerGate and the political sphere, it is necessary to note that online harassment has been normalized as "fair game" for any online and offline activity by women.

For example, in 2017 the female writers of the comedy show Rick and Moriarty were harassed and doxxed when they were credited for their work on two episodes. The harassers reacted negatively to the employment of women on comedy shows. Executive producer Mark Harmon publicly condemned the attacks: "I was familiar going into the third season, having talked to Felicia Day, that any high-profile women get doxxed, they get harassed, they get threatened, they get slandered. And part of it is a testosterone-based subculture patting themselves on the back for trolling these women. Because to the extent that you get can get a girl to shriek about a frog you've proven girls are girly and there's no crime in assaulting her with a frog because it's all in the name of proving something. I think it's all disgusting" (Hibberd 2017).

White male supremacists have also proposed a solution to online harassment of women. In words of commentator Milo Yiannopoulos: "Here's my suggestion to fix the gender wars online: Women should just log off. Given that men built the internet, along with the rest of modern civilisation, I think it's only fair that they get to keep it. And given what a miserable time women are having on the web, surely they would welcome an abrupt exit. They could go back to bridge tournaments, or wellness workshops, or swapping apple crumble recipes, or whatever it is women do in their spare time. I, Donald Trump and the rest of the alpha males will continue to dominate the internet without feminist whining" (Yiannopoulos 2016).

8.5   Online Consequences of GamerGate

After Gamergate, Twitter added a new feature that allows users to block multiple accounts at once by creating a block list (Zhang 2015). Twitter already had mute and block tools in place for individual accounts, but the block list feature lets users block people en masse. The block list was created for Twitter users who were dealing with higher volumes of negative and unwanted interactions, such as with GamerGate (Zhang 2015).

Users can create their own list of blocked accounts, export this list in their settings page, and then share the list with other users or groups. This tool is intended to help users who are being harassed by the same accounts to join forces and collectively block these users (Plante 2015).

Twitter grants the status of "authorized reporters" or "trusted flaggers" to certain users to identify and report inappropriate content. In November of 2014, Twitter granted Women, Action, and the Media (WAM), a non-profit organization, this status to conduct a pilot program to better respond to and help users with gendered harassment (Matias et al. 2015).

WAM's program created an online reporting tool to allow users to more easily report harassment, and for Twitter to respond more quickly to harassment—warning, suspending, or deleting accounts (Davis 2014). WAM collected harassment reports, assessed and analyzed them, streamlined reports to Twitter, and tracked Twitter's responses (Matias et al. 2015). The ultimate goal of WAM's program was to collect data that illuminated the intersections of gender and harassment, how this manifests on Twitter, and how Twitter can better combat it (Davis 2014).

In October 2017, Twitter introduced new user guidelines for unsolicited sexual advances, non-consensual nudity, hate symbols, violent groups, and tweets that glorify violence (Griffith 2017). Twitter did not ban pornography or specific groups, such as Nazis; instead, Twitter expanded the definition of "nonconsensual nudity" to include "creep shots" and hidden camera content (Griffith 2017). Twitter also announced it will hide hate symbols behind a "sensitive image" warning, though the company did not define what constitutes a hate symbol.

Christopher Poole, the founder of 4Chan, relinquished his role as administrator of 4Chan soon after GamerGate began proliferating on his site (Kushner 2015). Poole began receiving targeted harassment after he banned all Gamergate discussion from his site and posted the Digital Millennium Copyright Act policy to 4Chan in response to GamerGate (Kushner 2015). Poole had been considering leaving 4Chan for over a year, but the backlash and stress from GamerGate is what prompted Poole to finally depart (Kushner 2015). Poole handed over control of 4Chan to three anonymous moderators (Kushner 2015), although he himself had not been anonymous as a moderator.

Poole sold 4Chan to Hiroyuki Nishimura, the founder of 2Chan, which had inspired Poole to create 4Chan (Brandom 2015). 4Chan still doesn't require users to register, create an account, choose a username (even a pseudonymous one), or provide any personal information (4Chan 2017). Anyone can still upload content or comment on boards and threads with complete anonymity.

Poole's banning of GamerGate threads resulted in an influx of users to 8Chan, which has even looser moderation policies than 4Chan (Chiel 2016). Frederick Brennan, founder of 8Chan, actively publicized that former 4Chan GamerGate users could still post freely on 8Chan (Chiel 2016). During September of 2014, 8Chan's posts per hour increased on average from 100 to 4000 (Chiel 2016).

Tiffany Dohzen, Reddit's administrator, announced in March 2015 that Reddit posts and comment threads would now be embeddable (Brogan 2015). Previously, other websites used Reddit content without linking back to the original Reddit post (Brogan 2015). Dohzen explained that embeddable comments would allow users to have more control over the use of their content outside of Reddit (Reddit Blog 2015). Reddit also promoted embeddable posts as an easier way for users to share their content outside of Reddit-blogs, websites, etc. (Reddit Blog 2015).

Before the embedding feature was added to on Reddit, comments were only sharable via screenshots or copying and pasting The embeddable feature makes it possible for users to edit a comment after it had already been linked to a post, making it appear that users who had interacted with an earlier post were in fact interacting with the new one (Brogan 2015).

8.6 Offline Consequences of GamerGate

Over the nine months when the GamerGate hashtag was most active, numerous women and men reported a wide range of harassment to law enforcement. Attacks included threats of rape, death, and other violence; use of personal information to fraudulently open bank accounts, and false reports of serious emergencies designed to send SWAT teams to the target's address. As a result, many of the victims temporarily fled their homes, cancelled speaking engagements, and otherwise altered their lifestyles to deal with the fear from being targeted.

Yet months of investigation from the FBI never resulted in anyone being charged for the crimes. According to files released in January 2017, at least four men were identified and investigated in connection with the attacks, with two actually confessing to instigating the abuse. Yet prosecutors declined to bring the cases to court.

In some cases, authorities accepted the perpetrators excuse that their behavior was simply a joke, and let them off with a warning. Others were unwilling to dedicate already tight departmental resources to an issue that they believed could easily be handled by victims simply ignoring their abusers.

In large part, however, experts argue that current laws governing cyberbullying and other forms of online harassment are not adequate to deal with this type of mob behavior. With multiple individuals each contributing a small piece to the online torrent of abuse, law enforcement officials are stymied when they attempt to prosecute one person for the attacks.

"If you're going to be convicted of harassment, the state's got to prove that someone intentionally, repeatedly, [and] persistently targeted the person with speech that we can punish," University of Maryland professor of law Danielle Citron told Public Radio International in February 2016.

In addition, the global nature of the Internet makes it difficult for prosecutors to determine where to file charges against perpetrators. For example, FBI agents in San Francisco and Boston each felt they did not have the jurisdiction to prosecute in their own states, and recommended that the cases be administratively closed. Finally, records of the FBI investigation show that agents did not have the training necessary to untangle the proxy server chains and other methods GamerGate harassers used to hide their identities.

As a result, politicians demanded stronger enforcement of existing legislation and introduced bills in an attempt to close up loopholes in the current law. Among these was Rep. Katherine Clark of Massachusetts who convened Congressional briefings with GamerGate victims, urged the Justice Department to more strongly enforce existing laws against cyberbullying, and introduced several bills to specifically prohibit doxing, sextortion, and swatting. Sextortion is demanding sexual favors or money under threat of releasing compromising photos, and swatting is calling in a false report to law enforcement with the intent of causing police to send a SWAT team to an innocent victim.

Clark's most recent bill, introduced with Rep. Patrick Meehan of Pennsylvania and Rep. Susan Brooks of Indiana, combines all three of those crimes under one federal law. The Online Safety Modernization Act also provides millions of dollars in funding for police agencies to receive training on handling these offenses. Unfortunately, the bill—as did those before it—is languishing in committee.

For most people, GamerGate is over. Yet for those who endured the onslaught of abuse and harassment, the regular attacks have remained all too common. Many have chosen to continue working in the games community, either creating them or commenting on their social relevance, but do so now with an eye to helping others and attempting to change the environment that spawned such hatred.

Anita Sarkeesian, the blogger and YouTube producer whose now ended Tropes vs Women in Video Games arguably contributed to much of the anger that eventually bloomed into GamerGate, continues to be harassed and threatened in person at conferences where she speaks around the globe.

"They're playing for fun," she told Polygon after she dared speak back to a group of men who filled the first three rows of a panel talk on women's lives online at VidCon 2017 with the intent of taunting and intimidating her.

The men—largely YouTube personalities and bloggers who make a living attacking feminism, political correctness, and other progressive ideals—reportedly treated the event like a comedy club outing, calling out insults and filming Sarkeesian's comments for further attack online. They then complained when she called one of the ringleaders a 'garbage human' to shut down the attacks before they began, an incident that went viral on both sides.

"You have to be so far removed from the reality of what you're doing to engage in this behavior and call it 'playful trolling'," she continued in the Polygon interview. "This is harassment, pure and simple, with the goal of trying to scare and silence women who speak out against sexism in our culture."

VidCon responded by apologizing to Sarkeesian for the incident, increasing security at the remaining panels she attended, and offering her the opportunity to back out of any other public events she'd signed up for. She declined, saying that she didn't want the trolls to win.

This response by VidCon, while not perfect, is a sign that awareness of the issue is growing. Similarly, designers such as Matt Thorson, who included an homage to Sarkeesian with a positive representation of her in his recent video game, say her work has helped younger developers feel comfortable considering diversity and gender roles in their work.

Sarkeesian, who is attempting to move her legacy beyond GamerGate, is continuing to produce videos with her not-for-profit, Feminist Frequency, on popular culture's relevance to current events. She is also co-writing a book, Ordinary Women: Daring to Defy History, on 25 women whose accomplishments have been overlooked.

Zoe Quinn, meanwhile, continues to advocate for protections against online harassment in the courts, in Congress, and with the United Nations. Convinced that the current legal system could not protect her against online harassment, Quinn eventually dropped the criminal harassment case against Eron Gjoni, the former boyfriend whose 9,000 word screed about their failed relationship launched GamerGate. Nearly two years after the harassment began, Gjoni had become an internet celebrity with users dedicated to squelching feminism and its effects in the gaming industry, and Quinn said she simply wanted her life back and to get back to her love of developing games.

However, she has continued to fight for other victims of online harassment. Along with Sarkeesian, she has testified before Congress and given speeches at the United Nations to increase awareness of the problem and call on developers, lawmakers, and companies to strengthen protections for those affected by such abuse.

In addition, she and Alex Lifschiz launched Crash Override, a support network providing practical advice and assistance to victims of online abuse. The volunteer organization—fiscally supported by Sarkeesian's Feminist Frequency—produces general educational materials and creates individualized plans for victims. They also advocate with the criminal justice system and lawmakers in an effort to educate about the realities of online harassment while protecting genuine freedom of speech and access on the Internet.

Her memoir, Crash Override: How GamerGate (Nearly) Destroyed My Life, and How We Can Win the Fight Against Online Hate, continues the conversation by detailing her personal experiences in being the initial GamerGate target while providing practical advice for protecting oneself online and commenting on the current political environment. The book received positive reviews.

Finally, Brianna Wu decided to tackle the issue by running for Congress against Rep. Stephen Lynch in Massachusetts' 8th District (election scheduled for late 2018). Motivated in large part by Donald Trump's presidential win, Wu has argued that women in the gaming industry have not experienced the same support as those in entertainment. Her platform focuses on Internet privacy, online harassment., and greater economic opportunities for women, LGBTQ individuals, people of color, and the working poor.

Internet trolls have already begun personal attacks against Wu and her campaign, but she told the New York Times that GamerGate prepared her for what she might face. "The think Gamergate taught me is that there's nothing I can't handle," she said. "What is someone going to do: Call me ugly? Threaten to kill me? I already deal with all of that on a daily basis."

8.7   Scholarly Analysis of GamerGate

GamerGate served as an opportunity for various disciplines to look at its implications for gaming culture, in both broad and specific ways. Scholarship on the topic shows three overlapping areas of focus: (1) GamerGate's relationship to white, male misogyny and feminist activism, (2) GamerGate's illustration of how online structures and cultures in various contexts shape online behavior, (3) GamerGate's complexity and nuance. These trends in the literature are in no way exhaustive or mutually exclusive, but provide a basis to understand GamerGate in various contexts. This scholarly analysis will detail each area to shed light on the significant contributions that academics have offered to piece together the meaning of GamerGate for larger societal issues.

8.7.1   Misogyny and Feminism

Salter (2017) detailed how Western societies have masculinized computers in a way that supports events like GamerGate. In what Salter (2017) termed "geek masculinity," he explains a rationale for online behaviors that marginalize women due to the relationship between technological skill and manliness (p. 4). The integration of women into the gaming and technology culture has threatened this sense of masculinity, and it feeds into anti-feminist movements to preserve this identity (p. 5). While the media attention associated with GamerGate started a conversation about online acts of gendered hate, the underlying issues that spurred it are still present in technology culture (Salter 2017, p. 9). "Gamergate's core narrative is that treasured symbols of techno-masculinity, such as video games or the internet, are being destroyed in a "culture war" waged by feminists and progressives, and has merged with other reactionary masculine identity movements and taken on unexpectedly virulent forms" (Salter 2017, p. 9).

Scholars pointed out the larger implications GamerGate has for feminism both online and offline. Jane (2016) argued that GamerGate was one of the first instances of what she calls "gendered e-bile" that spills offline into the lives of the women involved (p. 286). She described a more recent event of an Australian female gamer taking the problem of online harassment into her own hands by contacting the underaged harassers' mothers in a vigilante-type crusade against misogyny (p. 284). Jane (2016) posited that this "digilantism" or "DIY" activism is ethically questionable because it encourages behavior that is also degrading to women, such as blaming a mother for her son's actions of online harassment (p. 292). "Yet, while highly individualized forms of feminism have the advantage of acknowledging and respecting difference, they are unlikely to solve a problem as broad and structural as gendered cyber-hate" (Jane 2016, p. 292). GamerGate was one of the first of its scale that highlighted significant questions about how feminists should organize to inspire practical and positive outcomes for their objectives in online and gaming contexts.

8.7.2   Structure and Culture of Online Platforms

While scholars agree that misogyny and feminism are certainly significant to Gamer-Gate, the focus of the various analyses differ. Massanari (2017) used actor-network theory (ANT) to conceptualize the importance of non-human aspects of online events such as GamerGate and The Fappening while specifically analyzing Reddit's social networking platform. The Fappening was an event similar in content and timing to GamerGate. Private celebrity photos of females, such as *The Hunger Games* star Jennifer Lawrence, were hacked and leaked onto 4chan and Reddit illustrating a very serious invasion of privacy that propagated long after the initial online spaces were taken down (Massanari 2017, p. 335). Essentially, Massanari posited that geek masculinity is absolutely pertinent to the analysis of these events, but that the culture created on Reddit contributed to the perpetuation of anti-feminist and techno-masculine rhetoric. "Both GG and The Fappening created an odd paradox, by which individuals associated with each event viewed their actions as somehow noble (at least in the case of the former) or at least unproblematic, while engaging in what even superficially could be considered unethical activity" (Massanari 2017, p. 341). To the outside world, online harassment is easily seen as an issue that needs to be addressed and eradicated. Yet, the culture and structure of these platforms as founded in a notion of geek masculinity, is what contributes to the participators' sense of virtue that accompanies their online actions (Massanari 2017).

A main tenet of geek culture apparent on Reddit is that specialized knowledge and interests that do not align with popular trends are coveted (Massanari 2017, p. 332). "But despite the ways in which geek culture may welcome and promote deep engagement with niche, often unpopular interests, it often demonstrates a fraught relationship to issues of gender and race." (Massanari 2017, p. 332). This paradox is complicated by structural and political elements of Reddit's platform that allow online, anti-feminist movements to fester. However, algorithms and policies specifically contribute to the perpetuation of online harassment that was the foundation for GamerGate and similar cases (Massanari 2017).

Massanari (2017) highlighted how Reddit's compilation of content is carried out primarily through upvotes and recent material, meaning that the most current and popular material gets more attention. This silences voices that might not be central participating actors or those who have different (i.e. non techno-masculine) views. Furthermore, Reddit's policies make it easy for users to post ethically questionable content. "Reddit's platform design also provides little support for discouraging material that might be objectionable or harassing. The only recourse administrators provide to users is the ability for individual accounts to report links and comments to moderators" (Massanari 2017, p. 338). This reliance on individual users to report content is complicated by the reality that if banned, making another Reddit account is simple (Massanari 2017, p. 339). Reddit has undergone policy changes to dissuade users from harassment activity (Massanari 2017, p. 342). Yet, the strong geek masculinity and bully culture is still present, as was seen in the online death threats that

Reddit CEO Ellen Pao received after firing a popular administrator (Massanari 2017, p. 342).

Salter (2017) also described how platform culture created breeding grounds for harassing, online behavior. He drew connections between particular platforms and the perpetuations of online harassment when noting "… it is not a coincidence that particular online platforms, particularly 4chan, 8chan, Reddit and Twitter, proved so conducive to Gamergate's misogynist campaigns" (Salter 2017, p. 2). Salter (2017) cited Marcuse's idea of "technological rationality" which explains that values and beliefs within technology normalize inequalities and perpetuate online harassment (p. 2). As an example, 4chan erases older posts to make room for newer posts possibly making people more likely to post without a sense of burden or regret (Salter 2017, p. 6). This lack of concern for posting questionable material is foddered by a libertarian culture that reveres freedom of speech (Salter 2017, p. 6). Furthermore, the primary platforms of GamerGate have little recourse for users to protect themselves from harassment, a point that some scholars agreed contributed to the perpetuation of this behavior (Massanari 2017; Salter 2017, p. 11). In addition to platform structure and online culture, there are additional cultural considerations that scholars have argued are essential to truly understanding the more broad trends and societal consequences of GamerGate and online harassment.

8.7.3 Additional Cultural Considerations: The Internet and Journalism

Cultural norms online have allowed misogynistic behaviors to perpetuate since the inception of the Internet. Hate and ignorance were spewed during GamerGate, but a unified community also emerged who will not accept these behaviors and attitudes.

Those who operate outside the accepted paradigms of gaming and challenge accepted social norms, have paid a heavy price. Social media and the internet have provided the perfect platforms, shielded by anonymity, for like minded people to come together and wreak havoc on the lives of others. Regardless of the intent and the level of involvement, communities like the Men's Rights Activists, who viciously attack their victims, have no regard for others. Anonymity makes it easier for a person to express views they may have otherwise kept hidden and GamerGate was and continues to be fueled by the nameless (Poland 2016, p. 17).

Participation of the masses is what helps to increase the harassment of a victim and to disseminate controversial views to as many people as possible, but it is not the involvement of the masses that is most concerning, it is the actions—or lack thereof—and behaviors of people in organizations and positions of authority that have the biggest influence and impact. People who create and publish content, provide support and legitimacy for ideas and help to incite the extreme actions of their followers.

The academic study by Perreault and Vos (2016), explored the significances of gaming journalists in Gamergate and "questioned the ethics of gaming journalism." (Perreault and Vos 2016, p. 2). Perreault et al., note that the negative treatment of women in gaming has had a long history, "Nintendo Power in the 1990s did not treat women as equal members of the gaming community. With this context in mind, this might be a reason for the early, cultivated and exclusionary masculine audience to feel threatened (Perreault and Vos 2016, p. 7). The current gaming industry is no longer solely by white straight males, and is being challenged across society at large. Those that have been discriminated against are pushing back. Perreault and Vos (2016) study analyzes the attempts of gaming journalists to "repair their paradigm," and examine how this process is a "standard feature in paradigm maintenance." (p. 3). A paradigm is a framework or established ways of thinking that have been agreed upon by the community.

During and after GamerGate, some journalists took a "paternalistic" stance and challenged the status quo of the industries traditional misogynistic attitudes and actions. Even those that took this stance took different approaches, some openly denounced the harassment, some chose to not give the attackers a voice, or a chance to spread their message. Journalists that took a traditional approach to the issue were willing to "go through great efforts to restore their own image and reputation", as a way to repair their paradigm (Perreault and Vos 2016, p. 3). They vehemently denied the harassment and chose to attack anyone they deemed necessary.

Opponents of "paternalistic" journalists questioned their "critiques about sexist and violent depictions in video games. Why, the critics asked, couldn't the journalists just focus on games for what they were – a type of technical pastime – and avoid political correctness altogether?" (Perreault and Vos 2016, p. 8). Gaming journalists play an important role because they are a part of an industry, profession and community that deals with large cultural and social issues, whether directly or indirectly. The gaming journalists no longer only provide "purchasing advice" but also "play a valuable role as citizen's guide." (Perreault and Vos 2016, p. 4).

Social media and the internet have helped to heighten the exposure and the reach of the hate and aggression surrounding Gamergate. It should serve as a reminder of the cultural norms that have long been accepted online and offline globally, but especially in the United States. The attitudes and actions of the gaming industry and its majority are not limited to a "subcultural drama" but instead largely reflect the dominant norms of society. Academic studies are being done on Gamergate and have been providing "significant contributions to piece together the larger social issues." According to a 2012 poll, by the University of Arkansas, "more than a quarter of all white men hold some sexist attitudes. Online no one needs proof: High profile stories of gender based harassment, abuse and bullying accumulate by the day" (Dewey 2016, p. 3).

Many of the participants of GamerGate do not see harm in the negative comments and hostility that occurs both online and offline. "Cybersexist's and sexists who operate offline tend to argue that something like a book, movie or video game is 'just entertainment', and, that seeing social patterns reflected within entertainment is the work of people who are looking to hard" (Poland 2016, p. 8). Cybersexism is the expression of prejudice, privilege and power in online spaces and through technology as a medium (Poland 2016, p. 3). Comments do not make people commit crimes, individuals may feel more empowered to if they know they are supported by a group of like minded individuals.

8.7.4 GamerGate's Complexity and Nuance

While some scholars viewed GamerGate as yet another example of white, male dominance or focused on the significance of structure or culture, Chess and Shaw (2015) argued that GamerGate was inspiring by a long standing marginalization of the gaming community. "For years those who have participated in gaming culture have defended their interests in spite of claims by popular media and (some) academics blaming it for violence, racism, and sexism" (Chess and Shaw 2015, p. 217).

The authors argued that there is something to be learned from GamerGate that extends beyond a simplistic frame of anti-female or pro-male inclinations. They described their experience hosting a "fishbowl" discussion of the Digital Games and Research Association conference (Chess and Shaw 2015). They hoped to encourage purposeful conversation about feminism in games, which quickly turned into an opportunity for harassers to extend similar behaviors as the participants of GamerGate (Chess and Shaw 2015). They used this example to help explain the intersections of feminism, academia, and the gaming community. Essentially, the Google document used for the fishbowl commenters spiraled into various academic, government, and feminist conspiracy theories expressed in harassing and violent ways (Chess and Shaw 2015).

> A perceived threat opens a venue for those who feel their culture has been misunderstood—regardless of whether they are the oppressors or the ones being oppressed. It is easy to negate and mark the claims of this group as inconsequential, but it is more powerful to consider the cultural realities that underline those claims (Chess and Shaw 2015, p. 217).

Questions about how GamerGate relates to feminism are not limited to how geek culture dominates gaming. Interestingly, some researched posited that the GamerGate culture's perspective helped them perpetuate a narrative with their participators as the victims.

Participants of GamerGate believed that they were taking action to continue their cultural ideals that were under attack from various groups (Mortensen 2016). "GG believed firmly in their own status as victims. The 'death of the gamer' articles confirmed this as attacks on their entire culture" (Mortensen 2016, p. 11). Mortensen (2016) further explained how GamerGate was an example of a highly complex series of events by noting that women participated in some of the harassment campaigns, further adding to the rationale as participants as victims (p. 11). "The bonding experiences of intense, often aggressive mass events are not reserved for men." (Mortensen 2016, p. 11). Women participated in GamerGate by defending the sexualization of victims with an aggressive stance that mirrored techno-masculine notions (Mortensen

2016, p. 11). Consequently, GamerGate cannot be neatly explained as a misogynistic movement or a lack of consolidated feminism because it has intersecting considerations that pervade multiple societal issues simultaneously. Furthermore, GamerGate's consequences transcend offline and online realities.

Gray et al. (2017) added another layer of analysis to GamerGate that draws connections between online and offline violence. First, the authors proposed their conceptualizations of violence and symbolic violence, where violence can be the act or verbal demoralization of another or the self and symbolic violence is the representation of threats and intimidation (Gray et al. 2017, p. 3). "Within this framing, violence doesn't have to be actual harm caused; but rather, the rhetoric alone can constitute violence" (Gray et al. 2017, p. 3). They argued that women in gaming and beyond still exist within archaic structures which perpetuate their marginalization in a multitude of contexts (Gray et al. 2017, p. 3).

The authors supported the notion that the masculinization of gaming is an important factor in an analysis, but posited that it is an online manifestation of how women are marginalized in the real world (Gray et al. 2017).

> Importantly, symbolic violence, while mostly invisible and ignored, creates the conditions of possibility for other more tangible and visible forms of violence (doxing, bomb threats, and so on). Understanding symbolic violence together with traditional discourses of violence is important because it provides a richer insight into the 'workings' of violence and provides new ways of conceptualizing violence (Gray et al. 2017, p. 6)

On social media and the internet, it can be difficult to differentiate reality from fiction. While some threats may go without action, this does not extend to all situations. Seemingly harmless comment can result in a woman being targeted, harassed, assaulted and forced to leave her home, "cybersexists utilize the same types of stereotypes, violence, and silencing tactics online that appear offline in order to achieve their goals and drive women away, especially from positions of prominence and power." (Poland 2016, p. 17).

The prevalence of the Internet and social media allows information to spread almost instantly. This extends to online harassment. Social media increases not only the opportunity for anonymity, but also the ability of harassers to target and carry out attacks on their victims. The goal of cybersexism is, "to build places in which women must either be silent or invisible, reinforce the sexist attitudes that see women's proper role as silent and objectified, and develop an Internet where men are not challenged on their use of stereotypes or violence against women" (Poland 2016, p 18).

People of different ages, races, religions, genders, ethnicities, education levels and employment types use the internet and social media. The University College London compared GamerGate users to typical Twitter users, and "25% of GamerGate's posts are negative compared to only around 5% for baseline users." (Chatzakou et al. 2017, p. 1). GamerGate users participate in cyberbullying in large numbers and exhibit aggressive behavior, spreading hateful and offensive posts, and sometimes perpetuating violence against women. The "harassment and abuse in these situations are intended to silence women entirely or force them to conform to men's chosen norms for a specific space (Poland 2016, p. 19).

As an additional consideration, to how online violence relates to offline violence, it is significant to consider the realities of United States culture for women in a more general way. Such considerations allow scholars to better explain the true impetus of GamerGate's harassment efforts.

8.7.5 Cultural Reality for Women in the United States

In the United States, women are not equally represented in legal and political arenas. Women occupy the lowest percentage of high ranking business positions and they make less money than men at various employment levels. Women also face the unfortunate reality that "stereotyping and gendered abuse are a common fact of life for women." (Poland 2016, p. 3). Negative portrayals of women that perpetuate stereotypical depictions help "to reflect and reinforce preexisting social beliefs." (Poland 2016, p. 7). Stereotypes make it harder for women to move forward, and abuse can have permanent effects. These stereotypes bleed into other spheres as well. In the larger entertainment industry, just as in the gaming industry, many women have few roles behind the camera, few participate in the writing process, and many often play highly sexualized and l roles. These roles fit into already established and accepted social norms about the roles of women, "the attitudes that result in violence toward women are an extension of the social, financial and political privileges already held by men – beliefs about the roles women should play in society, what can be done to keep them there, and what kinds of behavior are permissible in enforcing those roles." (Poland 2016, p. 12).

GamerGate is about something much bigger than what defines gaming or who is allowed to participate in gaming culture. The larger message is about, "how we define our shared cultural spaces, how we delineate identity, who is and who is not allowed to have a voice in mainstream culture. It is about that tension between tradition and inclusion and in that regard, Gamergate may be the perfect representation of our times" (Dewey 2016, p. 3). It is also an excellent example of how efforts of power and control are interconnecting, showcasing similar offline tactics to online contexts (Poland 2016, p. 17).

Intimidation and violence are ways to impose power onto others, and cybersexist harassment "is in fact intended to restore and reinforce the power and control of men – particularly straight, cisgender white men" (Poland 2016, p. 17). Gamergate helped to expose the gaming industry for its downfalls, but it also speaks to behaviors and patterns that exist in a larger national and social context.

References

4Chan (2017) GamerGate Wiki. http://thisisvideogames.com/gamergatewiki/index.php?title= 4chan. Accessed 16 Jan 2018

Alcid S (2013) The latest war on women: online harassment. EverydayFeminism.com, 26 Nov 2013. https://everydayfeminism.com/2013/11/war-on-women-online-harassment/. Accessed 20 Jan 2018

Al Jazeera News (2017) One in five women victim of online harassment. Aljazeera.com, 20 Nov 2017. http://www.aljazeera.com/news/2017/11/women-victim-online-harassment-report-171119201127598.html. Accessed 20 Jan 2018

Allen J (2014) GamerGate and the new misogyny. Medium.com, 15 Nov 2014. https://medium.com/@a_man_in_black/gamergate-and-the-new-misogyny-284bea6a8bb3. Accessed 9 Jan 2018

Anwar M (2014) #INeedDiverseGames is the perfect response to the mysogonistic video game culture. Bustle, 8 Oct 2014. https://www.bustle.com/articles/43346-ineeddiversegames-is-a-perfect-response-to-misogynistic-video-game-culture. Accessed 12 Jan 2018

BBC News (2007) Blog death threats spark debate. BBCNews.com, 27 Mar 2007. http://news.bbc.co.uk/2/hi/technology/6499095.stm. Accessed 20 Jan 2018

Berger V (2017) Mike Cernovich discusses his love of choking women and being arrested for rape (video). Twitter.com, 21 Nov 2017. https://twitter.com/vicbergeriv/status/933013953537552385?lang=en. Accessed 20 Jan 2018

Bokhari A (2017) Leftists think GamerGate caused Donald Trump; Maybe they're right. Breitbart.com, 22 June 2017. http://www.breitbart.com/tech/2017/06/22/leftists-think-gamergate-caused-donald-trump-maybe-theyre-right/. Accessed 20 Jan 2018

Boswell M (2017) What is YouTube and how do I use it. LifeWire, 27 June 2017. https://www.lifewire.com/youtube-101-3481847. Accessed 17 Jan 2018

Brandom R (2015) Christopher 'Moot' Poole on Gamergate and the future of 4Chan. The Verge, 22 Sept 2015. https://www.theverge.com/2015/9/22/9374643/christopher-m00t-poole-interview-4chan. Accessed 16 Jan 2018

Brogan J (2015) Reddit users should be very worried about changes to the site. Slate, 25 Mar 2015. http://www.slate.com/blogs/future_tense/2015/03/25/reddit_s_new_embeddable_comments_will_help_it_turn_its_users_into_commodities.html. Accessed 17 Jan 2018

Bruns A, Burgess J (2011) The use of Twitter hashtags in the formation of ad hoc publics. In: Proceedings of the 6th European consortium for political research (ECPR) general conference. University of Iceland, Reykjavik

Buncombe A (2017) Heather Heyer was buried in secret grave to protect it from neo-Nazis after Charlottesville, reveals mother. Independent.co.uk, 15 Dec 2017. http://www.independent.co.uk/news/world/americas/heather-heyer-grave-secret-hide-nazis-charlottesville-attack-mother-reveals-a8113056.html. Accessed 9 Jan 2018

Burgess J, Matamoros-Fernandez A (2016) Mapping sociocultural controversies across digital media platforms: one week of #gamergate on Twitter, YouTube, and Tumblr. Commun Res Pract 2(1):79–96

Carson E (2017) After years of GamerGate harassment, Brianna Wu's still fighting. CNET.com, 9 July 2017. https://www.cnet.com/news/after-years-of-gamergate-harassment-brianna-wus-still-fighting/. Accessed 9 Jan 2018

Chatzakou D, Kourtellis N, Blackburn J, De Cristofaro E, Stringhini G, Vakali A (2017) Hate is not binary. In: Proceedings of the 28th ACM conference on hypertext and social media. University College, London, pp 1–10

Chess S, Shaw A (2015) A conspiracy of fishes, or, how we learned to stop worrying about #Gamer-Gate and embrace hegemonic masculinity. J Broadcast Electron Media 59(1):208–220

Chiel E (2016) Meet the man keeping 8Chan, the world's most vile website, alive. Splinter, 19 Apr 2016. https://splinternews.com/meet-the-man-keeping-8chan-the-worlds-most-vile-websit-1793856249. Accessed 16 Jan 2018

Crecente B (2017) NBC News traces the link between GamerGate, Trump supporters, alt-right. RollingStones.com, 31 Oct 2017. https://www.rollingstone.com/glixel/news/tracing-link-between-gamergate-trump-supporters-alt-right-w510618. Accessed 9 Jan 2018

Daily Stormer (2017) Girl scouts warn parents: hugging Grandma leads to rape. DailyStormer.com, 28 Nov 2017. https://dstormer6em3i4km.onion.link/girl-scouts-warn-parents-hugging-grandma-leads-to-rape/. Accessed 9 Jan 2018

Davis C (2014) Twitter responds to #GamerGate harassment, employing a new quick response tool. Pajiba.com, 11 Nov 2014. http://www.pajiba.com/miscellaneous/twitter-responds-to-gamergate-harassment-employing-a-new-quick-response-tool.php. Accessed 15 Jan 2018

Dewey C (2016) In the battle of Internet mobs vs. the law, the Internet mobs have won [online]. The Washington Post, 17 Feb 2016. https://www.washingtonpost.com/news/the-intersect/wp/2016/02/17/in-the-battle-of-internet-mobs-vs-the-law-the-internet-mobs-have-won/?utm_term=.6fc41709a6a4. Accessed 20 Jan 2018

Dewey C (2018) The only guide to Gamergate you will ever need to read. Highbeam.com, 16 Oct 2014. http://www.highbeam.com/doc/1P2-37288329.html?refid=easy_hf. Accessed 12 Jan 2018

Duggan M (2017) Men, women experience and view online harassment differently. Pew Research Center, 14 July 2017. http://www.pewresearch.org/fact-tank/2017/07/14/men-women-experience-and-view-online-harassment-differently/. Accessed 20 Jan 2018

Gibbs S (2017) Facebook bans women for posting 'men are scum' after harassment scandals. TheGuardian.com, 5 Dec 2017. https://www.theguardian.com/technology/2017/dec/05/facebook-bans-women-posting-men-are-scum-harassment-scandals-comedian-marcia-belsky-abuse. Accessed 20 Jan 2018

Gray K, Buyukozturk B, Hill Z (2017) Blurring the boundaries: using gamergate to examine "real" and symbolic violence against women in contemporary gaming culture. Sociol Compass 11(3)

Griffith E (2017) Here are Twitter's latest rules for fighting hate and abuse. WIRED, 17 Oct 2017. https://www.wired.com/story/here-are-twitters-latest-rules-for-fighting-hate-and-abuse/?mbid=social_twitter_onsiteshare. Accessed 22 Jan 2018

Harveston K (2017) GamerGate, the ugly side of an industry built on fun. Headstuff.org, 24 Oct 2017. https://www.headstuff.org/gaming/gamergate-ugly-side-industry-built-fun/. Accessed 9 Jan 2018

Hemphill L (2014) #GamerGate vs #StopGamerGate2014 by the numbers [blog]. LibbyH.com. https://archive.is/Iw3zR. Accessed 20 Jan 2018

Hibberd J (2017) Rick and Morty co-creator slams trolls attacking their female writers. EW.com, 21 Sept 2017. http://ew.com/tv/2017/09/21/rick-morty-dan-harmon-female-writers/. Accessed 9 Jan 2018

Hunt E (2016) Online harassment of women at risk of becoming 'established norm', study finds. TheGuardian.com, 7 Mar 2016. https://www.theguardian.com/lifeandstyle/2016/mar/08/online-harassment-of-women-at-risk-of-becoming-established-norm-study. Accessed 20 Jan 2018

Jane E (2016) Online misogyny and feminist digilantism. Contin: J Media Cult Stud 30(3):284–297

Johnston C (2014) Chat logs show how 4chan users created #GamerGate controversy. In arsTechnica, 9 Sept 2014. https://arstechnica.com/gaming/2014/09/new-chat-logs-show-how-4chan-users-pushed-gamergate-into-the-national-spotlight/. Accessed 19 Jan 2018

Kidd D, Turner A (2016) The #GamerGate files: Mysoginy in the media. In: Novak A, El- Burki IJ (eds) Defining identity and the changing scope of culture in the digital age. Information Science Reference, pp 117–139

Kushner D (2015) 4Chan's overlord Christopher Poole reveals why he walked away. Rolling Stone, 13 Mar 2015. https://www.rollingstone.com/culture/features/4chans-overlord-christopher-poole-reveals-why-he-walked-away-20150313. Accessed 16 Jan 2018

Lees M (2016) What GamerGate should have taught us about the alt-right. The Guardian, 1 Dec 2016. https://www.theguardian.com/technology/2016/dec/01/gamergate-alt-right-hate-trump. Accessed 20 Jan 2018

Maiberg E (2017) Under Trump, Gamergate can stop pretending it was about games. Vice.com, 9 Feb 2017. https://motherboard.vice.com/en_us/article/bm5wd4/under-trump-gamergate-can-stop-pretending-it-was-about-games. Accessed 9 Jan 2018

Marantz A (2016) Trolls for Trump, meet Mike Cernovich, the meme mastermind of the alt-right. TheNewYorker.com, 31 Oct 2016. https://www.newyorker.com/magazine/2016/10/31/trolls-for-trump. Accessed 9 Jan 2018

Marche S (2016) Swallowing the Red Pill: a journey to the heart of modern misogyny. The-Guardian.com, 14 Apr 2016. https://www.theguardian.com/technology/2016/apr/14/the-red-pill-reddit-modern-misogyny-manosphere-men. Accessed 9 Jan 2018

Massanari A (2017) #Gamergate and the Fappening: how Reddit's algorithm, governance, and culture support toxic technocultures. New Media Soc 19(3):329–346

Matias JN, Johnson A, Boesel WE, Keegan B, Friedman J, DeTar C (2015) Reporting, reviewing, and responding to harassment on Twitter [online]. Women, Action, and the Media. http://womenactionmedia.org/twitter-report. Accessed 15 Jan 2018

McGuire P (2014) Elliot Rodger's online life provides a glimpse at a hateful group of "Anti-Pick-up Artists." Vice.com, 26 May 2014. https://www.vice.com/en_us/article/znwz53/elliot-rodgers-online-life-provides-a-glimpse-at-a-hateful-group-of-pick-up-artists. Accessed 9 Jan 2018

Molina B (2017) Reddit is extremely popular. Here's how to watch what your kids are doing. USAToday, 31 Aug 2017. https://www.usatoday.com/story/tech/talkingtech/2017/08/31/reddit-extremely-popular-heres-how-watch-what-your-kids-doing/607996001/. Accessed 19 Jan 2018

Mortensen T (2016) Anger, fear, and games: the long event of #GamerGate. Games and Culture [online]. http://journals.sagepub.com/doi/abs/10.1177/1555412016640408. Accessed 19 Jan 2018

Nussbaum E (2017) How jokes won the election. TheNewYorker.com, 23 Jan 2017. https://www.newyorker.com/magazine/2017/01/23/how-jokes-won-the-election. Accessed 9 Jan 2018

Perreault G, Vos T (2016) The GamerGate controversy and journalistic paradigm maintenance. Journalism: Theory, Practice & Criticism, 2016. http://journals.sagepub.com/doi/abs/10.1177/1464884916670932#articleCitationDownloadContainer. Accessed 19 Jan 2018

Perry M (2017) Why it's important to name the Nazis. Pacific Magazine, 17 Aug 2017. https://psmag.com/social-justice/naming-and-shaming-american-nazis. Accessed 9 Jan 2018

Philipson A (2013) Woman who campaigned for Jane Austen bank note receives Twitter death threats. Telegraph.co.uk, 28 July 2013. http://www.telegraph.co.uk/technology/10207231/Woman-who-campaigned-for-Jane-Austen-bank-note-receives-Twitter-death-threats.html. Accessed 20 Jan 2018

Plante C (2015) Twitter is letting you and your friends join hands to block trolls and miscreants. The Verge, 10 June 2015. https://www.theverge.com/2015/6/10/8761231/twitter-block-lists-share-import-export-social-media-trolls. Accessed 15 Jan 2018

Poland B (2016) Haters: harassment, abuse, and violence online. [ebook] Potomac Books. https://ebookcentral.proquest.com/lib/umdcp/detail.action?docID=4690661. Accessed 18 Jan 2018

Ratchford S (2017) I tried to find out if pick up artists are still influential in 2017. Vice.com, 24 Aug 2017. https://www.vice.com/en_au/article/j55bxd/i-tried-to-find-out-if-pick-up-artists-are-still-influential-in-2017. Accessed 9 Jan 2018

Reddit Blog (2015) Announcing embeddable comment threads. Upvoted, 23 Mar 2015. https://redditblog.com/2015/03/23/announcing-embeddable-comment-threads/. Accessed 17 Jan 2018

Reddit/RedPill.com (2016) Treating women badly because they deserve it. Reddit/RedPill.com, 30 Mar 2016. https://www.reddit.com/r/TheRedPill/comments/4ckvk1/treating_women_badly_because_they_deserve_it/. Accessed 20 Jan 2018

Romano A (2017) How the alt-right's sexism lures men into white supremacy. Vox.com, 14 Dec 2016. https://www.vox.com/culture/2016/12/14/13576192/alt-right-sexism-recruitment. Accessed 9 Jan 2018

Roosh (2015) How to stop rape. Rooshv.com, 16 Feb 2015. http://www.rooshv.com/how-to-stop-rape. Accessed 20 Jan 2018

Salter M (2017) From geek masculinity to gamergate: the technological rationality of online abuse. Crime, Media, Cult: Int J 3(3)

Sheer I (2017) GamerGate to Trump: how video game culture blew everything up. CNET.com, 27 Nov 2017. https://www.cnet.com/news/gamergate-donald-trump-american-nazis-how-video-game-culture-blew-everything-up/. Accessed 9 Jan 2018

Springer P (ed) (2017) Encyclopedia of cyber warfare. ABC-CLIO, LLC, Santa Barbara, CA

Stone J (2014) GamerGate's vicious right-wing swell means there can be no neutral stance. The Guardian, 13 Oct 2014. https://www.theguardian.com/technology/2014/oct/13/gamergate-right-wing-no-neutral-stance. Accessed 9 Jan 2018

Stuart B (2014) #GamerGate: the misogynist movement blighting the video games industry. The Telegraph, 24 Oct 2014. http://www.telegraph.co.uk/culture/culturenews/11180510/gamergate-misogynist-felicia-day-zoe-quinn-brianna-wu.html. Accessed 19 Jan 2018

Tunison M (2017) 13 things you never knew about 8chan, the controversial message board. The Daily Dot, 10 Sept 2017. https://www.dailydot.com/unclick/8chan/. Accessed 19 Jan 2018

Wofford T (2014) Is GamerGate about media ethics or harassing women? Harassment, the data shows. Newsweek, 25 Oct 2014. http://www.newsweek.com/gamergate-about-media-ethics-or-harassing-women-harassment-data-show-279736. Accessed 19 Jan 2018

Worley W (2017) Neo-Nazi website asks readers to target funeral of Heather Heyer who died in Charlottesville violence. Independent.co.uk, 15 Aug 2017. http://www.independent.co.uk/news/world/americas/america-top-neo-nazi-website-daily-stormer-orders-followers-harass-funeral-heather-heyer-victim-a7895496.html. Accessed 9 Jan 2018

Valenti J (2014) Elliot Rodger's California shooting spree: further proof that misogyny kills. TheGuardian.com, 25 May 2014. https://www.theguardian.com/commentisfree/2014/may/24/elliot-rodgers-california-shooting-mental-health-misogyny. Accessed 9 Jan 2018

Yiannopoulos M (2014) Feminist bullies tearing the video game industry apart. Breitbart.com, 1 Sept 2014. http://www.breitbart.com/london/2014/09/01/lying-greedy-promiscuous-feminist-bullies-are-tearing-the-video-game-industry-apart/. Accessed 20 Jan 2018

Yiannopoulos M (2016) The solution to online 'harassment' is simple: women should log off. Breitbart.com, 5 July 2016. http://www.breitbart.com/milo/2016/07/05/solution-online-harassment-simple-women-log-off/. Accessed 9 Jan 2018

Zhang X (2015) Sharing block lists to help make Twitter safer. Twitter Blog, 15 June 2015. https://blog.twitter.com/official/en_us/a/2015/sharing-block-lists-to-help-make-twitter-safer.html. Accessed 15 Jan 2018

Part III
Reactions to Harassment

Chapter 9
"The Continuum of Harm" Taxonomy of Cyberbullying Mitigation and Prevention

Zahra Ashktorab

Abstract In this chapter, I use the findings from a series of studies that explore cyberbullying to present cyberbullying mitigation solutions for designers of social media and other interactive platforms to consider as they address the bullying, harassment, and other negative content that plagues the Internet. The solutions presented throughout these studies are diverse and consider mitigation at various points of the "Continuum of Harm" of cyberbullying. I consider cyberbullying mitigation solutions through the "Continuum of Harm" framework, which consists of three types of prevention mechanisms: (1) **Primary Prevention**, in which the cyberbullying incident is prevented before it starts; (2) **Secondary Prevention**, where the goal is to decrease the problem after it has been identified, and (3) **Tertiary Prevention**, when intervention occurs after a problem has already caused harm. This chapter discusses the design of technological mechanisms to mitigate cyberbullying through Primary, Secondary, and Tertiary prevention.

9.1 Introduction

Cyberbullying is an umbrella term that captures instances of bullying, harassment, and intimidation through online social media platforms. With the growing popularity of social media and other forms of computer-mediated communication technologies, incidences of cyberbullying have significantly increased (Mesch 2009). At least 42% of teens in the United States have experienced cyberbullying (Lenhart 2007). Victims of cyberbullying experience emotional problems like anxiety and depression (Kim and Leventhal 2008; Hinduja and Patchin 2010). Teens who are bullied have a higher risk of suicide, which is currently the third leading cause of death among young people (Kim and Leventhal 2008; Kim et al. 2009; Hinduja and Patchin 2010).

The modes of cyberbullying (flaming, harassment, denigration, impersonation, outing and trickery, exclusion, and cyberstalking) are enacted based on the social and technical affordances of a given platform (Kwan and Skoric 2013; Nott J et al 2014).

Z. Ashktorab (✉)
IBM T.J. Watson Research Center, Yorktown Heights, NY, USA
e-mail: Zahra.Ashktorab1@ibm.com

© Springer International Publishing AG, part of Springer Nature 2018
J. Golbeck (ed.), *Online Harassment*, Human–Computer Interaction Series,
https://doi.org/10.1007/978-3-319-78583-7_9

Platforms that contain private messaging features enable outing and trickery by allowing a bully to take a private conversation/personal photo and sharing it with a wider audience. Among adolescents, there have been numerous examples of private content, such intimate photos shared between a couple, later becoming widely viewable on social media or through a texting chain, which may have significant social and emotional consequences for the involved parties (McLaughlin 2010). Addressing the cyberbullying affordances of some social media platforms becomes even more complicated when considering supposedly ephemeral communication platforms like Snapchat, which purport to delete a message after a specified number of seconds. However, there are several workarounds to capturing shared images and sharing them with a wider audience than the sender intended (Young 2014).

9.2 Iterative Succession of Cyberbullying Mitigation Studies

In my research on cyberbullying up-to-date, I began with a data-centric approach, attempting to find the motivation of the use of a social media platform associated with cyberbullying and ultimately building a classifier to detect it and various types of discourse (Ashktorab et al. 2017).[1] I then conducted participatory design which teens that ultimately led to a suite of cyberbullying mitigation prototypes (Ashktorab and Vitak 2016).[2] From each study, I gained an understanding of human behavior in the context of cyberbullying and introduce design recommendations for various cyberbullying mitigation tools. Cyberbullying is an all-encompassing term inclusive of various types of malicious interactions on various social media platforms. Some of the mitigation tools introduced in this thesis involve the prevention of cyberbullying—preventing aggressions before they even occur, while others focus on mitigating and promoting well being once cyberbullying occurs. In this chapter, I present cyberbullying mitigation through the "Continuum of Harm" framework for cyberbullying, a framework that considers the various stages of cyberbullying aggressions and prevention and mitigation during these different stages.

9.3 The Stages of Cyberbullying and Its Prevention: Continuum of Harm

Cyberbullying has a variety of negative influences on the emotional and physical well-being of victims. Cyberbullying has the potential to affect individuals at all

---

[1]This study was a collaborative project done with Jennifer Golbeck, Eben Haber and Jessica Vitak. It was presented at the 2017 ACM Web Science Conference.

[2]This study was collaborative project done with Jessica Vitak and was presented at the 2016 ACM CHI Conference on Human Factors in Computing Systems.

times of day regardless of an individual's location. Victims of cyberbullying are at higher risk for depression, anxiety, and suicidal ideation (Cowie 2013). Similarly, victims of cyberbullying have faced psychosomatic symptoms like sleeplessness and abdominal pain (Sourander et al. 2010). Victims of cyberbullying are also more likely to be involved in anti-social behaviors like alcohol consumption and drug-misuse (Hinduja and Patchin 2014). While there has been no in-depth longitudinal study of the relationships between the different symptoms of cyberbullying, literature informs us that emotional disturbance precedes behavioral and psychosomatic symptoms (Achenbach et al. 1987; Campo et al. 2004).

Similar to cyberbullying, domestic violence involves different stages by which the victim is affected. Prevention mechanisms have been outlined very clearly in domestic violence prevention. Wolfe et al. identify a health model which can be used to identify opportunities for domestic violence prevention along a "Continuum of Harm" (Wolfe and Jaffe 1999). At one side of the domestic violence "Continuum of Harm" lies gender-focused jokes and vulgarity, while physical force and rape lie at the other end of the spectrum. Similarly, I model a "Continuum of Harm" specific to cyberbullying. The continuum is triggered by cyberbullying. At one end of the continuum, there is damage to self-esteem, while suicidal ideation lie at the other end of the continuum. I use this continuum to evaluate the best point of entry for each of the intervention mechanisms we discover in our design sessions. For domestic violence, the "Continuum of harm" prevention includes a three-pronged approach: **Primary Prevention, Secondary Prevention, Tertiary Prevention.** Each of the design recommendations in the next section can be classified into one of these approaches with respect to the Cyberbullying "Continuum of Harm".

Cyberbullying mitigation solutions can be analyzed through a framework that considers the different stages of cyberbullying symptoms and is based on preventative measures aimed at mitigating the "Continuum of Harm" in domestic violence (Wolfe and Jaffe 1999) (see Fig. 9.1). Through this framework, the technological solutions resulting from the design sessions as well as design recommendations derived from the longitudinal study in Chap. 6 can be categorized through a three-pronged approach: (1) **Primary Prevention**, in which the cyberbullying incident is prevented before it starts; (2) **Secondary Prevention**, where the goal is to decrease the problem after it has been identified, and (3) **Tertiary Prevention**, when intervention occurs after a problem has already caused harm (Wolfe and Jaffe 1999). Two researchers who were involved in designing the participatory design sessions coded each

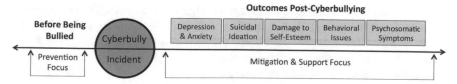

Fig. 9.1 The Cyberbullying Continuum of Harm describes the different types of emotional distress may follow cyberbullying

resulting solution based on this framework individually. Below we describe the solutions on which both researchers agreed regarding the prevention category in which they fell.

9.3.1 Primary Prevention

The goal of primary prevention is to stop cyberbullying before it happens. In the traditional non-technical realm, such a solution would include school-based programs that warn of the harms of cyberbullying (e.g., Beale and Hall 2007). However, "Exclusion Prevention" application, designed in the Participatory Design sessions to prevent purposeful repeated cropping on an individual on Instagram, is a strong example of a type of a cyberbullying preventive measure that aims to stop the incidence of cyberbullying before it can occur. While literature has discussed how to approach denigration and flaming (Dinakar et al. 2012), there are no academic research discussion issues related to exclusion online. In a *New York Times* parenting blog, the author said, "To be in a photo and to not be tagged is to be rendered socially invisible. Commenting on a party photo, my untagged daughter wrote, 'I was there too!'" (Milvy 2015). The "Exclusion Prevention" application aims to remedy the potential emotional damage of exclusion-based cyberbullying by presenting the potential bully with a reflective notification.

The main aim of primary prevention is to raise awareness about the potential harm that could be caused as a result of someone's actions. In "Exclusion Prevention", the bully decides whether she wants to continue with publishing data after the system warns the [potential] bully that she may be hurting someone by continuously cropping them out of photos. Ultimately, the decision of publishing the content lies with the potential bully. Dinakar et al. (2012) share examples of primary preventive measures when discussing reflective interfaces, which ask users to reflect on their behavior before publishing malicious content online.

From an implementation standpoint, preventative prevention requires some degree of monitoring since it is attempting to prevent the cyberbullying before it occurs. While privacy advocates may find this monitoring particularly troubling, many parents believe that they have the right to access and monitor their children's online activity (Barnes 2006). There are three notions of a reflective practitioner: "reflection in action", "reflection on action" and "ladders of reflections" (Schön 1983). Reflective user interfaces aim to prevent cyberbullying by asking the aggressor to reconsider their actions and reflect on them through showing potential consequences of their actions, flagging their content and notifying them of the potential harm they can cause. Since the main goal of Primary Prevention is to prevent the cyberbullying narrative from taking place, and the initiator of the cyberbullying narrative is the perpetrator, the perpetrator holds primary control over initiating the bullying after being presented with primary preventative measures.

9.3.1.1 Mitigation for Exclusionary Behavior

One common type of cyberbullying described by Willard et al. is "Exclusion", the act of purposefully excluding individuals through social media. In my 2016 participatory design study (Ashktorab and Vitak 2016), many respondents described instances of such behavior contributing to experiencing a negative social media experience for the week. This type of behavior occurred through various mediums: Snapchat and exclusionary Facebook posts. One participant reported, "Good friends always post exclusive pictures and it's annoying but not a big deal." In this particular case, the exclusion is occurring through photographs. Another participant described the exclusionary behavior as transcending beyond the online realm and translating into the offline realm, "seeing snapchat stories of people and events that I was not invited to". Sometimes the exclusionary behavior revealed a level of deception in which the subject was deceived about friends attending particular event and later on discovered the truth through social media content, "Friend said they weren't going somewhere and they went."

One type of "negative social media experience" that continuously reappeared in the weekly check-ins was related to exclusionary cyberbullying, cyberbullying that involves purposeful directed exclusion of individuals (Menesini et al. 2012). This cyberbullying manifested itself through different formats and on various platforms. While other types of cyberbullying are more discerning and can be more inflammatory, exclusionary cyberbullying is less obvious and thus creating mitigation tools to address this kind of cyberbullying are more challenging. In the prototype solutions in the participatory design study, clique-detection was suggested for victims of cyberbullying that were repeatedly cropped out of photos. The participants in the participatory design study suggested creating automated methods to detect exclusionary cyberbullying and present reflective interfaces to facilitate perpetrators of exclusionary behavior to rethink their actions.

9.3.1.2 Cyberbullying and the Dissolution of Romantic Relationships and Contextual Integrity

In an online survey we conducted asking about the nature of cyberbullying and online harassment faced by university students, many participants reported cyberbullying or online harassment occurring as result of the dissolution of a romantic relationship. Sas et al. make recommendations for managing the process of managing digital possessions after dissolving a romantic relationship: creating digital spaces for shared possessions, artifact crafting as sense making, incorporating tools for self control and harvesting digital possessions (Sas and Whittaker 2013). In the types of cyberbullying listed in the preliminary survey, many participants reported experiencing cyberbullying as a result of the dissolution of a relationship. One participant wrote, "There were a lot of subtweets about me after I broke up with my most recent relationship." Another participant said, "My friends ex sent her nudes into a group chat after the broke up. I confronted him but he didn't change."

Sas et al. recommend creating shared spaces for digital possessions. For example, a *relationship profile* would allow a couple to both celebrate a relationship and in the case of dissolution, delete content that would be painful to reflect on after the end of the relationship. While this method might be useful in aiding to forget a memory, such a design does not protect against more nefarious and malicious interactions that may occur after the dissolution of a romantic relationship, like the widespread publishing of content like explicit photos that were not meant for specific private audiences. In some instances, this type of sharing content is referred to as "Revenge Porn". "Revenge Porn" constitutes a violation of sexual privacy and involves the publication of non-consensual graphic images. The publication of such images can lead to emotional harms and even increase the risk of physical assault (Citron and Franks 2014).

One design recommendation which constitutes as Primary Prevention for social media platforms is adopting ephemeral interactions to prevent such interactions. Beyond ephemerality, social media platforms should opt to *notify* users if photos were screenshot on ephemeral technologies. Teens have turned to ephemeral communication on social media technologies (Charteris et al. 2014). Snapchat and Instagram allow the sharing of temporary photos and videos. Recently, iMessage and Facebook messages rolled out temporary messages (King 2016).

In these particular scenarios, *screenshot* detection serves as *primary prevention*, mitigation of potential cyberbullying. Snapchat allows users to circumvent automatic deletion of content by allowing screenshoting. However, users are notified if their photos have been screenshot (Xu et al. 2016). Xu et al. describe emerging norms on ephemeral communications that allow saving with a notification. To screenshot content that the poster would not like to be distributed would be violating the norms of snapchat. Nissenbaum describes the framework of contextual integrity. "Distribution" which refers to the movement of information depends on three factors: "actors (subject, sender, recipient), attributes (types of information), and transmission principles (constraints under which information flows) (Nissenbaum 2004). Since the default norm in ephemeral communications is ephemeral, Snapchatting and saving information is a violation of that norm. For this reason, social media platforms must notify users when Contextual Integrity is violated.

Screenshot detection and notification technologies in ephemeral communications serve as primary prevention of cyberbullying by notifying a user that their photo has been captured permanently by the recipient. Coupled with a reflective interface to reiterate that the once-ephemeral content has now been saved by the recipient, such a notification would make users reconsider sending explicit photos to a particular recipient who has violated the Contextual Integrity of the ephemeral communication platform, which might ultimately prevent any widespread publishing of such photos and further damage.

Beyond screenshot notification, reputations can be assigned for those who violate the Contextual Integrity of social media platforms. Reputation allows users to identify the standing of others and themselves on social media platforms. Keitzmann et al. describe "reputation" as one of the building blocks of social media (Kietzmann et al. 2011). Reputation depends on aggregated measures of trust-worthiness by users.

Fig. 9.2 Prototype of
reflective interface after
screenshotting a "secret"
Facebook chat

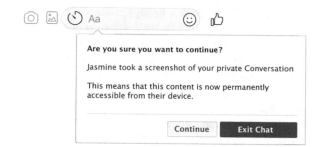

For example, LinkedIn assigns reputation based on endorsements (Bastian et al. 2014). StackOverflow assigns reputation based on up-votes on questions and other forms of interaction that contribute to the StackOverflow community (Nasehi et al. 2012). Such crowd-sourced ratings signal the trustworthiness of an individual and in turn influence how individuals interact with one another. As a *primary prevention* cyberbullying mitigation design recommendation, ephemeral communications should crowdsource reputations to measure users' adherence to the contextual integrity of the social media platform. In Fig. 9.2, symbols have been added next to Snapchat contacts in a prototype to demonstrate that an individual tends to screenshot photos. Such symbols would influence how users interact with one another.

9.3.2 Secondary Prevention

The aim of *Secondary Prevention* is to decrease the incidents of cyberbullying once it has already started. In the original "Continuum of Harm" pertaining to domestic violence, secondary preventative measures include home visits for high risk families to raise awareness of the harms of domestic violence. In the realm of cyberbullying prevention, *Secondary Prevention* manifests through cyberbullying applications which filter content or reporting content. A victim can choose to filter content once becoming aware of cyberbullying content. In the participatory design sessions, prototypes like "Watch Yo Profanity" and "SMILE," the victim decides if she would like some degree of filtering to be happening on his profile. In "Hate Page Prevention", a bystander or an automatic system flags the page and ultimately makes the decision to get rid of the data. In these types of cyberbullying design solutions, either a bystander or a third party automated system has ultimate control over the cyberbullying data being published. Control of solutions presented as a part of *Secondary Prevention* are held by the victim or a bystander of the cyberbullying since the victim is on the receiving end of the bullying.

In a study I conducted about young adult women's online harassment experiences (Vitak et al. 2017),[3] I recommended the use of custom filtering, since participants in this study reported being called names or receiving unwanted content online

---

[3] Study conducted in collaboration with Jessica Vitak, Kalyani Chada and Linda Steiner.

(Vitak et al. 2017). While language and machine learning tools are constantly improving to detect online harassment, language continues to evolve and online harassment can be contextual. Furthermore, cyberbullying and harassment might lack key features (e.g., expletives) that are required to automatically identify harassment and other malicious content (Dinakar et al. 2011). The prototypes resulting from the Participatory Design sessions describe the notion of user-centered custom filtering that allow users to identify the words that should be omitted from a user's timeline. After the publication of this work (Ashktorab and Vitak 2016) both Instagram (McCormick 2016) and Twitter (Newton 2017) adopted custom filtering, giving power to users to choose to identify words to be filtered from their social media platforms. Figure 9.3 represents a *Secondary Prevention* prototypes co-designed with teens in participatory design sessions that allow users to identify words that should be filtered from their platforms.

9.3.3 Tertiary Prevention

Tertiary Prevention is a preventative measure that occurs when the problem has already caused visible harm. From the suite of solutions produced in the participatory design sessions, many attempted to mitigate negative emotional outcome of cyberbullying by sending positivity. Since visible harm on the Cyberbullying Continuum of Harm is inclusive of behavior ills, psychosomatic symptoms, and suicide ideation, *Tertiary Prevention* can be initiated by bystanders or automated systems. In the cyberbullying domain, the "Positivity Generator" allows victims to replace malicious content on their profiles with uplifting quotes from their favorite celebrities. This particular solution aims to do more than just filter negative content, but provide support and encouragement to counter the negative cyberbullying content they have experienced.

9.3.4 "Continuum of Harm" and Prevention

In the domain of domestic violence Primary prevention aims to reduce the incidence of the problem even before it occurs. For different age groups, primary prevention for domestic violence looks different. Ultimately, the aim is to *educate* individuals about the harms of domestic violence and conflict resolution. Wolfe et al. describe the different types of public education of diminishing cyberbullying before it occurs (Wolfe and Jaffe 1999). For adolescents and high-school age youths (13–18 years), Wolfe et al. recommend school-based awareness and skill development. Communities should make a collaborative effort to teach awareness about violence and conflict-resolution skills (Wolfe and Jaffe 1999). Issues related to dating violence and forming healthy intimate relationships should be emphasized. For adults (18 years and older) Wolfe et al. recommend public education, media campaigns to promote awareness about domestic violence. For the primary prevention in the context of cyberbullying, we approach the prevention in terms of design and education. As primary prevention

Fig. 9.3 Example of SMILE application that reacts to cyberbullying once it has already occurred by omitting posts including user-defined words from a users' social media timeline

for domestic violence functions, schools should educate children about the harms of cyberbullying and online harassment in order to prevent such incidences.

For the domestic violence continuum of harm framework, secondary prevention which is targeted to individuals following early signs of domestic violence are offered community-based early intervention. For individuals exposed to violence aged 13–18, crisis support, individual counseling, and educational groups are offered with an emphasis on intimate relationships. For adults, individuals exposed to domestic violence are provided with coordinated services (Wolfe and Jaffe 1999).

9.4 Nudging and Cyberbullying Mitigation

Tertiary prevention mitigation systems remind users of the positivity or the existing social support on their social media platforms either by leveraging existing content on their social media profiles, or collaborative filtering as is the case in the Positivity Generator application. These systems fall under nudging policy, as they make assumptions about users' lack of knowledge of existing social support or ways they can promote their personal well-being. These *tertiary prevention* for cyberbullying mitigation make an assumption that the current state of the victims decision-making is mindless and passive (Thaler and Sunstein 2008).

When describing potential *primary prevention* mechanisms, I recommend screenshot detection as well as escalation detection. These mechanisms use boosting policies to inform users to make rational decisions about moving forward. Screenshot detection, both in the example described on Snapchat as well as Facebook messages, merely inform a rational user of an action that may have violated the contextual integrity of the ephemerality of the social media platform, and allow the user to proceed accordingly.

In *secondary prevention* mechanisms, *SMILE* and *WatchYoProfanity* are both human-centered mechanisms that depend on rational individuals to pre-determine a list of words that may be perceived as harmful towards the recipients. These mitigation mechanisms rely on the contextual nature of cyberbullying. Furthermore, by giving users the choice to determine the words that are being filtered, these mitigation mechanisms respect the individual sovereignty of users and treat them as rational individuals.

While a nudge is intended to steer someone's decision making and behavior in a particular decision, these tertiary prevention systems use positive memory to influence mood which in turn may influence behaviors that result from intense repetitive cyberbullying. A nudge utilizes empirically documented knowledge about human's cognitive capabilities and weakness and changes context to influence decision-making. While in the mitigation systems described above, users explicitly make decisions immediately when interacting with reflective interfaces, these tertiary prevention systems may be more subtle in their influence on an individual. While the goal is to improve mood, research shows as well as the data collected in this study that being reminded of dear friends and memories may cause an individual to communicate and seek social support from friends which will in turn ameliorate the negative effects of cyberbullying on well-being.

Nudge theory is the notion of utilizing positive reinforcement and indirect suggestions to influence decisions (Kosters and Van der Heijden 2015). It has been used in law and policy (Amir and Lobel 2008) and to influence behavior change (Leggett 2014). Thaler and Sunstein describe "libertarian paternalism", also described as "nudging" which helps people make decisions without compulsion (Thaler and Sunstein 2003). The "nudged" individual is given choices to move forward with his/her decision making. Many of the design recommendations for cyberbullying mitigation throughout this thesis tie in with "nudge theory", giving individuals the freedom to ultimately choose their course of action but also giving recommendations that may prevent cyberbullying along the "Continuum of Harm" described below.

Many of the design recommendations for cyberbullying mitigation rely on *nudging* policies, or creating a social environment within a platform to influence the behaviors of a potential bully or victim. Some critics and adversaries of nudging behavior conjure that nudging undermines human sovereignty since it exploits human weakness to influence behavior on social media platforms. Nudge policies undermine autonomy (Wilkinson 2013) since such policies change and alter contextual factors in order to influence decision-making. Critics stipulate that only "rational persuasion" can respect the sovereignty of individuals when they make choices (Hausman and Welch 2010), and nudging policies, or in this case, nudging design mechanisms do not constitute as "rational persuasion".

9.4.1 Boosting Policy and Cyberbullying Detection

Nudging and *Boosting* are two varying approaches aimed at influencing individuals to make better decisions that lead to a better outcomes (Grüne-Yanoff and Hertwig 2016). While nudging aims to co-opt systematic biases to influence behavior, boosting policies are more targeted to individuals who are competent and make informed decisions while increasing their skills (Grüne-Yanoff and Hertwig 2016). At this end, critics have rendered some nudging policies manipulative (Hausman and Welch 2010).

Furthermore, Grüne-Yanoff et al. describe the differences between nudges from boosts. Nudges and boosts differ in the "(i) immediate intervention targets, their immediate intervention targets, (ii) their roots in different research programs, (iii) the causal pathways through which they affect behavior, (iv) their respective assumptions about human cognitive architecture, (v) the reversibility of their effects, (vi) their programmatic ambitions, and (vii) their normative implications" (Grüne-Yanoff and Hertwig 2016).

Nudges operated under the heuristics and biases (H&B) research program (Gilovich et al. 2002) that concludes that human biases are flawed as are motivations which leads to poor choices and decisions. Boosts, according to Grune, operate under the simple heuristics program (SH) (Gigerenzer et al. 1999), which argues that humans are "boundedly rational decision makers" and given the tools and skills, can make "good enough decisions". The design recommendations made in this chapter to *prevent* and *mitigate* cyberbullying fall under the category of "boost" policy, not undermining the autonomy of users, but giving boundedly rational decision-makers the tools to make rational decisions. Below, I demonstrate how the various design recommendations in this chapter keep users informed and thus utilize "boosting" design mechanism to ultimately help make users sound decisions along the cyberbullying *continuum of harm*.

9.5   New Directions for Automatic Detection
of Cyberbullying

Human Centered Machine Learning is an emerging field that incorporates the knowledge garnered from ethnographic studies into machine learning algorithms and techniques. Cyberbullying detection is a vital component of cyberbullying mitigation (Ashktorab et al. 2014; Ashktorab and Vitak 2016). Many participants across all of the studies conducted cited exclusion as a type of cyberbullying they had experienced. Exclusion can be defined as directed repeated exclusionary behavior (Willard 2007). Participants reported experiencing exclusionary cyberbullying on Snapchat, Facebook and Instagram. In this section, I give examples of different types of exclusionary cyberbullying and provide recommendations for detecting exclusionary cyberbullying.

9.5.1   Exclusion Through Photo Cropping

Through the participatory design sessions, I provided a prototype for *Exclusion Prevention* as a cyberbullying mitigation prototype. *Exclusion Prevention* alerts a social media user when using the cropping feature on sites like Instagram and crop out one or more people in the picture. When considering technologies required to implement this feature, face-detection-technology (Rowley et al. 1998) and other image processing tools can help detect whether someone has been cropped out of a photo. In the reflective interface designed for *Exclusion Prevention*, (as seen in Fig. 9.4), a reflective message prompts the user to reconsider posting since exclusion has been detected. The user then decides whether they want to continue with posting the picture. While crop detection has not been an explored area of research, far more computationally difficult automated image processing tasks like achieving high accuracy when detecting the optimal photo crop based on subjects' facial gaze have been explored (Santella et al. 2006). A supervised image processing algorithm considering features like color, pixels, photo size, and number of people can potentially discover whether a photo has been cropped to exclude someone (Bezdek et al. 2006).

Additionally, exclusion prevention can be aided by social network analysis methods of groups and cluster detection (Du et al. 2007). The changing dynamics of visible social media interactions (likes, comments) of individuals in groups can be a considered feature in an exclusion detection algorithm. For example, Palla et al. develop an algorithm based on clique percolation (Derényi et al. 2005) to discover relationships that characterize the evolution of communities (Palla et al. 2007). Such methods can be applied to detect exclusion cyberbullying within mitigation tools.

Fig. 9.4 Prototype of reflective interface in "Exclusion Prevention" application

9.5.2   *Like Solicitation Exclusion*

The studies in this chapter reveal Like Solicitation exclusion across various social media platforms. On ASKfm, I discovered two types of discourse that exhibit qualities that allow "Like-for-Like" exclusion: *Like Solicitation and Rating Discourse* and *Listing All people You follow Discourse*. In *Like Solicitation and Rating Discourse*, the users ask that whoever "likes" the discourse will receive some sort of interaction on the website through "rating", "compliments", or reciprocated "likes". In *Listing All people you follow Discourse*, users ask a user to list everyone they follow on the site (via @username). This discourse type reveals "hidden" information as the site structure prevents users from seeing their followers list unless they receive a "like" interaction or are tagged in a discourse type like this one. Both of these types of discourse exhibit qualities that allow exclusionary behavior. To prevent this type of exclusionary behavior, users can be reminded through the social media platform to deliver on their Like Solicitation statuses. Figure 9.5 shows a notification to encourage a user to deliver on the promise of commenting in exchange for the like that has been redeemed.

Fig. 9.5 Prototype of notification interface to encourage Like-Solicitation exchange

9.6 Ethical Considerations for Designing and Implementing Cyberbullying Mitigation

With increasing use and analysis of big data, ethical considerations have received significant attention (Boyd and Crawford 2012), and the CSCW community has been at the forefront of discussions regarding ethical collection and analysis of user data (Fiesler et al. 2015). Ensuring the confidentiality of data and anonymity of participants is especially important when (1) analyzing adolescents and (2) analyzing sensitive events such as self-harm, bullying, and suicide. While standards vary across institutions and industries regarding what constitutes "human subjects data" researchers have a responsibility to take all necessary steps to protect the privacy and safety of individuals in a dataset.

Ethical considerations were built into the research design process to minimize any potential for harm. The researchers carefully weighed risks of data collection versus the potential benefits to the user population from this study. Scraping and data analytics in the aforementioned studies were only administered on public profiles. I do not present any information that could be used to re-identify an individual participant.

One of the biggest challenges in designing cyberbullying mitigations studies is minimizing the possibility that an automated response would have a negative effect on the recipient. Researchers working with automated response systems in any environment must consider all potential responses to content–no matter how banal in nature; with young people experiencing cyberbullying, this becomes even more critical. Future researchers should carefully consider how the systems they design may affect the intended audience, both for the better and for the worse. As important as this technology is, the well-being of the people on the receiving side is always paramount. The biggest ethical issue with the study is participant risk (e.g., bringing cyberbullying up during mitigation make victims feel worse).

9.7 Conclusion and Future Work: Measuring the Effectiveness of Cyberbullying Mitigation Solutions

While previous studies resulted in potential solutions for cyberbullying mitigation, much work lies ahead. I have proposed a number of potential mitigation solutions and the technologies required to implement these solutions. Future research should implement and evaluate these solutions with users through longitudinal studies to evaluate the behavioral impact they have on bullies, victims, and bystanders. In addition, future work should leverage the existing technologies to implement the proposed solutions which are a result of co-design between researchers and adolescents.

My analysis and categorization of the different preventative types allows me to consider additional research questions, such as which preventative solution is most effective for cyberbullying prevention and how can I accurately measure this effectiveness. Until this point, technological cyberbullying prevention mechanisms have not been evaluated for effectiveness. The framework presented in this chapter provides a straightforward way to begin to consider how one would compare different solutions. The ethical challenges of such a study are daunting, but would provide critical insights to preventing cyberbullying.

References

Achenbach TM, McConaughy SH, Howell CT (1987) Child/adolescent behavioral and emotional problems: implications of cross-informant correlations for situational specificity. Psychol Bull 101(2):213

Amir O, Lobel O (2008) Stumble, predict, nudge: how behavioral economics informs law and policy. Columbia Law Rev 2098–2137

Ashktorab Z, Haber E, Golbeck J, Vitak J (2017) Beyond cyberbullying: self-disclosure, harm and social support on ASKfm. In: Proceedings of the 2017 ACM on web science conference. ACM, pp 3–12

Ashktorab Z, Kumar S, De S, Golbeck J (2014) iAnon: Leveraging social network big data to mitigate behavioral symptoms of cyberbullying

Ashktorab Z, Vitak J (2016) Designing cyberbullying mitigation and prevention solutions through participatory design with teenagers. In: Proceedings of the 2016 CHI conference on human factors in computing systems. ACM, pp 3895–3905

Barnes SB (2006) A privacy paradox: social networking in the united states. First Monday 11(9)

Bastian M, Hayes M, Vaughan W, Shah S, Skomoroch P, Kim H, Uryasev S, Lloyd C (2014) Linkedin skills: large-scale topic extraction and inference. In: Proceedings of the 8th ACM conference on recommender systems. ACM, pp 1–8

Beale AV, Hall KR (2007) Cyberbullying: what school administrators (and parents) can do. Clear House: J Educ Strateg Issues Ideas 81(1):8–12

Bezdek JC, Keller J, Krisnapuram R, Pal N (2006) Fuzzy models and algorithms for pattern recognition and image processing, vol 4. Springer Science & Business Media

Boyd D, Crawford K (2012) Critical questions for big data: provocations for a cultural, technological, and scholarly phenomenon. Inf Commun Soc 15(5):662–679

Campo JV, Bridge J, Ehmann M, Altman S, Lucas A, Birmaher B, Di Lorenzo C, Iyengar S, Brent DA (2004) Recurrent abdominal pain, anxiety, and depression in primary care. Pediatrics 113(4):817–824

Charteris J, Gregory S, Masters Y (2014) Snapchat selfies: the case of disappearing data. In: Hegarty B, McDonald J, Loke SK (eds) Rhetoric and reality: critical perspectives on educational technology, pp 389–393

Citron DK, Franks MA (2014) Criminalizing revenge porn

Cowie H (2013) Cyberbullying and its impact on young people's emotional health and well-being. The Psychiatrist 37(5):167–170

Derényi I, Palla G, Vicsek T (2005) Clique percolation in random networks. Phys Rev Lett 94(16):160202

Dinakar K, Jones B, Havasi C, Lieberman H, Picard R (2012) Common sense reasoning for detection, prevention, and mitigation of cyberbullying. ACM Trans Interact Intell Syst (TiiS) 2(3):18

Dinakar K, Reichart R, Lieberman H (2011) Modeling the detection of textual cyberbullying. In: The social mobile web

Du N, Wu B, Pei X, Wang B, Xu L (2007) Community detection in large-scale social networks. In: Proceedings of the 9th WebKDD and 1st SNA-KDD 2007 workshop on web mining and social network analysis. ACM, pp 16–25

Fiesler C, Young A, Peyton T, Bruckman AS, Gray M, Hancock J, Lutters W (2015) Ethics for studying sociotechnical systems in a big data world. In: CSCW. ACM

Gigerenzer G, Todd PM, t. ABC Research Group et al (1999) Simple heuristics that make us smart. Oxford University Press

Gilovich T, Griffin D, Kahneman D (2002) Heuristics and biases: the psychology of intuitive judgment. Cambridge University Press

Grüne-Yanoff T, Hertwig R (2016) Nudge versus boost: how coherent are policy and theory? Minds Mach 26(1–2):149–183

Hausman DM, Welch B (2010) Debate: to nudge or not to nudge. J Polit Philos 18(1):123–136

Hinduja S, Patchin JW (2010) Bullying, cyberbullying, and suicide. Arch Suicide Res 14(3):206–221

Hinduja S, Patchin JW (2014) Bullying beyond the schoolyard: preventing and responding to cyberbullying. Corwin Press

Kietzmann JH, Hermkens K, McCarthy IP, Silvestre BS (2011) Social media? get serious! understanding the functional building blocks of social media. Bus Horiz 54(3):241–251

Kim YS, Leventhal B (2008) Bullying and suicide. A review. Int J Adolesc Med Health 20(2):133–154

Kim YS, Leventhal BL, Koh Y-J, Boyce WT (2009) Bullying increased suicide risk: prospective study of Korean adolescents. Arch Suicide Res 13(1):15–30

King H (2016) Facebook's 'secret conversations' mode deletes messages for extra security

Kosters M, Van der Heijden J (2015) From mechanism to virtue: evaluating nudge theory. Evaluation 21(3):276–291

Kwan GCE, Skoric MM (2013) Facebook bullying: an extension of battles in school. Comput Hum Behav 29(1):16–25

Leggett W (2014) The politics of behaviour change: nudge, neoliberalism and the state. Policy Polit 42(1):3–19

Lenhart A (2007) Cyberbullying. Pew Internet & American Life Project

McCormick R (2016) Instagram's anti-abuse comment filter is rolling out now

McLaughlin JH (2010) Crime and punishment: teen sexting in context. Penn St L Rev 115:135

Menesini E, Nocentini A, Palladino BE, Frisén A, Berne S, Ortega-Ruiz R, Calmaestra J, Scheithauer H, Schultze-Krumbholz A, Luik P et al (2012) Cyberbullying definition among adolescents: a comparison across six European countries. Cyberpsychol Behav Soc Netw 15(9):455–463

Mesch GS (2009) Parental mediation, online activities, and cyberbullying. CyberPsychol Behav 12(4):387–393

Milvy E (2015) Eavesdropping on the seventh grade instagram show

Nasehi SM, Sillito J, Maurer F, Burns C (2012) What makes a good code example? a study of programming q&a in stackoverflow. In: 2012 28th IEEE International Conference on Software Maintenance (ICSM). IEEE, pp 25–34

Newton C (2017) Twitter begins filtering abusive tweets out of your replies

Nissenbaum H (2004) Privacy as contextual integrity. Wash L Rev 79:119

Nott J et al (2014) Video gaming on the feminist frontlines

Palla G, Barabási A-L, Vicsek T (2007) Quantifying social group evolution. Nature 446(7136):664–667

Rowley HA, Baluja S, Kanade T (1998) Neural network-based face detection. IEEE Trans Pattern Anal Mach Intell 20(1):23–38

Santella A, Agrawala M, DeCarlo D, Salesin D, Cohen M (2006) Gaze-based interaction for semi-automatic photo cropping. In: Proceedings of the SIGCHI conference on human factors in computing systems. ACM, pp 771–780

Sas C, Whittaker S (2013) Design for forgetting: disposing of digital possessions after a breakup. In: Proceedings of the SIGCHI conference on human factors in computing systems. ACM, pp 1823–1832

Schön DA (1983) The reflective practitioner: how professionals think in action, vol 5126. Basic Books

Sourander A, Klomek AB, Ikonen M, Lindroos J, Luntamo T, Koskelainen M, Ristkari T, Helenius H (2010) Psychosocial risk factors associated with cyberbullying among adolescents: a population-based study. Arch Gen Psychiatry 67(7):720–728

Thaler RH, Sunstein CR (2008) Nudge: improving decisions about health, wealth, and happiness

Thaler RH, Sunstein CR (2003) Libertarian paternalism. Am Econ Rev 93(2):175–179

Vitak J, Chadha K, Steiner L, Ashktorab Z (2017) Identifying women's experiences with and strategies for mitigating negative effects of online harassment. In: Proceedings of the 2017 ACM conference on computer supported cooperative work and social computing. ACM, pp 1231–1245

Wilkinson TM (2013) Nudging and manipulation. Polit Stud 61(2):341–355

Willard N (2007) Educator's guide to cyberbullying and cyberthreats. Center for safe and responsible use of the Internet

Wolfe DA, Jaffe PG (1999) Emerging strategies in the prevention of domestic violence. In: The future of children, pp 133–144

Xu B, Chang P, Welker CL, Bazarova NN, Cosley D (2016) Automatic archiving versus default deletion: what snapchat tells us about ephemerality in design. In: Proceedings of the 19th ACM conference on computer-supported cooperative work and social computing. ACM, pp 1662–1675

Young D (2014) Now you see it, now you don't... or do you?: Snapchat's deceptive promotion of vanishing messages violates federal trade commission regulations, 30 j. marshall j. info. tech. & privacy l. 827 (2014). John Marshall J Inf Technol Priv Law 30(4):6

Chapter 10
Youth Perceptions of Online Harassment, Cyberbullying, and "just Drama": Implications for Empathetic Design

Abigail L. Phillips

Abstract Cyberbullying, cyberstalking, and similar forms of online harassment have become a point of concern among youth, parents, school administrators, and communities. Researchers have spent considerable time debating definitions, prevalence, predictors, and prevention and intervention strategies. In this chapter, the author will explore the multifaceted nature of cyberbullying among young adults/teens (12–18 years of age), particularly the complex nature of identifying as bully, victim, bully/victim, or bystander. Clearly, this is not easy to grasp, pinpoint, or even evaluate. Through semi-structured in-depth interviews and structured video autoethnographies, eight young adults discussed how they engage with social media, the toxicity of various platforms, experiences as cyberbully victims, bullies, and bystanders, "just drama" versus harassment, and seeking and providing support. The findings reveal suggestions for technological applications and resources to improve youth awareness of challenges when engaging online. Additionally, findings express a greater need for empathetic design within social networking sites and online safety education.

10.1 Introduction

Cyberbullying, cyberstalking, trolling, and similar forms of online harassment have become a point of concern among youth, parents, school administrators, and communities. Researchers have spent considerable time debating definitions, prevalence, predictors, and prevention and intervention strategies. For this chapter, cyberbullying refers to "any behavior performed through electronic or digital media by individuals or groups that repeatedly communicates hostile or aggressive messages intended to inflict harm or discomfort on others." (Tokunaga 2010).

A. L. Phillips (✉)
School of Information Studies at the University of Wisconsin-Milwaukee,
Milwaukee, WI, USA
e-mail: abigail.phillips@usu.edu

© Springer International Publishing AG, part of Springer Nature 2018
J. Golbeck (ed.), *Online Harassment*, Human–Computer Interaction Series,
https://doi.org/10.1007/978-3-319-78583-7_10

In this chapter, the author will explore the multifaceted nature of cyberbullying among young adults/teens (12–18 years of age), particularly the complex nature of identifying as bully, victim, bully/victim, or bystander. Clearly, this is not easy to grasp, pinpoint, or even evaluate. Cyberbullying is also not limited to the above age range; it can continue into college, adult social circles, and the workplace. However, teenagers, as heavy users of social media, have a greater likelihood of being cyberbullied, cyberbullying, or witnessing cyberbullying. Girls in particular report more instances of victimization (Lenhart 2007).

The trends of cyberbullying have shifted as new social networking sites (SNS) and apps have emerged and gained popularity while others sites and apps declined and become defunct. Ask.fm, a U.K.-based anonymous SNS, became notorious for incidences of cyberbullying linked to suicides. In the past, Ask.fm users, primarily teenagers, were encouraged to ask and respond to questions, sometimes leading to cruel and violent responses. Now this practice has changed, largely due to increasing occurrences of cyberbullying and aggression.

The multitude and variety of online platforms available have created and opened a realm for ways youth can both victimized and victimize. As the demographic of Facebook has changed and become older, youth and emerging adults have turned to more visual platforms such as Instagram, Snapchat, and Yeti. These platforms have been used to leave comments on images, create accounts that focus on attacking classmates, and spread videos of abuse and sexual encounters.

Yet there has been a growth of action and attention to improving online experiences and empowering youth to report instances of cyberbullying (Bilton 2014; Cybersmile n/d; Stopbullying.gov n/d). This chapter will delve into the complexities of cyberbullying including the overlap between school bullying and cyberbullying; and will conclude with potential directions for technical applications and tools for discouraging cyberbullying and other forms of online harassment. Finally, a brief discussion about empathic design which has strong implications for SNS and social media apps.

10.2 Literature Review

10.2.1 Academic Definition

Traditional bullying, characteristically, typically occur in the school. Olweus (1994, 1173) provided the standard definition of bullying, "a student is being bullied or victimized when he or she is exposed, repeatedly and over time, to negative actions on the part of one or more other students". These aggressive behaviors are limited to the school setting. However, due to its online environment, cyberbullying can exist anywhere, at any time, and occur anonymously. Table 10.1 provides key differences between traditional bullying and cyberbullying. Online disinhibition contributes to the lack of accountability and empathy among some digital youth. Since cyberbul-

Table 10.1 Definitional differences between traditional bullying and cyberbullying (Phillips 2014)

Traditional bullying	Cyberbullying
Power imbalance between bully and victim	Bully or bullies can remain anonymous
Bullying behavior is repeated over time	Bullying behavior is repeated over time
Intention to cause harm	Intention to cause harm
Perpetrated by an individual or a group	Perpetrated by an individual or a group
Face-to-face interaction	Bullying behavior occur through an electronic device or online
Largely confined to the school or school day	Can occur anywhere and at anytime

lies are able to hide behind a computer or smart phone screen, they do not receive the same visual feedback of causing pain and harm that they would when face-to-face (Accordino and Accordino 2011). To those cyberbullying, repercussions for actions appear non-existent. These and other characteristics of cyberbullying make it challenging to completely define.

Complicating the creation of an agreed upon definition for cyberbullying are the varying cyberbullying roles: cyberbullying victim, cyberbully, and bystander (Mishna et al. 2008). With traditional bullying, the labels are known and clear: bully, victim, and bystander. For teachers and school administrators, it is easier to identify which student is playing which role and either met out punishment or provide aid and support. These labels are more challenging to assign. Gámez-Guadix et al. and a few other researchers have noticed this uniqueness of the online "bully/victim". A youth can cyberbully a peer or peers while also being cyberbullies by another peer or peers. With the power imbalance of bullying replaced by anonymity, cyberbullying can be carried out more easily and spread more quickly than face-to-face bullying.

10.2.2   Young Adult Definition

During interviews with youth, Marwick and Boyd (2011) found that youth, in contrast to researchers, do not call teen conflict and fighting "cyberbullying". Instead, they use the word "drama". The differences between teen language "drama" and adult language "cyberbullying" or "bullying" contrasts sharply. Drama is, like much of social media, *performance based* and *active*, often involving some degree of conflict (Marwick and Boyd 2014). According to the researchers, "'drama' allows teens to distance themselves from practices which adults may conceptualize as bullying". When using the word drama, youth remove themselves from the stigma attached to bully or victim. Drama refers to anything form teasing, gossip, trash talk, joking, meanness, disagreements, or relational aggression, "a nonphysical form of aggression whereby the perpetrator's goal is to inflict or threaten damage to relationships" (Dailey et al. 2015, 79). Many of which could, from the adult perspective, fall into a bullying or cyberbullying label.

When older youth (16–19) reflect and comment on cyberbullying, they often refer to it as occurring more while in middle school or something that is grown out of after middle or high school. However, while still under-investigated, cyberbullying extends beyond sixth through twelfth grades, occurring among college students and adults (D'Souza et al. no date; Watts et al. 2017). Similar to young adults, these harassing behaviors are often not recognized as cyberbullying; Defaulting again to the joking, gossip, and teasing labels.

10.2.3 Online Is Everywhere: From the School to Home to Beyond

Once an image, video, or message is shared on social media, the reach is powerful and nearly impossible to stop. The classic characteristics of bullying—repetition, power imbalance, intentionality—appear morphed when researching cyberbullying (Cuadrado-Gordillo 2011). Repetition becomes hard to define. A single video spreads beyond an initial sharing among classmates on Instagram and moves to hundreds or thousands of people. The physical power imbalance that supported the stereotypical jock and nerd bullying becomes an internet savvy power imbalance. Anyone can become a victim (Cuadrado-Gordillo and Fernández-Antelo 2016).

There is still crossover from traditional bullying to cyberbullying (Juvonnen and Gross 2008). What happens during the school day appears on social media platforms like Instagram and Snapchat through anonymous or semi-anonymous posts. Schools struggle with how to stop cyberbullying when anonymity plays a strong role in aiding the its spread. Youth frequently know who posts the original images, videos, or messages (Juvonnen and Gross 2008). The cyberbullies are often their classmates and, sometimes, friends. However, anonymous users continue to share these posts far beyond the school social ecosystem.

The spread impacts the ability to delete or even moderate harassing posts. There is the potential that these cruel messages can be shared community-wide, state-wide, or even further. Although less common than reported in popular press, cyberbullying-related suicides (Stanglin and Welch 2013; Staff 2018) do occur. Much like traditional bullying, the effects of cyberbullying will continue to impact the victim beyond middle and high school. Because cyberbullying is a relatively recent form of harassment, youth who engaged, witnessed, or experienced cyberbullying are only now leaving higher education. The research is early but indicates that cyberbullying, for some youth, continues into higher education and beyond (Watts et al. 2017). Cyberbullying in the workplace, trolling, and cyberstalking are realties for adults although infrequently discussed openly (Bastiaensens 2014).

10.2.4   Early Prevention and Intervention

Without a firm definition or approach to accurately measure occurrences of cyber-bullying, the prevalence of cyberbullying and online harassment among youth can vary greatly anywhere between 4 and 46% (Biegler and Boyd 2010). Teens rarely report to adults when they are being cyberbullied or harassed online, leaning on close friends for support (Ackers 2012). Confiding in parents and other adults is usually the final option (Slonje et al. 2013). The young adults participating in this study viewed parents and other adults as not understanding cyberbullying or being aware of when cyberbullying is occurring.

Education is key to decreasing the likelihood of cyberbullying in schools and at a home (Meredith 2010). Some schools have modified traditional bullying intervention and prevention programs to fit cyberbullying (Slonje et al. 2013). For many school systems, digital citizenship training has become part of the curriculum. Digital citizenship concerns, "the norms of appropriate, responsible technology use." (Ribble 2015). Teachers, technology professionals, principals, police officers, and other school officials may provide some sort of digital citizenship education. However, as information professionals, school librarians often take the lead in providing consistent media use (Hollandsworth et al. 2011).

While traditional, face-to-face bullying was easier to identify and control, cyber-bullying is not. In school bullying, parents could consult with teachers and school administrators for assistance. However, cyberbullying often occurs off campus and sometimes anonymous. This leaves schools with the dilemma of who is responsible for stopping the bullying. As cyberbullying has becoming more common, parents, researchers, and school administrators have reached out to legislators for action. Currently, there are no federal laws regarding cyberbullying, only state mandates and school policies (Stuart-Cassel et al. 2011). For example, both the State of Washington and Utah both have recent legislation regarding the instruction of digital citizenship in public schools (Digital Citizenship, Media Literacy, and Internet Safety in Schools Act 2017; Safe Technology Utilization and Digital Citizenship in Public Schools Bill 2015). However, with only two states providing this guidance, cyberbullying remains inconsistently and ambiguously assessed, doing little to help the victims and prevent future bullying.

10.3   Research Questions

This study has three research questions:

RQ1: How do young adults define cyberbullying?
RQ2: What cyberbullying experiences have young adults had or witnessed?
RQ3: How would young adults seek support if they encountered cyberbullying?
RQ4: How do young adults cope with cyberbullying?

10.4 Method

10.4.1 Data Collection and Analysis

Participants were recruited through research flyers posted at locations young adults frequented (e.g. coffee shops, churches, libraries) and through snowball sampling. Recruitment took place in a single state within the Southeastern United States. Data collection took place over one month during the summer of 2015 and ended once saturation was reached. Youth participants have been assigned the pseudonyms in Table 10.2.

This study applied two methods: semi-structured interviews lasting approximately 30 min followed by structured video autoethnographies. Structured autoethnography allows for collection of an individual's (whether a researcher or participant) personal narratives and reflections through written, audio, and/or visual recordings (Coffey and Atkinson 1996).

In this study, structured autoethnography took the form of video entries recorded by seven rural young adult participants. These participants were given pre-written prompts to help guide the video responses they recorded. The video prompts included questions such as:

- "Have you experienced cyberbullying while on social media? If yes, what happened? Have you ever witnessed cyberbullying while on social media? If yes, what happened?"
- "What if you had a friend being harassed on social media, what advice would you give them to help stop it? How would you help this friend? Do you think cyberbullying can be stopped? Do you think cyberbullying can be prevented?"

Interview and video transcripts were analyzed using Charmaz's approach to grounded theory (2006). Following this approach, data was analyzed as it was collected. Being an exploratory study, codes and categories emerged from the data and were fine-tuned through multiple coding passes.

Table 10.2 Young adult participants

Participant pseudonym	Demographic information
Sarah	Female, Caucasian, Eighth grade, 14
Joshua	Male, Caucasian, Tenth grade, 15
Mary	Female, Hispanic, Graduated senior, 18
David	Male, Caucasian, Graduated senior, 17
Claire	Female, Hispanic, Eighth grade, 14
Emma	Female, Caucasian, Ninth grade, 15
Calvin	Male, Caucasian, Ninth grade, 14

10.5   Discussion

After analysis, four major themes emerged: defining cyberbullying, witnessing and experiencing cyberbullying, seeking (or not) support, and coping.

10.5.1   Defining Cyberbullying

Young adults spent a considerable amount of time delving into different aspects of cyberbullying classification. This includes male/female differences in cyberbullying, identifying "drama", dating and relationship conflicts, "toxic people" online, cyberbullying roles (victim, bully, and bystander), the dual nature of cyberbullying, and maturing out of cyberbullying. Discussions varied by gender, with girls more vocal and willing to share opinions and personal experiences and boys very direct and nonchalant about discussions of online harassment and cyberbullying.

Participants clearly differentiated between the classification of drama and cyberbullying, particularly when referring to relationship and dating conflicts. Joshua, a tenth grader highlighted this, "Frankly, it's mostly girls. You hear about guys talking about all that crap too. Guys are more likely to talk about fighting. It's more physical. With girls, it's more about talking behind each other's backs. It's often people causing drama at school." Several participants described "toxic people" who trolled, trash talked, or harassed friends and strangers while online. Toxic people and cyberbullies at times were one in the same.

However, in other instances, for example during online gaming, toxic people were described as limiting their harassment to single instances of mean or hurtful remarks instead of the consistent harassment typical of cyberbullying. One male interviewee describes the structure of an online gaming community in which he participated. Within this community, players could report occurrences of harassing behavior to the moderators. All of the participants had witnessed cyberbullying in some form but only two had experienced cyberbullying. Interestingly, none of the young adults acknowledged that they participated in any cyberbullying, but several did participate in attempts to end the cyberbullying of friends.

10.5.2   Witnessing and Experiencing Cyberbullying

The majority of the youth participants described witnessing cyberbullying, ranging from helping a friend manage to observing it in passing as part of a normal day. One participant, Mary, recounted seeing friends deal with bullying on Instagram. She pleaded with her friend to ignore the bullying and not feed into it by responding. Like the majority of the participants, Mary expressed her reluctance to seek the help of parents and instead relied on friends. She offered an explanation for why,

I think that it's common for teens to first ask friends for advice. We even talk about our parents to each other. Because especially stuff online, you want that separate from your parents. It's your own thing to be online and your own friends. When something bad happens, you don't want to go running to your parents, 'Mom, Dad, what can I do?'

Another teen, Sarah, described how she helped a friend being bullied on Instagram,

This one girl who didn't even go to our school started posting comments about how she (Sarah's friend) was ugly to my friend's Instagram page. This random girl. I said something to her (the bully). She tried to go on my page but since my page is private she couldn't do anything. She stopped eventually. We all just blocked her.

When friends encountered cyberbullying, many of the teens tried to help. Some common attempts at help included recommending privacy settings adjustment or saying to ignore and/or block the cyberbully.

Only one teen, Claire, a rising ninth grader, shared her experience with cyberbullying through Instagram. A group of girls at her middle school began harassing through comments and posts on Instagram, early in the school year. Like her peers and an example of dealing with "drama", Claire, in an interview, shrugged off the bullying, saying it didn't bother her. Unlike other teens being cyberbullying, Claire reached out to her dad who quickly contacted the principal.

10.5.3 Seeking (or not) Support

Friends were the first line of defense for the majority of the teen participants in cases of cyberbullying. Friends formed a support group to which teens could turn to for support if they were cyberbullied or harassed online. These friends included both face-to-face and online friends. Mary, a recently graduated senior demonstrated the importance of her friend support group, "One friend had the girlfriend of an ex-boyfriend commenting on her Instagram pictures. This person did it just because she could. My friend first reached out to our friend group through group chat. She said she didn't know what to do or say about these comments. We all told her not to get involved with it…it'll cause problems. But my friend started commenting back to the bully."

Friends were empathetic, offered advice, and provided support for cyberbullied friends. Yet, the participants' acknowledged that there was a limit to this help and stated that at times help from friends could be ineffective. Usually, teens would report to an adult in extreme cases, when it "crossed that line", became "too much to handle", or involved "self-harm". The teens pointed out that there were stigmas attached to seeking adult help, especially seeking help from a school counselor. Again, like with friends, teen participants acknowledged that there were limits to how much adults could help and that, at times, this help seemed ineffective.

The participating young adults offered many reasons why they would not seek help from adults. These discussions with teen participants included more emotional language and discussions of feelings. The teen participants saw themselves and their peers as being scared, ashamed, and wanting to appear perfect. The teens admitted that part of the reason they may choose not to report to an adult is because they want to seem mature and present themselves as an "adult". They also didn't want to "make a big deal" out of the cyberbullying and feared repercussions as a result of reporting to an adult such as getting in trouble, having their devices taken, or losing internet privileges.

10.5.4   Coping

The participants offered a range of coping mechanisms, male/female differences in coping and dealing with cyberbullying/drama, technical possibilities, and reporting routes to help deal with cyberbullying or drama. Teens often diminished cyberbullying, relabeling these behaviors instead as drama, "meanness", or "toxic" people. Several teens claimed that they didn't let it get to them or they didn't get involved with "that sort of stuff". Teens also offered, "not letting it get to you" and "not get involved" as advice for their peers to avoid cyberbullying.

David, a recently graduated Senior discussed how adults could support cyberbullied teens:

> People know cyberbullying is an issue, and it certainly is. The best information I could give to anybody is not to say, "Hey look. This has happened before." They're not looking for that type of answer. They're looking for someone who is going to support them personally. They're looking for some type of support. The best answer I could give is to suggest going to get that support. There are many venues and outlets for great support system out there.

Several other coping techniques were suggested such as dealing with it alone, ignoring it, and avoiding it. Young adult participants appeared mostly to want to deal with cyberbullying alone and keep it quiet or within their small social circle. Another quote from Mary, a recently graduated Senior, spoke to this feeling,

> For some teens they would push it until it became time for legal action. They think they can deal with it themselves. I'm like you're only 16 or 17. You don't know everything yet. I think maybe they think that dealing with that would be a symbol that they were grown up or proving to themselves that they could deal with this. Even though you're supposed to be older at that age, you shouldn't have to deal with things like that. Especially when you're a teenager and so vulnerable to what people say.

More so than the female teens, male participants suggested using specific features of social networking sites such as privacy settings, blocking, and unfollowing as ways to avoid or deal with cyberbullying. Overall, these were typically the first step these teens would take when encountering a cyberbully.

10.6 Implications for Design

The young adults discussed the techniques they employ to prevent and/or stop cyberbullying and other types of harassment. Many of these include privacy settings and ways to report cyberbullying within the SNS or app itself. The teens in this study had personal rules regarding how they used social media use such as avoiding "toxic people" and "not getting involved" in the drama. However, as indicated by the literature, teens are aware of privacy and security issues but are not fully informed of social media best practices.

School systems are attempting to fill this gap by teaching digital citizenship. Some states, such as Washington and Utah, are passing legislation that mandates digital citizenship be included in the curriculum. Frequently school libraries, as information specialists, instruct K-12 students about digital safety, responsible social media use, and online harassment (Oxley 2010). These are preventative measures that aim to encourage youth to reflect on their digital practices and become mindful about how they engage with social media. However, once cyberbullying has begun, the resources provide little support or guidance for the youth involved. Education about digital citizenship and responsible online use is often pushed off until middle or high school but must begin sooner (Common Sense Media 2018).

Social networking sites and apps have developed reporting systems and techniques that encourage users to stop and think before they post. The defunct anonymous, location specific app Yik Yak contained a hidden word filter that would recognize harmful and threatening language and warn the user that this could be offensive (Trevor 2014). Instagram allows user to turn off commenting on posts, filter comments, and has a website containing additional safety tips. Facebook and Twitter both have a complicated history with cyberbullying, trolling, and other types of online harassment (Ditch the Label 2017). On Twitter (2018) users can request offensive or aggressive accounts be taken down; blocking these users form creating new accounts. Users can also block or mute posts from malicious and harmful users. Facebook (2018) has a similar reporting system and allows for users to customize privacy settings. These techniques rely on users to report posts and accounts, sometimes involving a lengthy, confusing, and uncertain process.

This information gap leaves an opening other technological implications. One possibility is empathic design. This style of design gathers, analyzes, and applies information gathered from observing people as they work and live. Empathy, the ability to understand and learn from another individual's experiences, plays an important part in design (Kouprie and Visser 2009). It requires compassion and active listening. In the interviews, young adult participants frequently used the word "empathy" when referring to on and offline friends, peers, and adults. At times, teens experienced and performed empathy and compassion while online.

Through resources and tool empathically designed, early education on digital citizenship, and guidance and support from adults and peers, young adults have better chance at recognizing when cyberbullying is happening and how to seek help (Davis et al. 2015). Tools and settings built into a social networking site or app alone cannot stop online harassment like cyberbullying and trolling from happening. There must be a strong support system including parents, teachers, school administrators, and other community leaders.

10.7   Conclusion

This chapter discussed a study into how young adults understand, seek support, experience, and cope with cyberbullying. The differences between cyberbullying and traditional bullying were highlighted as well as the difficulties in truly understand why "cyberbullying" means from the perspective of youth. Implications regarding empathic design and other supports were detailed and offered for reflection.

Being a teenager is never easy. The digital world offers freedom, identity construction, and Online or offline youth encounter peers who are destructive, cruel, and, in some instances, unaware of the consequences of their actions and words. It is not enough to monitor online activities of youth. A conversation must be started about youth behaviors on social media that includes a focus on education, design applications, and peer and adult support. Additionally, youth input is critical. To fully understand how to help and support youth, we need to know how this help and support can be offered and how it will be received.

References

Accordino DB, Accordino MP (2011) An exploratory study of face-to-face and cyberbullying in sixth grade students. Am Secondary Educ 40(1):14–30

Ackers MJ (2012) Cyberbullying: through the eyes of children and young people. Educ Psychol Pract 28(2):141–157. https://doi.org/10.1080/02667363.2012.665356

Bastiaensens S, et al (2014) Cyberbullying on social network sites. An experimental study into bystanders' behavioural intentions to help the victim or reinforce the bully. Comput Hum Behav 31:259–271. https://doi.org/10.1016/j.chb.2013.10.036

Biegler S, Boyd D (2010) Risky behaviors and online safety: a 2010 literature review. Harvard University, Berkman Center for Internet & Society

Bilton N (2014) At Facebook, creating empathy among cyberbullying. The New York Times, 22 Oct. http://www.nytimes.com/2014/10/23/fashion/Facebook-Arturo-Bejar-Creating-Empathy-Among-Cyberbullying.html. Accessed 3 Nov 2014

Charmaz K (2006) Constructing grounded theory: a practical guide through qualitative analysis. Sage Publications, Thousand Oaks, CA

Coffey A, Atkinson P (1996) Making sense of qualitative data: complementary research strategies. Sage Publications, Inc

Common Sense Media (2018) Scope & sequence: common sense K-12 digital citizenship curriculum. Common Sense Education. https://www.commonsense.org/education/scope-and-sequence

Cuadrado-Gordillo I, Fernández-Antelo I (2016) Adolescents' perception of the characterizing dimensions of cyberbullying: differentiation between bullies' and victims' perceptions. Comput Hum Behav 55:653–663. https://doi.org/10.1016/j.chb.2015.10.005

Cuadrado-Gordillo I (2011) Repetition, power imbalance, and intentionality: do these criteria conform to teenagers' perception of bullying? a role-based analysis. J Interpers Violence 27(10):1889–1910. https://doi.org/10.1177/0886260511431436

D'Souza N, Catley B, Forsyth D, Tappin D (no date) Cyberbullying at work: towards a framework for advancing research. http://www.anzam.org/wp-content/uploads/pdf-manager/1651_ANZAM-2014-202.PDF

Dailey AL, Frey AJ, Walker HM (2015) Relational aggression in school settings: definition, development, strategies, and implications. Child Schools 37(2):79–88

Davis K, Randall DP, Ambrose A, Orand M (2015) I was bullied too: stories of bullying and coping in an online community. Inf Commun Soc 18:357–375. https://doi.org/10.1080/1369118X.2014.952657

Digital Citizenship, Media Literacy, and Internet Safety in Schools Act (2017). http://lawfilesext.leg.wa.gov/biennium/2017–18/Pdf/Bills/Senate%20Bills/5449-S.E.pdf

Ditch the Label (2017) The Annual Bullying Survey. London, U.K. https://www.ditchthelabel.org/wp-content/uploads/2017/07/The-Annual-Bullying-Survey-2017-1.pdf

Facebook (2018) Help center: bullying. https://www.facebook.com/help/420576171311103/

Hollandsworth R, Dowdy L, Donovan J (2011) Digital citizenship in K-12: it takes a village. TechTrends 55:37–47

Juvonnen J, Gross EF (2008) Extending the school grounds? Bullying experiences in cyberspace. J Sch Health 78:496–505

Kouprie M, Visser FS (2009) A framework for empathy in design: stepping into and out of the user's life. J Eng Des 20(5):437–448

Lenhart A (2007) Cyberbullying. Pew Research Center, Washington, D.C.

Marwick A, Boyd D (2011) The drama! Teen conflict, gossip, and bullying in networked publics. In: A decade in internet time: symposium on the dynamics of the internet and society, Oxford, England

Marwick A, Boyd D (2014) It's just drama: teen perspectives on conflict and aggression in a networked era. J Youth Stud 17:1187–1204. https://doi.org/10.1080/13676261.2014.901493

Meredith JP (2010) Combating cyberbullying: emphasizing education over criminalization. Federal Commun Law J 63(1)

Mishna F, Wiener J, Pepler D (2008) Some of my best friends—experiences of bullying within friendships. School Psychol Int 29(5):549–573. https://doi.org/10.1177/0143034308099201

No Author (2018) Suicide of Australian teen ad star sparks cyber-bullying campaign, The Straits Times

Olweus D (1994) Bullying at school: basic facts and effects of a school based intervention program. J Child Psychol Psychiatry 35(7):1171–1190

Oxley C (2010) Digital citizenship: developing an ethical and responsible online culture. in: Diversity challenge resilience: school libraries in action in proceedings of the 12th biennial school library association of queensland. Presented at the International Association of School Librarianship, Brisbane QLD Australia

Phillips A (2014) More than just books: librarians as a source of support for cyberbullied young adults. J Res Libr Young Adults, 4(1)

Ribble M (2015) The basics of digital citizenship, in: digital citizenship in schools. International Society for Technology in Education

Safe technology utilization and digital citizenship in public schools (2015). https://le.utah.gov/~2015/bills/hbillenr/HB0213.pdf

Slonje R, Smith PK, Frisén A (2013) The nature of cyberbullying, and strategies for prevention. Comput Hum Behav 29(1):26–32. https://doi.org/10.1016/j.chb.2012.05.024

Stanglin D, Welch WM (2013) Two girls arrested on bullying charges after suicide. http://www.usatoday.com/story/news/nation/2013/10/15/florida-bullying-arrest-lakeland-suicide/2986079/

Stuart-Cassel V, Bell A, Springer JF (2011) Analysis of state bullying laws and policies. Office of Planning, Evaluation and Policy Development, US Department of Education. http://eric.ed.gov/?id=ED527524

Tokunaga RS (2010) Following you home from school: a critical review and synthesis of research on cyberbullying victimization. Comput Hum Behav 26(3):277–287. https://doi.org/10.1016/j.chb.2009.11.014

Trevor (2014) Best Yik Yak Tips, Tricks & Secrets. Appamatix. https://appamatix.com/best-yik-yak-tips-tricks-secrets/

Twitter (2018) About online abuse. https://help.twitter.com/en/safety-and-security/cyber-bullying-and-online-abuse

Watts LK, Wagner J, Velasquez B, Behrens PI (2017) Cyberbullying in higher education: a literature review. Comput Hum Behav 69:268–274. https://doi.org/10.1016/j.chb.2016.12.038

Chapter 11
Avoiding Online Harassment: The Socially Disenfranchised

Xinru Page, Bart P. Knijnenburg, Pamela Wisniewski and Moses Namara

Abstract As social media increasingly mediate our relationships and social lives, individuals are becoming more connected and gaining social benefits. However, many are now experiencing online harassment. Avoiding or abandoning social media is one common tactic to cope with harassment. This chapter investigates the harassment-related motivations and concerns driving social media non-use, as well as the benefits and consequences that result from not using social media. This research sheds light on a previously underexplored type of non-user who faces social barriers to using social media (as opposed to functional barriers). This chapter explains how such individuals encounter social consequences whether they are on or off social media, resulting in a lose-lose situation that we term *social disenfranchisement*. Building on Wyatt's framework and the risk-benefits framework, we introduce this previously unidentified category of non-use as an extension to the commonly used taxonomy and provide a cohesive theoretical framework within which to understand various types of non-use. We then analyze the phenomenon of online harassment from the perspective of this non-use framework. Addressing the concerns of socially disenfranchised non-users is of utmost importance in the fight against online harassment. As others are increasingly connected, they are increasingly left behind and even ostracized. This chapter therefore concludes by providing design recommendations to alleviate the negative social consequences currently endured by socially disenfranchised non-users.

X. Page (✉)
Bentley University, Waltham, MA, USA
e-mail: xpage@bentley.edu

B. P. Knijnenburg · M. Namara
Clemson University, Clemson, SC, USA

P. Wisniewski
University of Central Florida, Orlando, FL, USA

© Springer International Publishing AG, part of Springer Nature 2018
J. Golbeck (ed.), *Online Harassment*, Human–Computer Interaction Series,
https://doi.org/10.1007/978-3-319-78583-7_11

11.1 Introduction

There has been a rapid proliferation of social networking sites (SNSs) in the past decade, with 73% of U.S. online adults now using SNSs (Duggan and Smith 2014). 79% of those SNS users are using Facebook. Other popular platforms like Instagram, Twitter, LinkedIn, and Pinterest are being used by about a third of SNS adopters (Greenwood et al. 2016). While just a few years ago only a minority of SNS users were logging in daily, now over two-thirds of Facebook's users sign on every day, many doing so constantly (Duggan and Smith 2014). Researchers identify many benefits to using social media such as increasing one's social capital, better life satisfaction, increased social trust, and even stimulating offline civic and political participation (Ellison et al. 2007; Park et al. 2009; Valenzuela et al. 2009).

However, as social interactions increasingly take place on social media, so do new forms of online harassment and bullying. While people vary to some degree in their views on what constitutes online harassment (Smith and Duggan 2018), online harassment is generally perpetrated with the purpose of attacking the victim's social, economic, and/or emotional well-being (Beran and Li 2005). Direct threats range in severity from spamming, bothering or insulting an individual, to causing physical or psychological harm. Indirect methods of harassment can take the form of social exclusion or spreading rumors about that person (Wang et al. 2009). Among children and adolescents the term cyberbullying is often used to describe such harassment (for an overview see Kowalski et al. 2014).

Harassment negatively impacts the target by invoking feelings of caution, stress, fear, loneliness, distrust, and lower self-esteem (Šléglová and Cerna 2011). It can even lead towards physical actions such as self-harm and aggression towards family and friends (Hinduja and Patchin 2010; Šléglová and Cerna 2011). Research points to key differences in cyber harassment that make it different in nature and perhaps more far-reaching than offline harassment. Specifically, the mediated interaction and anonymity may present a lower barrier to engage in harassment (Suler 2004), while the lack of geographic boundaries present the ability for the aggressor to affect a wider range of individuals (Mishna et al. 2009).

Less research has focused on coping strategies for harassment but found they can vary based on individual characteristics, past experiences, and other contextual factors (Šléglová and Cerna 2011; Smith and Duggan 2018). Some people try to use technical forms of coping such as reporting, blocking or unfriending the harasser. Others will engage in diversions such as a hobby or sport they enjoy in order to take their minds off the harassment. Still others will seek social support from friends or family and sometimes confront the bully or make light of the situation.

Finally, many choose *avoidance*, such as not using the account where the bullying is occurring. In the context of social media, this may mean not participating on the social media platforms (e.g. Facebook, Instagram, Twitter) that most people around them are using (Duggan and Smith 2014). However, the many social benefits associated with social media use, and its increasing prevalence in mediating our social relationships, may leave these social media non-users at a disadvantage.

Those who experience harassment are not the only ones to opt out of social media use. In fact, despite the prevalence of social media, there are many online adults who are not using it—27% in the United States (Duggan and Smith 2014). Reasons for non-use vary, as do the consequences. In fact, our research shows that the experiences of non-users due to harassment significantly differ from those of other non-users.

In this chapter we investigate the experiences of individuals who self-identify as "social media non-users", examining their motivations and highlighting the tensions between choosing to engage in versus abstain from social media. Drawing on our non-use framework (Page et al. 2018), we illustrate how the constraints and consequences for those avoiding online harassment are very different than for other non-users. While many individuals address their problems by avoiding social media, neither use nor non-use can successfully overcome social consequences for those trying to avoid harassment. This leaves them in an impoverished state of *social disenfranchisement*, where they cannot win on or off social media. This chapter concludes by suggesting how researchers and designers can support these socially disenfranchised individuals by designing for not only the user experience, but also the non-user experience.

11.2   Understanding Non-use and Social Media

Scholars have studied technology non-use in a variety of contexts including social media (Baumer et al. 2013; Lampe et al. 2013), the internet (Wyatt 2003), and technology in general (Satchell and Dourish 2009). Researchers have emphasized how understanding non-use can help us understand the role and boundaries of technology use (Satchell and Dourish 2009; Wyatt 2003). In fact, the typical view of technology adoption and acceptance as a desired outcome can obscure situations where non-use could be voluntary. Satchell and Dourish (2009) point out how there is a "utilitarian morality" where adopting technology is seen as a good. For instance, if one views internet usage and access as a privilege, than non-use could wrongly be associated with being deprived of access and impoverishment, a state of disenfranchisement (Wyatt 2003). Thus, several scholars have taken to understanding non-use as a productive mechanism for overcoming addictive tendencies and gaining control of one's technology usage, or as an act of resistance (Baumer et al. 2015a, b; Portwood-Stacer 2013; Schoenebeck 2014).

This section presents a synthesis of themes across the non-use literature as well as a review of the social media non-use literature.

11.2.1   Characterizing Non-use

Non-use research commonly asserts that non-use should be represented along a continuum, rather than the binary distinction of adoption and non-adoption (Baumer et al. 2013; Brubaker et al. 2016; Wyatt 2003). For instance, non-use may occur as a short-term break, such as giving up Twitter for Lent, or Facebook for "99 Days of Freedom" (Baumer et al. 2015b; Schoenebeck 2014). Second, non-use is not a "singular moment" but a temporal process, "involving layered social and technical acts" over time (Brubaker et al. 2016). For example, Rainie et al. (2013) examined the fluidity of Facebook users and found that 61% had taken a break in the past, 20% had previously used Facebook but since left, and 8% were interested in using Facebook in the future. For short-term and intentional breaks, frequency of past usage has proven to be a significant predictor of premature "reversions" (Baumer et al. 2015b).

Given the non-binary and temporally fuzzy boundaries of non-use, researchers have developed many orthogonal taxonomies of types of non-users. An early taxonomy of non-use, which is frequently cited in subsequent literature, varied along two dimensions: temporality and volition (Wyatt 2003). Individuals had either previously used the technology or not. Those who had not used as a result of their own choosing were considered *resisters* while those who chose to abandon were considered *rejecters*. On the other hand, individuals who were prevented from use by an external constraint were classified as *excluded* non-users, while those whose usage was disrupted were considered *expelled*. The barriers preventing use for these latter two categories of non-users were extrinsic constraints such as lack of access due to infrastructure or socioeconomic status.

Since then, others have explicitly and implicitly extended this taxonomy to other types of non-use. Table 11.1 integrates these various extensions from the literature within Wyatt's foundational classification. In addition to Wyatt's four categories, we identified four additional categories of non-use from the literature: (1) *laggards*, (2) *relapsers*, (3) *limiters*, and (4) *displaced*. For instance, the category *laggards*, which hails from diffusion theory, implies that non-users are simply future users who have not "yet" adopted (Satchell and Dourish 2009).

Table 11.1 also specifies the temporality of adoption for each non-user type, as well as the level of choice involved. For instance, Baumer et al. (2013) identified *limiters* as a type of non-user; yet, in terms of adoption these individuals were actually users in the past, present, and likely future. They limit their usage due to intrinsic motivations, such as attempting to reduce addictive behaviors (Baumer et al. 2013).

Narrowing our attention specifically to social media non-use, we find that much of the literature has studied individuals who are *rejecters* of a given social media service. In large part they focus on how Facebook non-users differ from Facebook users. For example, Facebook users have been found to be less likely than *quitters* to be conscientious, have privacy concerns, or be addicted to internet use (Stieger et al. 2013). Users may also have lower levels of social bonding capital than non-users (Lampe et al. 2013). The literature also reveals other configurations of non-use such as *abstainers* (Portwood-Stacer 2013), *leavers, relapsers, limiters* (Baumer et al. 2013), as well as *break-takers* (Baumer et al. 2015b; Rainie et al. 2013). A much smaller number of studies focus on non-use of other social media platforms. Some recent studies include pausing one's Twitter use (Schoenebeck 2014), avoiding location-sharing social media in general (Page et al. 2013) or even specific location-based dating platforms (Brubaker et al. 2016). However, an investigation of those who avoid all social media platforms is conspicuously missing.

Table 11.1 Integrating the literature on types of non-users

Non-user classifications	Sub-classifications of non-use and notes	Temporality of adoption	Level of choice
Resister: individuals who do not use a technology by choice (Wyatt 2003)	• **Active resistance**: outright refusal to accept technology (Satchell and Dourish 2009) • **Disenchantment**: unhappy with how technology changes how things used to be (Satchell and Dourish 2009) • **Disinterested**: simply uninterested or passive avoidance (Satchell and Dourish 2009; Wyatt 2003)	Past use: no Present use:no Future use: N/A	Intrinsic
Excluded: individual who do not use a technology due to external forces (Wyatt 2003)	Also known as "**disenfranchised**" due to external factors, such as the "digital divide" (Satchell and Dourish 2009)	Past: no Present: no Future:desire, implied	Extrinsic
Laggards: individuals who have yet to adopt a particular technology (Satchell and Dourish 2009)	Drawn from the theory of diffusion of innovation, the S-curve for adoption maturity would assume potential "future" use (Satchell and Dourish 2009)	Past: no Present: no Future: yes, implied	Both
Rejecter: individuals who have stopped using a technology by choice (Wyatt 2003)	• **Abstention**: discontinued use in objection to or support of a particular cause (Portwood-Stacer 2013) •**Leavers/Quitters**: Those who were active users but left indefinitely (Baumer et al. 2013; Brubaker et al. 2016; Stieger et al. 2013) • **Break-takers**: Those who left a technology platform only for a given time period (Baumer et al. 2015b; Schoenebeck 2014)	Past: yes Present: no Future: no, implied	Intrinsic
Relapser: individuals who intend to stop using a technology but ultimately return (Baumer et al. 2013)	Another term used in the literature was "Reversions" for people who came back from a break earlier than intended. This type of non-use was often discussed in relation to addictive tendencies (Baumer et al. 2015b)	Past: yes Present: yes Future: yes, implied	Intrinsic

(continued)

Table 11.1 (continued)

Non-user classifications	Sub-classifications of non-use and notes	Temporality of adoption	Level of choice
Limiter: individuals who use social media but within specific parameters (Baumer et al. 2013)	This category illustrates the notion that non-use is not a binary "yes or no" adoption decision	Past: yes Present: yes Future, yes, implied	Intrinsic
Expelled: individuals who had previously adopted but stopped involuntarily (Wyatt 2003)	These individuals may also be considered "**Disenfranchised**" (Satchell and Dourish 2009) depending on the circumstances	Past: yes Present: no Future: desire, implied	Extrinsic
Displaced: individuals who use technology indirectly as a service (Satchell and Dourish 2009)	Also discussed as "**Indirect Use**" as a secondary use though others (Wyatt 2003). In terms of specific social media platforms, such as Facebook, displacement could also refer to using other platforms as an alternative (e.g., Google+) (Baumer et al. 2015b)	Past: N/A Present: yes, indirect Future: yes, indirect	Both

The literature further identifies common reasons that contribute to social media abandonment (Baumer et al. 2013, 2015b; Lampe et al. 2013; Page et al. 2013; Portwood-Stacer 2013; Rainie et al. 2013; Schoenebeck 2014; Stieger et al. 2013). They have helped us better understand the motivations and context in which non-use occurs. Barriers to use can be triggered by worries about one's data being misused and privacy violations. It can also arise from social considerations such as feeling like one is being manipulated or judged, avoiding excessive drama and gossip, preferring a different communication style, or other boundary regulation concerns. For some it can be as simple as feeling disinterested in the content and seeing it as a waste of time. It can even result as an act of political resistance.

The boundaries between many of these non-use concepts and motivations are blurry. To provide more clarity, we map these empirically driven findings into a cohesive framework based on Wyatt's taxonomy. We extend the framework to account for an additional temporal dimension we identify from the literature—that of (constrained) current and future adoption. Figure 11.1 illustrates a more holistic view of the non-use literature, highlighting examples from social media non-use research (figure originally appeared in Page et al. 2018).

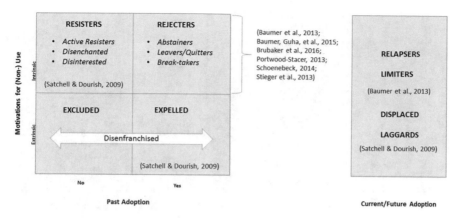

Fig. 11.1   Extending Wyatt's non use framework

11.2.2   Accounting for Online Harassment

While the social media non-use literature adds a richer understanding of technology avoidance, this chapter sheds light on a dimension of non-use that has not been considered previously. Unlike previous platform-specific non-use research, we investigated those who have abandoned or abstained from *all* social media platforms. In doing so, we found that fear of (and experiences with) being harassed on social media or in the offline world was a common theme for these individuals. In fact, this group differed from the *resisters* and *rejecters* commonly studied in the literature in that social media non-use for this population was mostly driven by *social engagement* barriers rather than *functional* barriers.

For example, Interviewee N (a postal worker in his sixties) explained, "I grew up in a time where there were no computers, so all the bullying I received was physical." Now as an adult, he is civically active and once again, "I seem to be a target…That is one reason I haven't embraced the whole social media aspect." This *social engagement* barrier is a fear of being harassed by others online. He received enough offline harassment and did not want to expose himself to more of the same in another medium.

Compare this experience with interviewee O, an elementary school classroom aide in her sixties whose son thought she would enjoy keeping in touch with people and set up her Facebook account. After the first day she stopped using it, un-intrigued by all the "day to day stuff…'I have a headache'. I don't want to hear that. It turns me off completely. That's a waste of my time." This *functional* barrier was a desire not to waste time and be bombarded with what she perceived as useless information. Interviewee O was *happy* to stay off social media and felt that solves her functional problem. In contrast, interviewee N felt compelled to avoid social media due to harassment, and thus *involuntarily* missed out on opportunities for social interaction on social media.

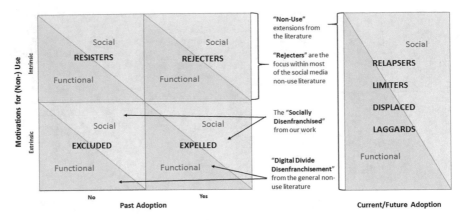

Fig. 11.2 Empirical and theoretical extensions to Wyatt's non-use framework

Acknowledging this important distinction, we have further extended Wyatt's (2003) taxonomy along this dimension to show that the driver behind non-use can be categorized as either due to *functional* barriers or *social engagement* barriers. Figure 11.2 (as originally introduced in Page et al. 2018) provides a cohesive theoretical framework that includes these dimensions. This distinction is critical in that the consequences from *functional* barriers to non-use can be resolved satisfactorily upon avoiding social media. Not so with *social engagement* barriers to non-use—in fact, in our analysis of our interview study data, we demonstrate that the consequences of being off social media can be just as bad as being on it. We thus identify a new sub-class of expelled and excluded non-users who are subject to social engagement barriers rather than functional barriers, and thus become *socially disenfranchised*.

We now illustrate by presenting the results of an interview study of social media non-users. This allows us to unpack how these types of non-use differ, and in this chapter we focus on those deterred from social media because of harassment.

11.3   A Study to Understand Social Media Non Users

We conducted a study that focused on social media non-use across all social media platforms (originally described in Page et al. 2018, summarized in this chapter). We interviewed seventeen adults who self-identified as "social media non-users" to understand whether they had previously used social media, their motivations for use and/or non-use, and their perceived and/or real benefits, risks, and concerns associated with social media use versus non-use. We further probed on if and why they would anticipate using social media at some future point. We drew on Wyatt's taxonomy (2003) to analyze the interviews based on whether non-use is intrinsically or extrinsically motivated, while also considering the *temporal* dimension of whether they had adopted the technology in the past or not. This analysis uncovered an additional dimension that should be considered when understanding use and non-use decisions, the *type* of adoption barrier. We found that adoptions barriers could be characterized as either *social engagement* barriers or as *functional* barriers. We uncovered this crucial distinction when we discovered that many of our interviewees who self-identified as "non-users" were still on social media to accomplish *functional* tasks for work even though they avoided using it for their own personal or social needs. Their conception of being a social media user consisted of using it for social reasons and they expressed social engagement-related barriers to doing so. This observation led us to uncover a stark difference between the experience of those who faced social engagement barriers in comparison with those who encountered only functional barriers.

Furthermore, by analyzing the interviews through the lens of privacy calculus theory (Laufer et al. 1973; Laufer and Wolfe 1977), we identified both the negative and positive forces that drive use or non-use. Weighing benefits and consequences (both perceived and actual) allowed us to understand how these factors drive users' adoption decisions. We found that when social reasons motivated these individuals to use social media (such as wanting to connect with friends), it wasn't enough to motivate them to continue using or to start using. Rather, perceived social engagement barriers (such as harassment) always outweighed the social benefit they were seeking. However, several interviewees felt that they may use social media in the future under a limited capacity, only to achieve functional goals (such as being able to get announcements from their work, school, or ecclesiastical organizations that were central to their lives). Indeed, several "non-users" already did engage in this type of occasional functional usage.

These insights lead us to describe a "non-use calculus" that describes how non-users weigh the costs and benefits of (not) using social media. It turns out that there are drawbacks experienced by this newly identified class of users whether they use social media or not. This creates a class of *socially disenfranchised* social media non-users who seek the social benefits that can come from being on social media, but are kept from those benefits as a result of social and emotional barriers. Ironically, being off social media does not keep them from experiencing those social consequences—it actually also worsens their state of social deprivation by introducing additional social consequences. For example, becoming a social media user can lead to social consequences such as harassment. However, as we will illustrate, staying away from social media can trigger other types of harassment. By exploring the different circumstance of those who face social engagement barriers, we bring to light the unique needs of this population. Moreover, by showing that they are deeply affected whether on or off social media, we point to the role of designers as designing and impacting not only their users, but their non-users as well. It is essential to make design decisions that will empower these individuals, who are currently stuck in a state of social deprivation.

11.3.1 Data Collection

We conducted semi-structured interviews about social media attitudes and usage with individuals in the United States who were at least 18 years old. A subset of those participants identified themselves as non-users of social media (N = 17). We focus on these individuals in this chapter. Interviewees were asked about their attitudes and any previous usage of social media. We explained social media by giving examples of popular platforms that are considered social media in recent Pew studies (e.g., Facebook, Instagram, Twitter, Snapchat, LinkedIn) (Greenwood et al. 2016). To reach a diversity of participants in terms of age and socioeconomics, we recruited participants from several sources: a mid-sized private university in the Northeast, the local community and industry, and the extended social networks of the researchers. We also utilized a snowball sampling approach to reach non-users, which turned out to be more difficult to find than users. Participants were asked about past usage, motivations, attitudes about social media, perceived benefits and drawbacks. These non-user interviews took place in 2016 during the summer.

11.3.2 Data Analysis

Drawing from our framework extends Wyatt's (2003) taxonomy (see Fig. 11.1), we conducted a thematic analysis. We first considered *temporality of adoption* by exploring interviewees' past usage, current non-usage, and possible future usage. We also asked about *motivations* behind each use/non-use decision, and classified these as intrinsic needs or extrinsic constraints. Finally, we drew on the privacy calculus framework (Laufer et al. 1973; Laufer and Wolfe 1977) that analyzes disclosure decisions as the outcome of weighing costs against benefits. The privacy calculus has been used in prior social media non-use (Baumer et al. 2015b; Lampe et al. 2013) as well as adoption (Xu et al. 2009) studies. However, we focused beyond privacy-related motivations and treated it as a broader "non-use calculus". That is, privacy was only one of many possible factors to weigh when considering the costs, risks and benefits of non-use. We used open coding to identify these non-use factors (i.e. potential/actual benefits and costs) and motivations for previous, present, and future use or non-use. Two researchers independently coded the interviews. Any coding conflicts were discussed and resolved.

11.4 Characterizing Social Media Non-Users

11.4.1 Participant Characteristics

Table 11.2 summarizes characteristics of our participants, who represent a variety of socioeconomic backgrounds and age ranges. All participants identified themselves as social media non-users; however, during the interviews we commonly found that interviewees actually used one or more social media platforms. It turned out that participants viewed their usage of these services as serving a *functional* purpose (e.g. to communicate with someone in an organizational context) and not a way to engage with others socially. This led to the realization that non-users perceived "social media users" as those who use it to cultivate *social engagement*. Based on this finding, we classified interviewees' actual and anticipated social media non-usage as *social* or *functional* to more clearly illustrate the type of usage they engaged in. Table 11.2 also categorizes participants based on Wyatt's (2003) dimensions of past usage as well as *intrinsic* versus *extrinsic* non-use motivations.

Our participants each represent one of Wyatt's four types of non-use (2003): *rejecters, resisters, excluded, and expelled*. It is important to note that these classifications refer to non-use as a result of social barriers as opposed to more functional, socio-economic constraints. All of the interviewees could afford and had access to smart phones with data plans as well as home computers and other devices. Most of them had used social media in the past and did not experience any technical barriers. Even those without social media experience were capable of using other technologies and expressed no anxiety around doing so. Rather, it was often the anxiety around social consequences that led half of these interviewees to choose to be *displaced* non-users, occasionally getting indirect access to social media via a family member. A few interviewees infrequently used social media for functional purposes, but not for social engagement. This emphasizes how their Wyatt classification reflects social usage, not functional. Finally, all participants described how they were surrounded by social media users, usually including their spouses and their closest relationships.

11.4.2 Motivations for Use, Non-use, and Potential Future Use

Here we describe what motivated some of our participants to use social media in the past, their reasons for discontinuing, and what, if anything, would motivate them to start using social media in the future.

11.4.2.1 Why Non-users Engaged in Social Media in the Past

Most of our interviewees had engaged with social media in the past. Some were motivated by intrinsic, social engagement factors, such as the desire to engage with their friends, or keeping updated about how others are doing. A *rejecter*, D, explained how he was motivated to join Facebook to be "able to connect with some people that I haven't seen for a long time." On the other hand, some interviewees were extrinsically nudged by their loved ones such as an adult child or a close friend. L, an *expelled* interviewee explained that "my youngest was going off to college, and I was going

Table 11.2 Self-identified non-user participant profiles

ID	Gender	Age range	Occupation	Past use	Non-user type
A	M	20's	Computer programmer	Facebook*, Twitter, Snapchat, LinkedIn, etc.	Expelled (being a good soc. media citizen, false sense of community, change who I am, data privacy)
B	F	20's	Youth counselor	–	Resister (too much useless info)
C	F	20's	Dance student	Facebook (1 day), Instagram*	Expelled (bullied)
D	M	30's	Legal field	Facebook	Rejecter (too much useless info, misleading info, data privacy)
E	F	30's	Attorney	Facebook, LinkedIn*	Expelled (being a good soc. media citizen, misleading info)
F	F	30's	Government	Facebook*, Instagram*	Excluded (being a good soc. media citizen, change my identity)
G	M	40's	Finance	Facebook*, LinkedIn*	Rejecter (too much useless info)
H	M	40's	Scientist	Facebook, MySpace, LinkedIn*	Rejecter (too much useless info, data privacy)
I	F	40's	Secondary school teacher	–	Excluded (false sense community, data privacy)
J	F	40's	Researcher	–	Resister (too much useless info, data privacy)
K	M	50's	Civil engineer	–	Resister (too much useless info, misleading info)
L	F	50's	On disability	Facebook (1 day), Twitter*	Expelled (being a good soc media citizen, bullied, false sense of community)
M	F	50's	College coach	LinkedIn*	Resister (data privacy)
N	M	60's	Postal worker	LinkedIn*	Excluded (bullied, misleading information)
O	F	60's	Classroom aide	Facebook (husband now uses the account)	Rejecter (too much useless info)
P	F	60's	Multi-level sales	–	Excluded (being a good soc. media citizen)
Q	F	60's	Retired	Facebook (1 day)	Expelled (change who I am)

*An asterisk denotes that the usage of the platform was purely for functional purposes. Those who are excluded from social uses of social media may still have used for functional purposes

to miss her a lot. And so, she said, you need a hobby or something. You take care of your kids all your life, and there's nothing left…So she said to go on Facebook." These individuals signed on to social media at the encouragement of those interested in their social well-being.

In contrast, those who were functionally motivated treated social media as a tool to accomplish some more practical, often work-related goals. This type of use could also be classified as driven by extrinsic or intrinsic factors. For instance, G, a *rejecter* treated LinkedIn as a Yellow Pages: "I really don't use it as a social media site…I really don't look at the connections. I don't contact anyone in LinkedIn. But I'm there in case people want to connect with me." Some interviewees were personally motivated to use Facebook or LinkedIn to spread the mission of their organization. E, an *expelled* participant would occasionally think to "share media campaigns that are part of some policy reform effort that we're doing. But that's different, that's not personal, that's just for work." Occasionally, functional use was pushed onto individuals. For instance, several past users had to sign up for certain types of social media accounts to use third-party services. Social media was also often used as the primary communication mechanism at work or for community, religious, and other organizations central to the individual's life. In these cases, a heightened burden was introduced through extrinsically-driven functional use. For example, F, an *excluded* interviewee, describes how her old school "put our whole class on Facebook…all of a sudden I started getting these like emails like friend requests [and] I was so livid I literally called Facebook headquarters and was like, I want you to take everything down." This frustration was echoed by those trapped into using social media to perform everyday tasks and goals.

11.4.2.2   Why They Disengaged

The literature has often focused on *rejecters* and identified a number of reasons that cause them to leave social media. These are similar to the more functional concerns we identified, including informational data privacy (from government, future employers, etc.) (Baumer et al. 2015b; Lampe et al. 2013; Stieger et al. 2013), accuracy of social media such as "fake news" or others' unresearched opinions (Baumer et al. 2015b), or being subjected to a flood of uninteresting or overly dramatic posts (Baumer et al. 2013; Rainie et al. 2013). While non-users of every type vocalized these concerns, we were able to uncover several additional motivations for non-use that were very different in nature and that came largely from socially *excluded* and *expelled* non-users, which had not been previously identified in the literature. These motivations for non-use trace back to social media's negative influence on one's relationships as well as ability to shape one's identity. We describe four of these non-use motivations here. Three of these reasons for disengagement were expressed by both those who experienced online harassment and those who did not, although the impact of each of these was more severe for those experiencing harassment. The last category (bullying) was unique to those who had been harassed. Interestingly, even though bullying was triggered by an intent to harm, the other causes consist of unintentional harmful behaviors by others. This illustrates how other's unintentional behavior can lead to the same types of problems as intentional harm (or harassment).

Being a model citizen on social media. Several interviewees held high expectations about what it means to use social media. They felt like they had to maintain an active presence, keeping all of their posts and information up-to-date, as well as reading others' posts. These non-users were overwhelmed at the thought of keeping up with everyone's lives and maintaining their own presence. *Expelled* participant E explained:

> It felt like something I just can't accomplish...If you really want to do Facebook right you really feel like you need to be on top of it, checking it on a daily basis...There's a ton of posts...and that's something that I have to admit I just kind of feel like I can't even get through it all so why bother...that's just a lot more time that I don't have.

When she gave up Facebook, E often missed life events of good friends such as the birth of a child. Several times she "engaged temporarily only to get overwhelmed by the amount of content and disengaged again." The effort to stay active and maintain a presence was so burdensome that non-users like E felt they should not be using social media at all. In fact, they expressed that a poor presence on Facebook would damage their relationships and so they might as well avoid it completely. These individuals realized that being on social media creates an implicit expectation that they will keep everyone updated and stay updated on everyone's posts as well. These non-users pointed to how friends would operate under the assumption that they saw posts, an unintentional pressure that led to these feelings of anxiety. Some interviewees were internally driven to excel: "[If I] got on Facebook, I would want to make it like the most, you know, informative, pretty page. And then I would spend more time on the computer than I already do looking 'oh, what is everybody else doing' and it would suck me in." This *excluded* non-user, F, acknowledged her own inclinations to be a model social media citizen.

However, this pressure manifest in a more negative way for those exposed to harassment such as A: "The deciding factor in my abandonment of social media is the fact that when I was trying to use it, it caused me great amounts of stress...situations like 'This person I knew in high school sent me a friend request, I liked them then, but haven't talked to them in ten years, do I accept them or not?' ridiculously uncomfortable for me." Being afraid of acting in a socially unacceptable way was a hindrance to being on social media at all for this individual.

Lured into a false sense of community. Although several interviewees wanted to feel connected with others on social media, they came to the realization that only superficial connections are created. D explained how rather than connecting with his friends, "It was kind of a waste of my time. Because I didn't really talk to the other people that I knew very often, and neither did they talk to me." However, some who were harassed described how there was a deeper problem even when people did connect on social media: "[People] have 'friends' that they block (but don't actually unfriend) because they actively dislike them, but feel some sort of social obligation to have them as friends...This creates a sense of false community...it lets people pretend to be connected to others when they aren't really…I think social media is a plague. I think it lets people pretend to be connected to others when they aren't really." Here, A was looking for a community but expresses extreme discouragement when he realizes that the relationships are actually rather empty.

Negatively shaping who I am. Several non-users expressed concerns about how social media would negatively shape who they are and encourage unhealthy behaviors. I, an *excluded* interviewee, decried how people are relying on their social media networks for advice to tell them how to feel, rather than learning to be self-reliant:

> [If] I have a bad day, I can say some four-letter words, throw something down, and I start working myself out of it…[if] I put it in writing, people are going to continue that bad moment by having it come back at me [reinforcing how bad it is]…You don't learn to rely on your own [character]….where is the time where you can become yourself?…If you're told how to do something all the time, and for years, you're always going to look for the instruction of how to do things.

This interviewee felt she would lose her personal character and independence if she joined social media. Having others shape how she thinks by reinforcing negative emotions is a drawback. Although these other people may not have an intent to harm her, their behavior could be viewed as something that causes unintentional harm—it reinforces and brings about negative emotions—although that may or may not be the intent of the poster. On the other hand, some harassed participants focused on how social media develops maladaptive traits in others, such as promoting gossiping or cyberstalking. Negative behavior such as gossiping could be considered an indirect way of inflicting harm and lead to similar consequences as harassment.

Dealing with bullying. Social media could serve as an opportunity to find support for individuals who are bullied offline. Unfortunately, bullies followed some participants onto social media despite privacy controls to hide content or other features designed to help people reject friend requests. L explained how her daughter helped her set up her account to only be viewable by friends, but somehow her sisters-in-law still found out what she had posted:

> My husband came home mad. 'My sister's mad. You put something on there.' And I'm like, I didn't put anything on there, except for, you know, who I am and what I like, or something, you know?… So they tell him what I can and can't do and whatever, and he goes along with it. So my daughter said, 'You're right. This is not going to be pretty for you, so let's just get you off.'

This example illustrates that even what might seem like a lighter form of harassment at face value, such as being judged, can be detrimental and trigger additional offline forms of harassment by others. In this case, judgements by L's sister-in-law triggered offline harassment from her husband. Just one episode was enough to make her discount the social benefits of being connected to old friends and renewing social connections now that her daughter would be leaving to go to college.

Several interviewees similarly described using technical features to prevent information from getting to the wrong person, but were bewildered about the complex display logic on these platforms when it still somehow fell into the wrong hands.

Nonetheless, even when it was clear how the privacy feature worked, there were social barriers to using them. For example, C described how she would not consider blocking or unfriending people who bullied her:

[If I] see the friend request initially, [it] would probably spark some anxiety within me. Like reopening the old wounds from middle school that I've healed and don't want to necessarily remember. And even though they were unkind to me, I still have an issue being rude to somebody...I don't want to hurt their feelings, because I wouldn't want anybody to feel the way that that person made me feel. But at the same time, I just don't want to be in contact with them, or anything remotely close to contact.

This non-user realized that she would encounter past bullies and present-day critics of hers on social media which "would be another way to hurt my self-esteem." However, her sense of humanity prevented her from saying no to friend requests. This illustrates how settings that can technically accomplish a task do not necessarily constitute a socially acceptable solution. A common refrain from our non-users was that they wanted to be conscientious. Designers should consider the social meanings and implications behind any features designed to allow this population to become users.

Furthermore, sometimes interviewees would encounter distress without anyone intentionally inflicting harm. Rather, it was the platform's algorithm that unwittingly committed the violation. For instance, Facebook would make friend suggestions and pictures of former bullies would appear. A feature meant to offer serendipitous rediscoveries of past connections or of second- or third-degree relationships becomes a way to perpetuate harassment over time, without any person actually instigating. A context collapse is created by shrinking the geographic and relationship distance between people on social media, which leads to improper intersection of different social circles and contexts (Marwick and Boyd 2011; Vitak 2012). This makes it easier for past harassment to resurface.

11.4.2.3   Why They Might Rejoin

Interestingly, participants who left social media to avoid negative consequences never expressed a desire to rejoin social media for socially motivated reasons. Instead, they anticipated missing out on some social benefits due to their absence from social media. Those who did express an interest in rejoining did so due to intrinsic motivations that were purely functional and fully anticipated negative social repercussions and emotional distress. However, the need for addressing certain functional needs warranted taking these risks. Specifically, concerns about keeping a child safe online overrode personal anxieties about being on social media for several non-users who might use social media in the future to monitor their child's account. Participant N, who became an *excluded* non-user due to bullying, said he might rejoin social media to help his organization share their uplifting messages, despite anticipating "negative responses" targeted personally at him. This highlights the catch-22 for individuals facing online harassment—opting out of social media is often not a viable option in today's society that relies so much on social media as a communication channel.

One cannot simply avoid social media to prevent online harassment because another form of harassment, the type that perpetuates through exclusion, becomes imminent. For instance, many websites now ask users to log in using their social media accounts, which creates a barrier to entry for those who do not have or have closed their accounts. Indeed, even A, one of the *expelled* interviewees who has experienced frequent harassment for being *off* social media, had to create a social media account to fulfill his job duties. In such cases, non-users must become compulsory users. This means enduring online harassment as a necessary evil if they want to accomplish everyday tasks.

11.4.3 Linking the Past, Present, and Future

We found that the motivations behind past usage seemed to predict current and future non-use. Drawing on Wyatt's (2003) taxonomy, we grouped participants' motivations to use social media by the dimensions of intrinsic (e.g. "I wanted to keep in touch" or "I wanted to promote this cause") versus extrinsic motivation (e.g. "my daughter thought I would like to be connected" or "the organization asked that we communicate this way"). We then further categorized the participants based on the dimension of *social engagement* versus *functional use*. We found that intrinsically motivated functional use was the only type of usage likely to persist over time. Even though these users identified as "non-users" given their social disengagement, some were still functional users, and functional reasons could trigger them to consider using social media in the future. As discussed earlier, two participants expressed that they would use social media to monitor their children once they became social media users. Otherwise, they both said that no socially motivated reasons were compelling enough to make them rejoin. Extrinsic motivations also appeared to be less influential than intrinsic reasons for rejoining. Most of the extrinsically motivated functional use failed to keep users engaged with social media over time. This demonstrates how intrinsic motivations are generally a stronger driver, unless one is physically (or digitally) compelled to use social media. The only extrinsically motivated use that continued was a computer programmer who worked with social media sites and needed to test his code using a Facebook account. Even though this represented an extrinsic functional motivation, it was one that was consistently required over time due to his job. Most other participants only needed to be on social media intermittently for their jobs.

11.4.4 Articulating a Non-use Calculus

We introduce a "non-use calculus" framework to better understand how interviewees weighed the positive and negative consequences associated with being on or off social media. This calculus tended to work against social media usage, resulting in limited functional usage or complete disengagement from social media.

11.4.4.1 Weighing the Benefits of Use Against Non-use

Non-users who previously used social media perceived few social or functional benefits of social media use. However, many had originally hoped for social benefits. Many acknowledged that social media is like a virtual phone book; several individuals valued that others could reach them through their social media accounts. Several interviewees also appreciated being able to promote their organizations or a cause by posting to social media. Participants also discovered they could be included on event invitations by being on social media. Yet, to these non-users, the benefits of non-use outweighed that of use. Overwhelmingly, the amount of information on social media was too much and interviewees felt they saved a lot of time by steering clear of social media. They no longer had to worry about personal data breaches or online privacy issues. Additionally, they did not have to constantly assess the authenticity of information or people—instead, they felt that they were able to rely on more reputable sources for news and opinions in the offline world.

By leaving social media, non-users reported that all of the functional concerns and consequences of use were resolved. The functional concerns and consequences simply translated into benefits of non-use. Those who never used social media also voiced concerns that corresponded to actual consequences experienced by other study participants, which leads us to infer that non-users who have never engaged with social media are fairly perceptive about how using social media would negatively affect them.

The social benefits of non-use were equally compelling. Avoiding judgement and criticism from social media was a huge benefit for non-users who were already subjected to offline bullying in their youth, or even now as adults. Participants commonly alluded to this non-use benefit by saying it made "life simple." They were also relieved not to have to constantly update their profiles or keep up with what others posted. Furthermore, they felt less pressured by their social networks to think or behave a certain way.

11.4.4.2 Social Consequences of Non-use

However, negative social consequences of social media non-use persisted. Almost every individual that was driven towards non-use by a particular social concern also experienced a social consequence from being off social media that corresponded to that original concern. Furthermore, it was mainly *expelled* and *excluded* non-users who vocalized these social concerns and consequences of non-use. They felt alienated from social media but were also now experiencing negative consequences from not being on social media. By choosing not to engage in social media, others were now shaping their online identities for them. They felt socially isolated due to lost social connections, and many still had to contend with offline bullying without any online social support to counteract these negative experiences. Specifically, those previously facing online harassment experienced more severe consequences of non-use than other non-users. Ultimately, they just could not win. This lose-lose phenomenon of social media non-use (i.e., *social disenfranchisement*) has not been widely recognized in the literature until only recently (in Page et al. 2018). It represents a critical problem that has not been addressed within the online harassment literature, as individuals cannot simply disengage from social media to avoid online harassment. We illustrate each of these themes in more detail below.

Losing control over my identity. Interviewees explained that their friends who were social media users often posted about and tagged them, even though they were not able to curate this content. Consequently, non-users' identities were then being shaped by others. Even though non-users often left social media due to identity management and social concerns, those around them were still engaging in maladaptive social behaviors that implicated them, such as gossiping and creating other online drama. Social media users can thus shape the non-user's identity *despite* their absence from social media. Even worse, by not being present, it was even harder for non-users to manage harmful or misrepresented content that involved them. Some interviewees worried about family members posting unflattering pictures of them, and non-users who previously experienced online harassment were concerned about even more extreme forms of unwanted (mis)representation. For instance, A described how his friends created a social media profile for him without his consent: "Actually, now that I think about it I have a Facebook profile under my name that I don't even have the login info for. My friends created it to troll me for refusing to be on Facebook myself. They'll check 'me' into mildly embarrassing places and post things pretending to be me." This illustrates how non-users may lose control over how they present themselves on social media.

Missing social connection and a sense of community. Despite realizing that there is a false sense of community on social media, several non-users also reported losing real social connections and a sense of community offline. Many expressed sentiments of being "left behind" and losing friends who chose to build stronger bonds with others through social media, drifting apart from the non-user. This is especially true for several of the harassed non-users. C sadly explains:

> I have a friend group that I've been friends with for about a year now, and they've recently stopped, like, inviting me to come to stuff, because they all have a Facebook page together and they all tell each other through Facebook. And so, they just either forget to invite me or don't tell me outside of Facebook. So, I've, you know, sadly had to lose a few friends because of it too. They have a big group message and they send each other stuff through that and, like, they're—it's pretty much constant contact between that group. And just, you know, they forget that I don't have Facebook, and they don't necessarily seem to care.

Expelled and *excluded* interviewees commonly expressed this feeling of being left behind. Although they hoped for more in-person interactions with others by leaving social media, it did not happen. One interviewee felt like, "I have something else to compete with; not just the TV or the newspaper, but Facebook." Instead of socializing with her, people were socializing on social media and "sucked into their phones." Non-users seemed so few and far between that offline relationships without an online component seemed rare, giving non-users a sense of social isolation. Even offline social events were problematic since the invitations came through social media and non-users were often forgotten or found out at the eleventh hour. They were also the last to find out how others are doing. They felt that previous channels of communicating social news have been replaced by social media. Christmas cards, family pictures, and bridal shower invitations now rarely come through postal mail, photo-sharing websites such as Flickr, or even email. Therefore, they missed out on a number of important announcements, such as births, graduations, marriages, and deaths, all momentous events that they would have liked to share with their friends.

Offline bullying. Disengaging from social media did not solve issues related to bullying for our non-users. Worse yet, they missed out on benefitting from online social support that could have offered relief. L expressed how she "probably would have stayed on there if it wasn't for the harassment of my relatives…. I feel like I don't have a life… I don't have a job, I can't go anywhere," and she still had "in-law issues on a daily basis, of them calling, harassing." She felt social media would be "fun, seeing how people who've been in your life before [are doing], and you wonder where they are."

In summary, functional consequences could be resolved by avoiding social media, but when it comes to issues related with social engagement, non-users ended up in a lose-lose situation where they encountered problems regardless of whether they were on social media or not.

11.4.5 Surviving in a Social Media-Dominated World

Although interviewees were surrounded by users connected through social media, some found ways to mitigate the effects of their own non-use. Many *expelled* and *excluded* interviewees occasionally engaged in secondary or displaced use, relying on a family member to share social news with them. Although scholars have largely viewed displaced use as extrinsically-driven (e.g. Satchell and Dourish 2009), we found that in our sample it was mostly an intrinsically-motivated decision. These participants chose not to be on social media and to rely on an intermediary. They hoped to benefit by staying in the loop, but avoiding the negative social consequences of using social media.

However, their intermediary still served as an external constraint in achieving this balance of non-use and being socially connected. The intermediary had to initiate by informing the non-user when there was something of interest. If the intermediary forgot or was not diligent about sharing such content with the non-user, they missed out. This could be especially tough for the individuals dealing with harassment. L pointed out how even though she would like to know much more about her friends and former social connections, it really depended on whether her husband remembered to let her know: "Every once in a while, he will show me some of my old students or friends or something. He will say, do you want to see them? And he'll show me once in a while." Whether L was on social media or off, for her husband "it's a control thing." On social media, her sister-in-laws would tell her husband what L should be doing and he would follow along. Off social media, he controlled what she can see on social media, creating real-world relationship tensions between her online contacts, her husband, and herself. She can't get away from negative consequences regardless.

Some had faith that their friends would remember to communicate with them via email or phone calls. However, this approach was nowhere near foolproof. An *excluded* participant, F, felt that she always eventually receives an invitation in email, but sometimes it would be very short notice and she already had other plans. It was especially problematic for A, who was already experiencing harassment for not being on social media. He explained: "I get a lot of flak for not being on Facebook... A lot of people use Facebook to invite people to things like parties. Often I'll not get invited because they'll send out invitations via Facebook and forget that means I won't see it. I get 'What do you mean you didn't know about the party? Oh yeah, I keep forgetting you aren't on Facebook. Sorry about that.' a lot." Even though people did not intentionally exclude these non-users, the result was that they were often not included in time, which left them out of real-world events where they would have garnered benefits of socially engaging with others.

Several interviewees felt that others would call them or directly reach out to them if it was important; yet, they found that social media has become the go to channel for broadly disseminating good and bad news, superseding, e.g., traditional birth announcements on paper or even via email and photo sites. Non-users were left with no way to receive this news. As a result, many felt socially ostracized or isolated, which we identified as a new sub-class of social media non-use: *social disenfranchisement*.

11.5 Implications of Non-Use

11.5.1 Social Media Use that Is not Social

We presented and examined different types of non-use that arise from Wyatt's (2003) original framework. The results of our study further suggest that the framework should be extended to account for the dimensions of *social engagement* versus *functional* motivations and barriers to usage (Fig. 11.2). By partitioning non-use in this way, it is clear that scholars have largely focused on *rejecters* who have voluntarily abandoned social media when it comes to those motivated by social engagement reasons (Baumer et al. 2013, 2015b; Brubaker et al. 2016; Lampe et al. 2013; Portwood-Stacer 2013; Schoenebeck 2014; Stieger et al. 2013). In regards to functionally-motivated usage, scholars in the "digital divide" and digital literacy literature have largely focused on those who are barred from social media use because of functional barriers such as technology access or financial hardships (Satchell and Dourish 2009; Wyatt 2003). However, researchers have not focused on two octants. Particularly, *excluded* and *expelled* non-users as a result of extrinsic social barriers (i.e., *social disenfranchisement*) have not been explored in depth. This study addressed this gap by focusing on social barriers such as concerns around shaping one's social identify or being bullied. These social barriers can arise as a result of intentional harassment, but also from unintentional pressures coming from others. Moreover, the barriers and severity of consequences are greater for those who face harassment.

11.5.2 Does Social Media Perpetuate Harassment?

Our research demonstrates how avoiding social media also allows non-users to avoid functional problems such as being inundated by too much useless social information. However, social issues cannot be completely avoided by staying off social media. In fact, it is just as bad if not worse in some respects. Non users continue to search for a sense of community while they are left behind by social media users who are building stronger relationships amongst themselves. Non users continue to be bullied offline. They even give up their claim to a digital identity which is now being shaped for them by other social media users. In short, these non-users are left in a state of social disenfranchisement where they can't win.

Sadly, we find that this is especially true for those who deal with harassment. While those who deal with unintentional pressures do encounter some challenges, those who experienced harassment faced consequences off social media that left them in an emotionally and socially impoverished state. For example, while L is harassed by her in-laws and husband if she goes on social media, now that she is off social media she needs to rely on that same husband to occasionally share social news from his feed. She feels isolated by not being able to know what her friends are up to. However, even when she experienced social media, she felt left behind upon seeing pictures of everyone's busy, interesting social lives: "I mean, I'm happy for them. But then I kind of feel sad. Like, everybody's got this life—they're all going on with their lives, and I'm not part of their lives."

Even more surprising, we see that being off social media can *lead* to harassment. A was forced off social media by unintentional pressures such as anxiety about being a good social media citizen, as well as disenchantment at the false sense of community on social media. He stopped using all social media just to have his friends "troll" him by creating an account for him and regularly making embarrassing posts. This expectation to be on social media leads to the other extreme of being harassed for not following the norm.

11.5.3 Looking Forward

Our research focuses on trends and patterns of use and non-use across an initial sample of social media non-users. Importantly, we focus on a new class of *socially disenfranchised* non-users, who left social media to avoid negative social consequences, but experience additional problems due to their absence. Their impoverished state may or may not reflect the experiences of others, such as those who continue to use social media despite experiencing harassment. Future research should investigate whether similar social barriers and consequences manifest for those who may still use social media in some (perhaps limited) social way. Furthermore, future larger scale studies can help us understand to what extent social disenfranchisement is a problem and whether users with certain characteristics or from certain demographics are more at risk.

We also discovered that the types of features and social interactions valued by social media users may directly conflict with non-user concerns. Unfortunately, non-users are in a lose-lose situation where avoiding social media also leads to negative social consequences. As a result, we urge designers and developers to think about ways to improve the *non-use experience*. Rather than pushing non-users towards using social media at the risk of online harassment, we suggest building a bridge between users and non-users which would bring value to both groups while lifting non-users out of a socially impoverished state. Here are some possible solutions that are in line with our findings:

- *Let non-users consume without being producers of social media content.* Some non-users are anxious about having to produce content (e.g., constantly updating their social media status), but still have a desire to consume content posted by friends and family. Social media that do not emphasize reciprocal relationships, such as Twitter, set expectations about asymmetrical information-sharing better than reciprocal networks like Facebook. However, taking it a step further and allowing a "follow only" option that does not require the creation of a profile could allow consumption-only interactions that meet the needs of some non-users.
- *Provide a way to address violations.* Non-users are sometimes mentioned, or even misrepresented, by social media users. While social media users can monitor and mitigate such events, even setting privacy settings to manage when they are "tagged," non-users have a harder time finding out about and mitigating such situations. To address this limitation, social media platforms could alert non-users when others mention them on social media (akin to Google Search's "Alerts" feature), and give them a way to provide feedback to the author or report a violation to have content removed. The alert should be communicated through another channel such as email. In this way, social media platforms could empower non-users, making freedom from harassment a right for all people, not just their users.
- *Integrate other channels for social media event notifications.* Interviewees in our study complained about missing invitations and announcements. Social media are replacing other communication channels. Providing ways to share posts or other social news through email or other channels would allow non-users to be included.

For example, an *excluded* interviewee explained how this type of feature used to be available in Facebook and allowed her to stay in the loop. But once it disappeared, she no longer had a way to stay connected.

- *Suggest new connections and bring up past memories with caution.* As we see from the experiences of those who are bullied, negative connections on social media can cause undue stress and alarm. For example, features that suggest new friends to connect with may bring up the memory of someone who has harmed you in the past. Bringing up those emotional associations can be damaging, and a cause for avoiding social media. Extreme cases demonstrate this, such as a rape victim who received a recommendation to friend his rapist (Kantor 2015). Similarly, features like Facebook's "See Your Memories" that show users a picture from their past can feature events or people whose relationship with the user has now changed, triggering negative emotions. Such features need to be more selective about what or whom they feature, and easy to turn off. Even for relationships that do not have a negative tenor, a feature that implicitly pushes users to make a choice about friending someone (e.g. Facebook's "People You May Know") can unintentionally put pressure on these individuals and cause them social anxiety about making that decision.

These suggestions arise from our understanding of the non-user experience. Future research should validate to what extent these mechanisms could alleviate some of the concerns and problems faced by non-users.

11.6 Conclusion

Researchers may be keen on addressing online harassment as it occurs to users of social networks. We argue that victims of online harassment can also be found among non-users, and that the consequences of harassment do not simply go away as users leave the network. Our work identifies a category of non-users we call the *socially disenfranchised*. The pervasive socialization that occurs via social media leaves these individuals at a loss for solutions, as they face negative consequences regardless of whether they are on or off social media. Furthermore, we find that those facing harassment are impacted to an even greater degree by social disenfranchisement, and have a much harder time overcoming the consequences of both use and non-use. One approach could be to address these concerns by improving designs to mitigate drawbacks of using social media. We suggest an alternative approach that would instead empower non-users in their decision to disengage from social media. Platform designers can do this by designing for non-users in a way that mitigates the social consequences of non-use. In considering the problem of online (and offline) harassment, our research makes a paradigmatic shift: Rather than solving the problem of non-use and encouraging user adoption, we can concentrate on how to support both users and non-users alike.

References

Baumer EPS, Adams P, Khovanskaya VD, Liao TC, Smith ME, Schwanda Sosik V, Williams K (2013) Limiting, leaving, and (Re)Lapsing: an exploration of Facebook non-use practices and experiences. In: Proceedings of the SIGCHI conference on human factors in computing systems. ACM, New York, NY, USA, pp 3257–3266. https://doi.org/10.1145/2470654.2466446

Baumer EPS, Ames MG, Burrell J, Brubaker JR, Dourish P (2015) Why study technology non-use? First Monday 20(11). https://doi.org/10.5210/fm.v20i11.6310

Baumer EPS, Guha S, Quan E, Mimno D, Gay GK (2015) Missing photos, suffering withdrawal, or finding freedom? how experiences of social media non-use influence the likelihood of reversion. Soc Media Soc 1(2). https://doi.org/10.1177/2056305115614851

Beran T, Li Q (2005) Cyber-harassment: a study of a new method for an old behavior. J Educ Comput Res 32(3):265–277. https://doi.org/10.2190/8YQM-B04H-PG4D-BLLH

Brubaker JR, Ananny M, Crawford K (2016) Departing glances: a sociotechnical account of leaving Grindr. New Media Soc 18(3):373–390. https://doi.org/10.1177/1461444814542311

Duggan M, Smith A (2014) Social media update 2013. Pew Research Center. http://www.pewinternet.org/2013/12/30/social-media-update-2013/

Ellison NB, Steinfield C, Lampe C (2007) The benefits of Facebook Friends: social capital and college students' use of online social network sites. J Comput Mediated Commun 12(4):1143–1168. https://doi.org/10.1111/j.1083-6101.2007.00367.x

Greenwood S, Perrin A, Duggan M (2016) Social Media Update 2016. Pew Research Center. http://www.pewinternet.org/2016/11/11/social-media-update-2016/

Hinduja S, Patchin JW (2010) Bullying, cyberbullying, and suicide. Arch Suicide Res 14(3):206–221. https://doi.org/10.1080/13811118.2010.494133

Kantor K (2015) People You May Know. https://www.youtube.com/watch?v=LoyfunmYIpU

Kowalski RM, Giumetti GW, Schroeder AN, Lattanner MR (2014) Bullying in the digital age: a critical review and meta-analysis of cyberbullying research among youth. Psychol Bull 140(4):1073–1137. https://doi.org/10.1037/a0035618

Lampe C, Vitak J, Ellison N (2013) Users and nonusers: interactions between levels of adoption and social capital. In: Proceedings of the 2013 conference on computer supported cooperative work. ACM, New York, NY, USA, pp 809–820. https://doi.org/10.1145/2441776.2441867

Laufer RS, Proshansky HM, Wolfe M (1973) Some analytic dimensions of privacy. In: Küller R (ed) Proceedings of the lund conference on architectural psychology. Hutchinson & Ross, Lund, Sweden, Dowden

Laufer RS, Wolfe M (1977) Privacy as a concept and a social issue: a multidimensional developmental theory. J Soc Issues 33(3):22–42. https://doi.org/10.1111/j.1540-4560.1977.tb01880.x

Marwick A, Boyd D (2011) To see and be seen: celebrity practice on Twitter. Convergence 17(2):139–158. https://doi.org/10.1177/1354856510394539

Mishna F, Saini M, Solomon S (2009) Ongoing and online: children and youth's perceptions of cyber bullying. Child Youth Serv Rev 31(12):1222–1228. https://doi.org/10.1016/j.childyouth.2009.05.004

Page X, Knijnenburg BP, Kobsa A (2013) FYI: communication style preferences underlie differences in location-sharing adoption and usage. In: Proceedings of the 2013 ACM international joint conference on pervasive and ubiquitous computing. ACM, New York, NY, USA, pp. 153–162. https://doi.org/10.1145/2493432.2493487

Page X, Wisniewski P, Knijnenburg B, Namara M (2018) Social media's have-nots: an era of social disenfranchisement. Internet Res

Park N, Kee KF, Valenzuela S (2009) Being immersed in social networking environment: Facebook groups, uses and gratifications, and social outcomes. CyberPsychology Behav 12(6):729–733. https://doi.org/10.1089/cpb.2009.0003

Portwood-Stacer L (2013) Media refusal and conspicuous non-consumption: the performative and political dimensions of Facebook abstention. New Media Soc 15(7):1041–1057

Rainie L, Smith A, Duggan M (2013) Coming and going on Facebook. http://www.pewinternet. org/2013/02/05/coming-and-going-on-facebook/. Accessed 12 Feb 2017

Satchell C, Dourish P (2009) Beyond the user: use and non-use in HCI. In: Proceedings of the 21st annual conference of the australian computer-human interaction special interest group: design: open 24/7, New York, NY, USA, ACM, pp 9–16. https://doi.org/10.1145/1738826.1738829

Schoenebeck SY (2014) Giving up Twitter for lent: how and why we take breaks from social media. In: Proceedings of the SIGCHI conference on human factors in computing systems. ACM, New York, NY, USA, pp 773–782. https://doi.org/10.1145/2556288.2556983

Šléglová V, Cerna A (2011) Cyberbullying in adolescent victims: perception and coping. Cyberpsychology J Psychosoc Res Cyberspace 5(2). https://cyberpsychology.eu/article/view/4248

Smith A, Duggan M (2018) Crossing the line: what counts as online harassment? http://www. pewinternet.org/2018/01/04/crossing-the-line-what-counts-as-online-harassment/. Accessed 26 Jan 2016

Stieger S, Burger C, Bohn M, Voracek M (2013) Who commits virtual identity suicide? differences in privacy concerns, internet addiction, and personality between facebook users and quitters. Cyberpsychology Behav Soc Netw 16(9):629–634

Suler J (2004) The online disinhibition effect. CyberPsychology Behav 7(3):321–326. https://doi. org/10.1089/1094931041291295

Valenzuela S, Park N, Kee KF (2009) Is There social capital in a social network site?: Facebook use and college students' life satisfaction, trust, and participation. J Comput Mediated Commun 14(4):875–901. https://doi.org/10.1111/j.1083-6101.2009.01474.x

Vitak J (2012) The impact of context collapse and privacy on social network site disclosures. J Broadcast Electron Media 56(4):451–470. https://doi.org/10.1080/08838151.2012.732140

Wang J, Iannotti RJ, Nansel TR (2009) School bullying among US adolescents: physical, verbal, relational and cyber. J Adolesc Health Off Publ Soc Adolesc Med 45(4):368–375. https://doi. org/10.1016/j.jadohealth.2009.03.021

Wyatt SME (2003) Non-users also matter: the construction of users and non-users of the Internet. Non-users also matter: the construction of users and non-users of the internet, pp 67–79. MIT Press. http://dare.uva.nl/search?metis.record.id=220721

Xu H, Teo H-H, Tan BCY, Agarwal R (2009) The role of push-pull technology in privacy calculus: the case of location-based services. J Manag Inf Syst 26(3):135–174. https://doi.org/10.2753/ MIS0742-1222260305

Printed in the United States
By Bookmasters